RHUBARB IN THE CATBIRD SEAT

Red Barber
and Robert Creamer

Afterword to the Bison Books Edition
by Bob Edwards

University of Nebraska Press
Lincoln and London

⊚ The paper in this book meets the minimum requirements of American
National Standard for Information Sciences—Permanence of Paper for
Printed Library Materials, ANSI Z39.48-1984.

First Bison Books printing: 1997
Most recent printing indicated by the last digit below:
10   9   8   7   6   5   4   3   2   1

Library of Congress Cataloging-in-Publication Data
Barber, Red, 1908–
Rhubarb in the catbird seat / Red Barber and Robert Creamer; afterword
by Bob Edwards.
p.   cm.
Originally published: Garden City, N.Y.: Doubleday, 1968.
ISBN 0-8032-6136-5 (pbk.: alk. paper)
1. Barber, Red, 1908–   .   2. Sportscasters—United States—
Biography.   I. Creamer, Robert W.   II. Title.
GV742.42.B35A32   1997
791.44′5—dc20
96-41632   CIP

Reprinted from the original 1968 edition by Doubleday & Company,
Inc., Garden City, New York.

To

LYLAH

And for

SARAH

RHUBARB IN THE CATBIRD SEAT

Red Barber sat next to the small pool behind his house on Key Biscayne, across the water by the Rickenbacker Causeway from Miami. It was early in December 1965, and we had been talking for several hours in his office, which is only a step or two from the lovely, screened-in area around the pool. Gardeners were planting small trees and bushes in the yard, and every now and then Lylah, Red's wife, would call him and he would excuse himself for a few minutes to supervise a planting. The Barbers had been living in Key Biscayne only a few months. They had moved south, back to Florida, that autumn after having lived in or near New York City for more than a quarter of a century. He was not retiring, Red had explained earlier. But with their daughter Sarah, their only child, grown and out on her own teaching school, he and Lylah had bought this house with an eye on the day he *would* retire. Florida is their home state and, after all, Red was fifty-seven and he had been doing play-by-play broadcasts of major league baseball every season since 1934. It was getting close, that time to retire. He grinned as he said it. Less than a year later he *was* retired, forcibly, when the New York Yankees fired him. But he was ready. Key Biscayne was ready. He had his memories—no one else had ever broadcast baseball play-by-play for thirty-three consecutive seasons—and he found that he enjoyed being around the house, living like a normal human being, traveling when he felt like it, writing a column for the Miami *Herald* once a week, doing a broadcast now and then, reading, fooling around in an eighteen-foot outboard.

That day in December, before all this, before the turmoil of the Yankee dismissal, he had relaxed beside the pool and explained why he wanted this book written. A man wants something tangible, he said. If an engineer creates a bridge or an architect a building, the bridge and the building are there for people to use and admire. A composer's music is played over and over; an artist's painting is hung in a museum. A singer can be recorded, an actor can be filmed. All have tangible evidence of their work, something to show their children, material evidence of what they have done with their lives. But a broadcaster's work, however well it is done, is gone an instant after it has come into being.

"I don't know how many words I have spoken into a microphone," Red said, "but it must be in the hundreds of millions. And where are they? All gone. I want something I can see. Something my friends can hold. Something my daughter can have in her hands all her life."

I found it hard to understand what he meant, really. To me, his monument is himself. I am middle-aged, only fourteen or fifteen years younger than Barber, but I cannot get rid of a sensation of awe at being close to him, talking with him, sharing this book with him. You have to understand that he was one of the heroes of my youth, one of the magic names. I suppose the heroes you have when you are young are your heroes all your life. I know that I have been acutely and continually aware of Red Barber since the spring of 1939, when I was sixteen and Larry MacPhail brought him into New York—or, more accurately, Brooklyn—to broadcast Dodger baseball games. MacPhail had taken over the moribund Dodgers and had borrowed money, bought ballplayers, hired Leo Durocher to manage, and put Red Barber on the air.

The three of them, MacPhail, Durocher, and Barber, revolutionized baseball in 1939, and Barber's part in the revolution was by no means the least important. Other major league teams had been broadcasting their games (Barber had done play-by-play in Cincinnati from 1934 through 1938), but often on a sporadic, now-and-then schedule. And there had been no baseball broadcasts in New York City, except at World Series and All Star time. After Barber and the Dodgers exploded into prominence, baseball broadcasting became as integral a part of a major league club's operation as the third-base dugout; but when MacPhail declared that he was going to have the Dodgers' games broadcast, the New York Yankees and the New York Giants were aghast. They followed MacPhail's lead, but reluctantly and angrily. The old curmudgeons who ran those two richer and more successful clubs hated the idea; they watched their meager attendance figures year after year and were appalled at the idea of "giving away" baseball over the radio.

MacPhail knew better. He was the shrewdest executive in the history of the game, I believe; it is startling to realize that he accomplished all that he did in only eleven seasons: three with Cincinnati, five with Brooklyn, and three with the Yankees. When I was sixteen, car radios were coming in, and portables, and small "kitchen" radios instead of those big bombs that sat like Grant's Tomb in front parlors. People were listening to radios all over the place. To MacPhail, play-by-play broadcasting advertised baseball, promoted it, stimulated it. And of course he was right. In the half dozen years before 1939 the Yankees had won three American League pennants and finished second three times, yet their average season attendance in the biggest city in the country had averaged only 860,000. The Giants had won three National League pennants in the same half dozen seasons, and they had been in the thick of the pennant race every year; their average attendance was 770,000. The Dodgers, poor souls, had been in the second division six straight times and their attendance averaged barely 500,000, though they drew 660,000 in 1938, MacPhail's first season as general manager. But in 1939, with Durocher driving the players that MacPhail had got for him and, significantly, with Barber broadcasting every game, the Dodgers finished third and their attendance jumped to 955,000. They outdrew the pennant-winning Yankees by nearly 100,000 and the Giants by a quarter of a million.

Attendance in Brooklyn went up again in 1940, and in 1941 (the most exciting baseball season ever in my memory: the

Dodgers fighting their way to their first pennant in twenty-one years, Joe DiMaggio hitting safely in fifty-six straight games, Ted Williams batting .406, the Yankees and Dodgers meeting in the Mickey Owen World Series), it soared to 1,214,000. Only once in all the years before the MacPhail-Durocher-Barber triumvirate had the Dodgers ever drawn a million; now, except for two seasons during the war, they would never again fall below it.

Lord, those years were exciting. Everybody talked baseball. If a million people went to Ebbets Field to see the Dodgers play, ten million listened to Red broadcast their games. I was a Yankee fan in those days—I rooted for the Yanks when they played the Dodgers in the 1941 World Series—but I never listened to Yankee ball games. I listened to Barber and the Dodgers. Everybody did. In the summer of 1941 you did not need to own a radio to hear Red broadcast. You could walk up a street and hear the game through one open window after another and never miss a pitch. You could thread your way through the crowd on a beach and get the game from a dozen different portables. In traffic you'd hear it from a hundred different cars.

Barber's impact on New York was extraordinary. Everybody knew who Red Barber was, even my maiden aunt—literally. The language he used in his broadcasts became part of everyone's speech. James Thurber used some of it in a memorable short story that was later made into a motion picture. Much of it sounds dated now—sittin' in the catbird seat, tearin' up the pea patch, walkin' in tall cotton, we got a rhubarb growin' in the infield, the bases are FOB: full of Brooklyns—but a cliché is essentially a phrase that is so good everybody keeps repeating it. And Barber was good. Mixed in with all that southern corn were felicitous phrases like "advancing to third on the concomitant error," which flattered his ever-more-knowledgeable audience, an audience that was ever more knowledgeable primarily because of him.

He created fans. They learned about the game of baseball by just listening to the old redhead sitting in his catbird seat tearing up the pea patch. I remember so vividly the mother of a close friend of mine, a lady whose practical knowledge of baseball before Barber was about the same as my present understanding of the political situation in Upper Volta. My friend and I were listening to a Dodger game one afternoon as Red described a play in which the opposing team had a man on first base with no one out. The batter hit a ground ball to shortstop. Pee Wee Reese took it and tossed it to Billy Herman at second for the forceout, but the batter beat Herman's relay to first. The crowd yelled when the double play seemed imminent—the roar of the crowd at Ebbets Field was always shaking the radio—and my friend's mother came hurrying in from the kitchen, carrying a half-peeled potato and a paring knife. Paying no attention to us, she cocked her head to listen. Then she muttered, "Oh, well. We got the front man," and trotted back into the kitchen.

Red Barber did that. He did it to me, too, and I thought I knew baseball. He did it by reporting the game—colorfully, brightly, excitingly, and always factually. He loved Brooklyn, but on the air he was a reporter. He told you about the *game*. He told you about it fairly and accurately, and he interpreted it, and in doing so he set standards of excellence that have never been surpassed, and seldom, if ever, equaled.

If a man like that feels he needs a book to be remembered by, okay. I hope this one is it.

When Red and I began our interviews for the book, I knew these general facts about him. He was from the South. He had broadcast in Cincinnati before going to Brooklyn. He did play-by-play for the Dodgers from 1939 through 1953 and then switched over to the Yankees. He was a very active layman and a lay reader in the Episcopal Church. He had been seriously ill a couple of times. That's about all. I didn't know, for instance, that he was a writer.

He told me, "Our association—the two of us together doing this book—is something that has taken me some years to come to. It evidences an increased awareness of my own shortcomings and my own peculiar temperament, because for years and years I told Doubleday that if I ever wrote this book I would write every word of it myself. Until now I have written every word that I have ever used. That doesn't include play-by-play, of course, or impromptu interviews on the air. But I have written all my radio shows myself and all my television shows. I wrote a book on the Dodgers called *The Rhubarb Patch* with Barney Stein, the photographer. The photographs are Barney's, but every word in the book is mine. In 1950, when Bill Corum, the columnist, took a leave of absence from the New York *Journal-American* to go run the Kentucky Derby, I took his place, and even though I was broadcasting Dodger games at the same time I wrote a daily column called "Sitting in the Catbird Seat" that appeared in the *Journal-American* six days a week for nine straight weeks, from the middle of March until Bill came back in the middle of May. Every word in that column was mine.

"But when I tried to write this book, I couldn't get it done. Too many things interfered, and I kept getting sidetracked. I tried twice. I finally realized that to get it done, I needed a professional in the field. That's you."

And so the professional in the field sat back and listened, while the writer who didn't have time to write talked. He talked first about Brooklyn.

RED	①								
BARBER									

I hope I can put this in the proper focus. I was one of many people involved in what could be called the rise of the Dodgers in 1939 and 1940 and 1941, and I received a lot of undue credit for the impact they made. I happened to be the person who spoke into a microphone, and so it was through my voice and my words that millions of people heard about what was going on over there in Brooklyn. But, my goodness, this whole thing had been building. It was the product of something that had been building for years and years, for forty years at least.

There were so many things involved in it and so many people. The millions of people who lived in Brooklyn were a big part of this, and I'm not being sentimental. It's a fact. There were nearly three million people in Brooklyn, and if every one of them wasn't rooting for the Dodgers, every one *seemed* to be. People around the country were hoping the Dodgers would win for Brooklyn's sake, for the sake of that downtrodden three million. These were the masses, subjects of the glittering city of New York, across the river.

You could win money betting that Brooklyn had more people than Manhattan did. That surprised people, but it was true. Someone once pointed out that if you could tow Long Island a couple of miles out to sea so that it would be completely separate from New York, Brooklyn, on the western end of the island, would be the second biggest city in the country. And Chicago would be first, not New York. But you couldn't tow Long Island out to sea, and Brooklyn had to stay where it was. It was an official part of New York City, the most populous of the five boroughs, but to the world Manhattan, with its tall buildings, was New York. Brooklyn was just a subservient area.

This galled Brooklyn. Brooklyn had been an independent city for years and years. It wasn't until 1898 that it was made part of the City of New York by an act of the state legislature. Manhattan, Brooklyn, the Bronx, Queens, and Staten Island were made boroughs, and together they comprised one city. The people of Brooklyn hated the idea. They felt they had been forced into it by the legislature, and they resented it. When I got to Brooklyn in 1939—forty-one years later—the resentment was still there, and it was a genuine resentment. You could feel it. They say that to this day in England there is a feeling against redheaded people (the traditional idea that redheads have terrible tempers is part of this), and that this feeling is part of a subconscious heritage that has been handed down over the centuries. It goes back to the terrible fear the Anglo-Saxons had of the redheaded Danes who used to invade them regularly back before A.D. 1000 and lick the tar out of them.

In Brooklyn in 1939 the resentment was not subconscious. It was very much on the conscious level. After all, someone who had been twelve years old in 1898 was barely in his fifties when I got to Brooklyn. A boy of twelve feels things strongly, and nobody in Brooklyn has ever been famous for keeping his feelings to himself. As that boy grew older and voiced his resentment, his children heard him; they heard him talk about it all their lives. He hated New York, and they hated New York.

It established the Brooklyn character. If you were from Brooklyn you were outspoken and you were truculent. During World War II, Brooklyn, with its huge population, had more men in the armed forces than any one of some thirty-eight states. And every one of them said he was from Brooklyn. He didn't say New York. He said Brooklyn loud and clear, and as a result there wasn't a movie, a novel, a story about World War II that didn't have a character from Brooklyn involved in it. Somebody even wrote a song during the war called, "Give Me the Moon Over Brooklyn."

Brooklyn's resentment at being treated like a poor relative was real. It had the bridge, but Manhattan had the skyscrapers, the theaters, Wall Street, the landmarks. The great ocean liners docked in Manhattan; Brooklyn got the cargo ships. Broadway was a glamorous name; Flatbush Avenue sounded funny. Brooklyn became a joke; the laughingstock of comedians. Say "Brooklyn" and you got an automatic laugh.

Brooklyn was suffering from a borough-wide inferiority complex. That complex was compounded by the fact that so many people there felt they were foreigners. They talk about America being the melting pot. Brooklyn was, and it still is. There were more different racial and national strains in Brooklyn than anywhere else, and a lot of those people didn't speak English too impeccably, if they could speak it at all. Especially the older people. The children were different and I suppose by now a lot of them have made money and moved out of Brooklyn. But the original immigrants tended to band together in groups and in neighborhoods. Some people who emigrated from Europe came through Ellis Island, went over to Brooklyn to join friends or relatives, settled in a certain neighborhood, and never left that neighborhood for the rest of their lives. When I came to Brooklyn in 1939—and I know this for a fact—there were people living in Brooklyn who had never once been to Manhattan. If these people had to go downtown they might go to Flatbush Avenue or one of the other big streets in Brooklyn. Manhattan was another country. But these people who thought in terms of their own group and then their own neighborhood began to think in terms of Brooklyn. This was their town—not New York.

The feeling extended into sports, specifically baseball. Brooklyn had had professional baseball since the 1860s, and it had been in the National League continuously since 1890. In fact, in 1890, when there were three major leagues (the National, the American Association, and the Players' League), Brooklyn had a team in each league. It won the National League pennant that year, and it won again in 1899 and 1900. The Giants had won only two pennants up to that time, and the Yankees and the American League didn't even exist.

But after John McGraw took over the Giants in 1902, Brooklyn's fortunes sagged. In the next thirty-five years, from 1903 through 1937, the Giants won thirteen pennants and finished in the first division thirty-two times. The Dodgers won only two pennants and finished in the second division twenty-eight times. Then in 1920 the Yankees got Babe Ruth and they began to win a horde of pennants. Brooklyn kept finishing sixth.

Until the Yankees got Ruth, and even for a while afterward, the Giants were the big club in baseball, and particularly in New York. They had money and a fine big ball park and they had the carriage trade. They used to start their games after three o'clock. They waited for the elevated train that came up from Wall Street after the stock market closed at three. They were still starting games at three-fifteen in New York—and in Brooklyn, too, for that matter—when I got there. I asked why they started them so late and they told me it was because of the fellows from Wall Street. I said, "This thing has gotten bigger than that, hasn't it?" They said, "Well, that's how it started, and we haven't changed it yet." Larry MacPhail changed it. He moved his time up and the others had to follow him because we were all broadcasting and they couldn't stand the idea of having MacPhail on the air ahead of them. Wherever MacPhail went, the others had to follow. They got madder and madder, too, but that was all right with MacPhail.

But the Giants did have the carriage trade, and they had the money and the big ball park and the fine ball club. The Dodgers didn't. A good part of the reason why they didn't traced back to their ball park, Ebbets Field, because Ebbets Field was the thing that set in motion the terrible division in ownership that left the Dodgers almost immobile for so many years. Charles Ebbets had bought the Dodgers in the 1890s, and Ebbets was a man who believed strongly in the future of baseball. He built Ebbets Field as a showcase—it was opened in 1913, and a Mr. Casey Stengel got four hits in the first game ever played there— and for those days it was a marvelous, modern stadium. Yet Ebbets was severely criticized for building such a big park. People said it was too big, far bigger than would ever be needed. Ebbets replied that that was not true and he made the famous statement that has come down to this day: "Baseball is in its infancy." He was a prophet, but he didn't live to see his prophecy fulfilled. In fact, he went broke building Ebbets Field and had great trouble finding someone who would lend him money to finish it. He finally worked out a deal with Stephen McKeever, who said, "All right. I'll *give* you the money to finish it. But you give me 50 per cent of the ball club."

Ebbets agreed, and that is how the exact 50–50 split in ownership between the Ebbets and the McKeevers came into being. Ebbets died in 1925, and his heirs and the McKeevers could agree on nothing. Neither side had control because of the 50–50 split, and nothing got done. The ball club stumbled along, and the beautiful modern ball park turned into a rundown old dump. After 1920 the Dodgers did not win a pennant. The Giants won seven in sixteen years, which rubbed the salt a little deeper into Brooklyn's wounds.

Everything seemed to aggravate the situation. The Brooklyn manager from 1914 to 1931 was Wilbert Robinson, old Uncle Robby, a big fat fellow who had been a butcher as a young man and who visited with the fans and roared and hollered on the field. He fit Brooklyn, and Brooklyn liked him, so much so that the Dodgers were almost universally known as the Robins during the years that Uncle Robby managed. And he hated John McGraw. He and McGraw had played together on the famous Baltimore Orioles of the 1890s, and later Robby had served as a coach under McGraw. But they had had a falling out over something, and now there was a genuine dislike between them. That dislike extended to the two ball clubs and to the fans, and it was important. Maybe it wasn't too important in Manhattan, but it was in Brooklyn. Brooklyn cared deeply.

All this came to a lovely head in 1934, an explosive head. McGraw and Robinson were both gone by then, and Bill Terry was managing the Giants and Casey Stengel the Dodgers. Terry had won the pennant and the World Series with the Giants in 1933 and during the off-season, at a press conference, he was talking about the season ahead and the teams he thought would give the Giants the most trouble. He felt he had a winning ball club in New York, but I guess he offered some favorable comment on the Chicago Cubs, who were perennially strong then, and perhaps on the Pittsburgh Pirates and the St. Louis Cardinals.

Someone asked him, "What about Brooklyn?"

Terry, not realizing what in the world he was starting, tossed off a little quip. He said, "Brooklyn? Is Brooklyn still in the league?"

It got a little laugh. It was just a wisecrack and everybody let it go at that. Except for one man, and he added to it more than he had any idea he was adding. That was Roscoe McGowen of the New York *Times*, who wrote up the press conference and included Terry's remark. He didn't make a big to-do over it, but he did include it in his story. It ran the next day, and seldom has a sports story been picked up and quoted and requoted as much as that one of Roscoe McGowen's. Pretty soon everybody knew that Bill Terry of the New York Giants had said, "Brooklyn? Is Brooklyn still in the league?" It was all that three million already-angry-at-Manhattan-New York-McGraw-Giants-Terry Brooklyn fans needed. They took Terry's wisecrack and made it their war cry. Is Brooklyn still in the league? We'll show you whether we're still in the league.

Now we come to the last couple of games of the 1934 season. That was the year the St. Louis Cardinals won the pennant, with the famous Gas House Gang. It was my first year broadcasting in the majors—I was at Cincinnati—and I remember that season well. I would say that the 1934 Cardinals were the most colorful ball club for getting into trouble, a pleasant, cheerful sort of trouble, of any ball club that ever existed. They were lively. They were spirited. They had personality. That club had Dizzy Dean and Paul Dean and Leo Durocher and Rip Collins and Pepper Martin and Joe Medwick and Dazzy Vance and Jess Haines and Wild Bill Hallahan and Tex Carleton and Jack Rothrock and Bill Delancey, and, oh, I can't remember all the names. Frank Frisch was the manager. It was a collection of museum pieces. They were colorful. They did things. They got into everything. They had style. There was no false modesty on that club. They were great names. Dizzy Dean would pop off— or you thought he was popping off—about something he was going to do, and then he would go out and do exactly what he said he was going to do. He stood on the mound in the 1934 World Series and laughed at Hank Greenberg, who had hit .339 that year. Then he struck Greenberg out. Pepper Martin,

Medwick, Frisch—this wasn't just a collection of museum pieces, this *was* a museum, a movable museum, moving all the time. On the ball field, in hotel lobbies, on trains. They never stood still. They were fabulous. They were the Gas House Gang, and they have come down to us as a legend. Whenever people get to talking about great ball clubs they almost automatically include the Gas House Gang.

But they were not a great ball club. Colorful, sure. Great, no. To me, the measure of a great ball club is not just what it does in one season but whether it throws off a series of winners. It has to be the dominant club in the league over a number of seasons. The 1927 Yankees were great, but they won pennants the year before and the year after. McGraw's Giants won four straight pennants, and for nine straight years finished first or second. McCarthy's Yankees won seven pennants in eight years. The Dodgers won six in nine years in Brooklyn with pretty much the same cast of players, and then went out to Los Angeles, rebuilt, and won four more, three in four seasons. Casey Stengel won ten pennants in twelve years at New York.

The Gas House Gang won only one pennant, and they won it largely because Roscoe McGowen quoted that flip remark of Bill Terry's. As the 1934 season came down to its last days, the Gas House Gang was in second place, despite being the Gas House Gang. They were playing the Reds at home in St. Louis the last weekend of the season. The Reds were a last-place team—on merit. I know that because I watched them all season long. The Reds left town to go to St. Louis to meet the Cardinals, and Powell Crosley, the Cincinnati owner, was distressed. His team was so inept, and here it was going into St. Louis to play the Gas House Gang at this critical moment. The Cardinals had been on a September surge, just marvelous, marvelous. Dean was winning everything—that was the season he won thirty games —and they were moving, but they were still in second place behind the Giants. And the Giants were closing the season at home against the Dodgers, who were, as usual, in sixth place.

I ran into Mr. Crosley in the corridors of the radio station in Cincinnati. He was deeply concerned. He said, "There must not be any question in anybody's mind but that we are going to do our very best against St. Louis." Now, Paul Derringer, the big pitcher, was one of the two or three genuine ballplayers on the Reds. He had worked hard that season (he won fifteen games and lost twenty-one for a last-place team), and Charlie Dressen, who was the manager, had been quoted in the papers as saying he was undecided whether or not to pitch Derringer against St. Louis. Mr. Crosley said to me, "We *must* be able to say that we've done our best. I feel so strongly about this that I am going to do something I've never done before. I'm going to send Dressen a telegram, and I'm going to tell him that he must pitch Derringer in the first game, that he has to lead with our best."

He sent the telegram, and Dressen did pitch Derringer. The Reds did do the best they could. It's important to know this, and to know how Crosley felt and what he did, how he *tried*, because the Reds went into St. Louis to play four ball games and with consummate ability and consistent artistry managed to lose all four.

That meant, in turn, that the Giants had to beat their second-division rivals, the Dodgers, in their last two games in the Polo Grounds. What could have been a quiet season-ending set between a pennant winner and a sixth place also-ran was suddenly something crucial. And Brooklyn was ready for it. The Brooklyn fans, with their stored-up hatred and anger and resentment, came pouring across the bridges and through the tunnels into Manhattan and up to the Polo Grounds. There must have been thousands and thousands of Giant fans there, too, but they tell me that all you could hear was Brooklyn. They shouted and they yelled and they threw firecrackers. They really tore up the pea patch. When Bill Terry appeared outside the center-field clubhouse they booed him all the way into the Giant dugout.

With that kind of support, what happened seemed inevitable. All that the Dodgers did was beat the Giants two straight, knock them out of the race, and give the Gas House Gang the pennant. And all that the Brooklyn fans yelled, raucously, over and over, was, "Is Brooklyn still in the league? *Hey, Terry!* Is Brooklyn still in the league?"

But, of course, the Giants came back and won pennants in 1936 and 1937 and were contenders every season. And the Dodgers couldn't even get to .500. They lived for years on that one wild, exultant triumph over Terry and the Giants in 1934, but otherwise Brooklyn was still second-division, second-rate, inferior.

The Dodger front-office situation, always bad, was getting worse. The Ebbets and McKeever heirs were still split, and the ball club was foundering and in debt. In effect, it was in hock to the Brooklyn Trust Company, and the bank had the ball club in its basement. A very similar situation had existed in Cincinnati when MacPhail had moved in there, and he straightened that one out in a hurry. The Brooklyn thing had become alarming to the bank—and to the National League, too—and it became obvious that something had to be done, that strong measures had to be taken. I wasn't around the club then and I don't know all the details, but from what I have heard MacPhail say, the most important man involved in straightening out the mess was Ford Frick, then president of the National League. The next most important man was the chief executive officer of the Brooklyn Trust Company, George V. McLaughlin, who was a rockcrusher. When McLaughlin wanted to move, he moved, and now he had decided to move. Frick and McLaughlin cracked the whip on the embittered, divided owners, who weren't even speaking to each other and who couldn't agree on anything. Frick and McLaughlin told them they were *going* to agree on one thing, and they were going to agree right away. And that was that a Mr. Larry MacPhail was going to come in and be general manager. *He* was going to run the ball club. He was going to run it for their sake, for the league's sake, for the bank's sake and for baseball's sake.

And so MacPhail came in. Now, Larry was not only dynamic and forceful and hot-tempered, he was also a beautiful, working, practicing diplomat. He got into no feuds with either faction of owners. Instead, he honey-toned both sides. He buttered up the Ebbets heirs and he buttered up the McKeever heirs, and pretty soon both factions were equally fond of him. Eventually, they got to fighting over who loved him the most.

Very quickly, MacPhail got this jumbled mess working like a well-oiled sewing machine. He moved. He had been brought in by the bank because it had a dying ball club on its hands as security for huge loans, but the first thing MacPhail did was go to the bank and borrow more money. He wanted to paint the ball park and clean up the rest rooms and generally freshen and tidy things up.

The bank thought, well, okay. That's that. Now we won't have to bother with him any more. But MacPhail came right back in and made them give him some more money, and he went off and bought Dolf Camilli from the Phillies. That bank found out about MacPhail in a hurry. If they were going to get their money back, first they were going to have to send some more in where it was.

Camilli was Larry's first major move (he had hit .339 with the Phillies the year before, and in 1941 when the Dodgers won that pennant Dolf was named the Most Valuable Player in the National League), but it wasn't long before General Mills, which made Wheaties and sponsored baseball games practically every other place but New York, began talking to Larry about broadcasting the Dodger games. They had worked with him in Cincinnati, and they knew him. MacPhail was violently pro-radio. He knew it was the strongest single promotional tool he could have, and he wanted it. The five-year anti-radio ban then in existence among the three New York clubs was expiring after the 1938 season, and almost before MacPhail had warmed the executive chair at 215 Montague Street in Brooklyn he notified the Giants and the Yankees that he was not going to renew it. He was going to broadcast in 1939. They protested but MacPhail told them flatly that he would not be a party to another five-year ban, he would not be a party to a five-month ban, he would not be a party to a five-minute ban. He was going to broadcast.

It created a big rhubarb. The Giants and the Yankees blustered and threatened. They said, "We'll run you out of town if you broadcast." MacPhail said, "You go right ahead and run me out of town all you want to. *I'm* going to broadcast. Next season, 1939."

And he did, and this is where I came in. I'll go into the details of my getting the Dodger broadcasting job later, but for now let's just say I got it. In March of 1939 I left my friends and associates at the radio station in Cincinnati and drove with Lylah and the baby down to Clearwater, Florida, where the Brooklyn club was training. I was to spend a couple of weeks with the team to get acclimated and then I was going to drive on up to New York and get settled before the ball club got there.

I have gone on at this length about the background of the situation in order to make clear what was happening when I reached the place in 1939. The season before, 1938, the people of Brooklyn had been given MacPhail, their first, genuine, talented, all-out champion. Uncle Robby had been well-loved, but he was far from being a great manager. Babe Herman had been colorful, and he could hit, but people thought of him as a clown. It was great beating Terry, but that was a one-shot act.

But now they had MacPhail. They had nothing else when he got there, but they had him, and he was the best. He suited the Brooklynites to a T. He was loud. He was truculent. He was mad. He hated the Giants. He didn't like the Yankees. He had no use for the tall buildings of New York—or so they thought in Brooklyn—and he snapped his fingers under Terry's nose.

McPhail did things. He cleaned up that filthy old ball park. He got the Dodgers some ballplayers. After his first year he made Leo Durocher the manager, and Leo was the ideal man for the job because *he* was loud and *he* wasn't afraid of anybody. MacPhail put in night baseball. He decided to broadcast the games over the radio. He brought me in to broadcast, and that was important to Brooklyn because I was an established major league broadcaster. I had done the last four World Series. I knew how to do the job.

You see what MacPhail was doing for the borough? He was moving Brooklyn up. In 1939 his Dodgers finished third, and Brooklyn had a first-division team. MacPhail was named the major league executive of the year. Durocher was named manager of the year. The park looked beautiful. The broadcasts were major league. All of a sudden Brooklyn was even with everybody in the world. Nobody was better than Brooklyn.

In Clearwater one day that spring MacPhail and I had been sitting out in the sun watching practice, not saying much of anything, and when it was over he got up to leave. On the spur of the moment, I asked, "Larry, do you have any instructions for me about this job in Brooklyn?"

When you look back at it, that was a pretty fair question. I was going to New York, the big town, a town I had never been in except for a few brief trips. I was going to work for a fellow I had worked for before, but I would be working for him in an entirely new area. I would be doing play-by-play broadcasts where they had not been done before. But Mac-Phail just said, "No," and started to walk away. He had never given me an instruction in Cincinnati as to how he wanted a broadcast done, and never in the years to come at Brooklyn did he ever give me an instruction.

He walked away about ten or fifteen feet and then—I can see it now, just as it happened—all of a sudden he whirled around and his face was furious. He came striding back to where I was and he bellowed, "Yes! Yes, I have!" The veins in his neck were standing out and his voice was hoarse. He was raging. Larry MacPhail angry is an unforgettable sight. If you have ever seen it, you know precisely what I mean. He roared, "When I told the Yankees and the Giants that I was *not* going to be a party to that anti-radio ban any more and that I *was* going to broadcast, that Brannick [he meant Eddie Brannick, secretary of the Giants] said to me, 'If you dare broadcast, if you *dare* break this agreement, we'll get a fifty-thousand-watt radio station and we'll get the best baseball broadcaster in the world and, MacPhail, we'll blast you into the river.'"

MacPhail's face got even redder, and the veins stuck out another inch or two, and he yelled, "That's what that [and I won't quote exactly what he called him] Brannick said to me. He *threatened* me! Now, yes, I have an instruction for you. I've *got* a fifty-thousand-watt radio station: WOR. Whether you know it or not, that's fifty thousand watts, and there's not a bigger one. And I've got *you.*" He let that sink in, and then he said, "And I don't *want* to be blasted into the river."

He glared at me and then he spun around and walked away. This time he kept walking.

That was the only instruction Larry MacPhail ever gave me in my life on how to broadcast, and I like to look back and think that he *wasn't* blasted into the river. As a matter of fact, for a couple of years there after we all got going, the Giants and the Yankees couldn't come up with sponsors and *they* went off the air. As Casey Stengel would say, you could look it up.

Because, you see, none of this fascinating Brooklyn story had been on radio before. When people talk about what I did for the Dodgers, they forget that. Sure, I was the medium that brought the continuing excitement of the story to millions of listeners and, sure, yes, I did a good job. I was a professional broadcaster. But the thing was there. I didn't create it. All I did was reflect the atmosphere. At any rate, I certainly tried to.

Between Innings: THE CATBIRD SEAT

We are all creatures not only of our heredity but of our environment. Most of the phrases that I used in broadcasts and which became fairly popular are simply phrases that I heard and picked up and began to use. There were a few, like the bases are FOB: full of Brooklyns, that I did coin, but most just came naturally into my speech. I like words, I like colorful language. I think most people do, and that is probably the reason why things like "rhubarb" and "the catbird seat" and the others became so popular. Incidentally, both "Rhubarb" and "The Catbird Seat" are copyrighted as titles, but not by me. James Thurber wrote a short story for *The New Yorker* called "The Catbird Seat" and some Hollywood outfit bought the movie rights. In 1953 when Barney Stein and I did our book on the Dodgers we wanted to call it *The Catbird Seat.* It seemed like a natural, since the phrase was so closely associated with me and with the Dodgers. But Hollywood owned the title, and we couldn't use it. So we called the book *The Rhubarb Patch. Rhubarb* is a title, too. H. Allen Smith wrote a comic novel called *Rhubarb* in 1946. It was about a volatile cat that was named Rhubarb because he was always creating a disturbance, which is what "rhubarb" means, of course. Smith mentioned me in the book and gave me credit for popularizing the word but he pointed out, quite accurately, that I had gotten it from Garry Schumacher, who is out in San Francisco now with Stoneham and the Giants but who was a New York sportswriter in those days. Garry got it from Tom Meany, another old sportswriter, who died a few years back. And Tom, in turn, got it from a bartender. There was a famous incident—and a true one that dramatized the intensity of feeling between Giant and Dodger fans in those days—that happened about 1937 or 1938, before I got to Brooklyn. Some fans got into an argument in a bar; one of them, a Giant fan, ragged a Brooklyn fan so unmercifully that the Brooklyn fan left, got a gun, came back, and shot the Giant fan in the stomach. Well, according to the story as I know it, Tom Meany stopped in a tavern the day after this thing happened—I think it was the very place where the shooting had occurred—and the bartender said, "We had quite a rhubarb last night, Mr. Meany."

Tom told that to Garry, who fell in love with the word. When I came east a year or so later I heard Garry use it, and I began to toss it on the air whenever the fur began to fly or the air turned blue. At first, I always said, "As Garry Schumacher says, we've got a rhubarb!" Finally, I went ahead and just used it without the credit to Garry.

It caught on, and now it's in the dictionaries. World War II was the thing that really popularized it—after all, Brooklyn was in every part of the armed forces. I know that it kept popping up in war communiques and dispatches.

So, I borrowed "rhubarb." But "the catbird seat" is different. I bought that. I bought it in Cincinnati. Lylah and I were playing penny ante poker with some friends, and I sat there for hours and couldn't win a pot. Finally, during a round of seven-card stud, I decided I was going to force the issue. I raised on the first bet, and I raised again on every card. At the end, when the showdown came, it was between a fellow named Frank Cope and me. Frank turned over his hole cards, showed a pair of aces, and won the pot. He said, "Thank you, Red. I had those aces from the start. I was sitting in the catbird seat." I didn't know the derivation of it, but I didn't have to be told the meaning. And I had paid for it. It was mine.

RED	1								
BARBER	②								

Larry MacPhail was an absolute genius in the art of public relations; there was no question about it. He knew how to use radio. He knew how to spruce up a ball park. He established season-ticket plans. He put in night baseball. His ability to get the public interested in his ball club was extraordinary. Nobody else was close to him.

When you stop to realize the things MacPhail did in baseball you wonder why he hasn't been put in the Hall of Fame in Cooperstown long ago. He took the Cincinnati ball club when it was dying, and he put it on its feet. The Reds won two pennants and a World Series with the basic club MacPhail put together; he had gone on to Brooklyn by then, but they won with the ballplayers MacPhail had set in motion. His decision to put in lights was revolutionary. People forget that before 1935, when Larry started night ball at Cincinnati, every single ball game that had ever been played in the major leagues had been played in daylight. Baseball could not operate now without lights, but when Larry put them in he did it despite strong objections from important baseball people.

He came east and took over the Brooklyn club when *it* was dying, and in his second season he had the Dodgers in third place and outdrawing both the Yankees and the Giants. He put lights in at Ebbets Field, in the face of even stronger objections, this time from the powerful Yankees and Giants. With typical MacPhail flair, or luck, or simply because the gods liked to smile on him, he managed to have Johnny Vander Meer pitch his historic second successive no-hitter in the first night game ever played at Brooklyn. He brought radio broadcasting into New York—again, over vociferous objections—and forced the Yankees and Giants into a position where they had to broadcast. The first major league game ever televised was televised in Ebbets Field. Try to imagine where baseball would be today without radio and TV. When he took over Yankee Stadium after World War II he put lights in there and helped set off the tremendous postwar boom in baseball. He was extraordinary. He has been out of baseball for twenty years, and yet his impact on the game is so great you would think he had left it only last week.

MacPhail could judge a ballplayer, too, and he could judge people. The more you look at it, the more you realize that MacPhail and Rickey were the two men whose influence on baseball is most in evidence today. I worked with them both and loved them both, and I say that advisedly. There was nothing I would not have done for Rickey when he was alive, and there is nothing that I would not do right now for MacPhail. I would take the word of either of them to the ends of the earth. If either of them said it, that was it.

Each of them flattered me in my job by paying me the supreme compliment of acknowledging that I was a grown man who knew his business, and they left me alone to do it. Of course, in doing this they made me want to work as hard as I could. You didn't count the hours—and the extra hours—that you put in for MacPhail and Rickey. Your only thought was to get the job done and done right. I had the full strength of these men behind me, and they were strong men. MacPhail told me, "When you're broadcasting and you think this club ought to be burned, you burn it. You do the job the way you think it ought to be done. I don't care how it comes out. If you have to rip the club, rip it."

In other words, MacPhail was strong enough not to worry about every word a broadcaster said. He told me to report the games. Report what I saw and heard. Report what I felt. Let him worry about the quality of the team on the field. Larry knew you couldn't fool the fans. Real baseball fans spend half their time criticizing the teams they love. What Larry wanted was to have those fans talking about his team, thinking about it. That's why he liked radio and the exposure it gave to his ball club.

When Lylah and I left Clearwater to come up to Brooklyn in 1939, the Dodgers were getting ready to play exhibition games in Florida. MacPhail wanted me to get to New York so that I could start broadcasting these exhibition games from Western Union wire reports. He was always so far ahead of everybody. The Yankee-Giant broadcasts weren't going to start until Opening Day, and they sneered at the idea of putting exhibition games on the radio. But do you see what happened? This was the first year the anti-radio ban was off and when MacPhail broadcast Dodger exhibition games, it meant that the Dodgers reached this fresh, expectant audience in New York weeks before the Giants and Yankees ever began. It was a novelty. You didn't have to be a Dodger fan to want to hear the Dodger baseball broadcast. MacPhail gave us a big jump in grabbing the audience.

But we had problems. When the team was still in Florida, things were fine. Western Union had experienced men down there who were accustomed to sending what they call Paragraph One— or play-by-play—accounts of baseball games. But when the team broke camp and started north, it was different. This was back in the days when the teams left the training camps fairly early and spent perhaps two weeks barnstorming their way home, playing exhibition games in one minor league town after another. The first stop the Dodgers made was in a small city in South Carolina. The local Western Union operator was to send the play-by-play description to us in the WOR studios in New York.

I was standing by the microphone in the studios when the description began to come in. It was marvelously confusing. The receiving operator, who was with me in the studio in New York, kept breaking into the sending operator, the fellow in South Carolina, to ask questions about what had been sent and to request more information. I never could tell a dot from a dash, so I didn't know exactly what the operator with me in the studio was getting or what he was asking, but he began to go wild. He even had trouble getting the batting orders.

The game began, and now I was on the air, waiting for the

skeletal information from which I would build my re-created broadcast of the game. The way it worked ordinarily was for certain basic facts to come in: a certain hitter was up; the first pitch was a strike; the second pitch was a ball; he hit a fly ball to the left fielder and was out. And so on. On the first hitter this day, the wire clicked and the receiving operator, translating for me, somewhat desperately typed out the message: HIT TO SHORT. I assumed the batter had beaten out a grounder to shortstop, and I put him on first base. The second batter came up, and the message was: HIT TO CENTER. It didn't say that the first runner had gone around to third, so I played it safe and held him at second. The third batter was up and the message said: HIT TO THIRD. It didn't say whether it was a bunt, or a topped grounder, or a hit off the fielder's glove, or whether a run had scored. I was greatly perturbed. My every inner sense was telling me that something was sadly amiss, but I didn't know what I could do. Here I was standing in a studio in New York, and the ball game was being played in South Carolina.

Then, stunningly, came the startling announcement that the other team's first batter was up. I had the bases loaded and nobody out and wondering whether the man on third had scored or not, and now, suddenly, I've got a different team at bat. The wire started to click, and it was the same thing, only it went from bad to worse. I finally realized that when this poor inexperienced operator in South Carolina sent HIT TO SHORT he meant the ball had been hit to the shortstop and the short-stop had thrown the batter out at first. Or else he had caught a line drive. Or a pop up. In any case, the batter was out. It wasn't a base hit, and neither were the other two. Knowing that helped, but not much. I couldn't begin to broadcast a ball game from the report that was coming in. I had to quit. We waited a bit, but then I said to the audience, "Folks, I'm very sorry, but we are unable to get the Western Union report on this game," and we packed it in. I walked out of the studio.

It was the only time in my life that I was ever defeated on a broadcast. The studio was upset, and Western Union in New York was wild. But not as wild as I was. I got in touch with the sponsors over at the Knox Reeves advertising agency, which handled the General Mills account, and they were wild. But *they* weren't as wild as I was. After all, I had had the ignominy—and I learned the meaning of the word that day— of starting a baseball broadcast on a fifty-thousand-watt radio station and then having to walk away with three men on base and nobody out and the wrong team at bat in the first inning.

We found out afterward that while the poor fellow in South Carolina was a competent telegrapher, he had never sent a ball game play-by-play before. When we notified Western Union earlier that we were going to broadcast the game, they simply notified their office in whatever town it was to cover it. Period. Well, it was covered.

But it left us with a serious problem. What could we do to avoid a similar disaster in the other towns the ball club would be playing in on the way north? Somebody suggested that we ask Western Union to assign an experienced man to travel with the ball club. But there was so little money involved in baseball broadcasts in those days that it was impossible for Western Union to spend what it would cost to have a special operator travel with the Brooklyn Dodgers for two weeks just to send descriptions of the ball games to the studios in New York. We were stuck. We had to have the broadcasts—they were a tremendous promotional plus for us—but we could not take a chance on another fiasco.

Then I remembered something. I remembered hearing one of the baseball writers who traveled with the Dodgers say once, in passing, that he had put in a lot of years as a telegrapher on a railroad out in the Midwest someplace. It was Roscoe McGowen of the *Times*—and so twice Roscoe figured significantly in this great upsurge of interest in the Dodgers. I suggested we try him. The meeting at Knox Reeves exploded with relief, anxiety, effort. There was a great deal of long-distance phoning back and forth, questions being asked, permission being obtained. Yes, it turned out, Mr. McGowen was indeed a full-fledged dot-and-dash man. And, of course, as was evident, he was a thoroughly experienced baseball man. If anybody knew the Brooklyn Dodgers, Roscoe McGowen did. And yes, for a modest fee, Mr. McGowen would himself send, beginning the very next day, the full Paragraph One report of Dodger games for the rest of the barnstorming trip. He did, and he sent it impeccably, and our broadcasts went over beautifully. That was the beginning of a very warm friendship between Roscoe and me that did not end until his death more than a quarter of a century later. McGowen went through a terrible siege with a desperately ill wife, whom he attended all through her last years, and then he himself put up as game a fight against illness as I've ever known a human being to make. He was dying of cancer and he knew it, but he never quit, never felt sorry for himself, never lost his spirit.

Roscoe saved us in 1939. Without him I don't know what we would have done about getting the Paragraph One games on the air. With him we did, and the public response was excellent. That was a stimulating time, those first few weeks in New York. I was broadcasting. Lylah and I were busy finding a place to live. We were *there*. It was an extraordinary sensation to realize that we were bonafide members of the great metropolitan complex that is New York City. You cannot know what that feels like unless you came, as we did, from far away from New York. It was exciting, very exciting.

The teams came back north and we got ready to open the season, and now the great Giants and Yankees condescended to begin *their* broadcasts. After McPhail broke the radio ban, the Yankees and the Giants joined forces and worked out a combination deal. They would share one station and use the same announcer. The way the major league schedules worked out then, the Giants and Yankees were never home in New York at the same time. They decided they would broadcast all home games from Yankee Stadium when the Yankees were in and all home games from the Polo Grounds when the Giants were in. The man brought in to be principal announcer—for both Yankee and Giant games—was a good man and a good friend of mine named Arch McDonald. Arch had been doing play-by-play in Washington for several years, and before that he had broadcast in Chattanooga. We had known each other well for five years, and we continued to like each other right up to the time Arch suffered a heart attack and died many years later. There was never any antagonism between us, never any *personal* antagonism.

But he was coming in now, ready to broadcast. The season was ready to begin. Then *Time* magazine, which likes to tell the world and the reading public that it covers all the news and covers it better than anybody else, came out with a story just two or three days before Opening Day that I will remember as long as I live. It was in the Radio section of the issue of April 17, 1939. Somebody handed the magazine to me and said, "Here, take a look at this."

There was a story of some length on the coming season and the new broadcasts of the Giants and Yankees in New York—the beginning of baseball broadcasting in New York—and it reported that as of Opening Day in New York all sixteen major league teams would be broadcasting for the first time in history. It said that the broadcaster for the New York teams would be Arch McDonald, and it went on for about a column and a half —the bulk of the story—on how skillful this man McDonald was. They even ran his photograph. *Time* said he was the best, and it went on to tell about the things he had done in Washington, his figures of speech, how he approached a broadcast. It went to some length about how he had challenged certain disreputable and abusive listeners to meet him somewhere and fight. It said the vice president of the United States had called him the world's greatest baseball broadcaster. It was a long and impressively complimentary story about the outstanding new announcer in New York named Arch McDonald.

I got to the end of the piece, and I suddenly realized that this great newsgathering magazine had not even mentioned that there was going to be another broadcast in New York as well, and another broadcaster. It had nothing at all about Brooklyn, much less anything that said a fellow named Red Barber was going to broadcast in Brooklyn.

I don't know when I have ever been as mad. I thought it was the damndest thing I had ever experienced in my life. It's not that I thought *Time* had been kind to McDonald, and unkind to me. Kindness has nothing to do with a news medium. But, as far as I was concerned, *Time* had given me the ultimate insult. It had ignored me. It had ignored Larry MacPhail, the man who was responsible for breaking the radio ban. It had ignored the Dodgers. It had ignored Brooklyn. It had ignored our fifty-thousand-watt radio station. It had ignored the games we had done already during spring training.

When a newsmagazine ignores you completely in a situation like that, they can't do anything more to you. Even if they mention you derogatively they do you a favor—at least you know they know you're alive, and maybe you could even sue them and at least have the satisfaction of getting into a rhubarb. But when they don't even mention your name, that means you don't exist. And to tell that to a human being, especially, a young, excited, ambitious, redheaded one who was taking on the biggest job of his life, you can't do anything worse to him.

Seriously, the theologians say that man's great trouble is when he gets lost from God, when he comes to the conviction that he has no God and is alone in creation, or when he feels that God doesn't know about him or care. A man can stand anything as long as he feels that God knows him and knows where he is. He wants people to know about him, too, and *Time* sure didn't know about me. To be blunt, they didn't know much about Arch McDonald either. Arch was an excellent announcer for certain areas, but not New York City. He couldn't cut a ripple in New York. Arch knew it, and he was unhappy. After one season he went back to Washington. He wanted to go back. He was well liked there, the tempo was slower and the competition was not nearly so aggressive. The sponsors were perfectly willing for him to go and leave the New York scene to other people.

Looking back now, I realize that for all the resentment I felt at the moment, *Time* and Arch McDonald did me a great favor. If I needed anything to lock me into Brooklyn, to make me one with Brooklyn, me, a stranger in the flesh who had drifted within the month into New York and who, when I read the article in *Time*, had been in the borough of Brooklyn only once—I rode out and back on the subway one day, just to see the ball park and look at where I was going to broadcast—if I needed *anything* to make me completely at one with the three million Brooklynites who hated and resented New York and Manhattan and the Giants and the Yankees, this complete rebuff was it. My reaction was pure Brooklyn: "Oh, yeah? I'll show 'em." I started to work harder than I ever thought I could.

With all this resentment and ambition burning in me, I got myself to Brooklyn for Opening Day. The Dodgers were playing the Giants. I hadn't planned to do anything on Opening Day except go over to Ebbets Field, sign the game on the air, broadcast it, and sign off. But after this thing with McDonald and *Time*, I thought, "We've *got* to do something extra." When you're motivated like that you start walking around in a tight circle, thinking. You start asking yourself questions, and you find yourself answering them, aloud. I said, "We got to do something, right?" And I answered, "Right!" Then I went off and got hold of somebody at WOR and asked if I could have ten minutes of extra time before the game began.

They said sure. Everybody was so ecstatically happy about breaking the ice and starting the baseball broadcasts that they would have done anything. Also, air time didn't mean quite so much in those days. They gave me fifteen minutes. They got me a cord with a little microphone on it, and I went down *on* the field with it. That sounds like ho-hum news today, but it was pretty special then. I went to the Giant dugout, and I went to the Brooklyn dugout. And if you like talent, the only people I had on this pregame broadcast were Bill Terry and Leo Durocher. Terry was the big manager in the National League just then; he had won three pennants and a World Series in six seasons. He was also the big villain as far as Brooklyn was concerned because of that crack in 1934. Terry had a reputation for being a cold, tough man, but it was not true. It is always wise, when you hear something about a man, to remember who told you and why he told you. Newspapermen created Terry's reputation. Not all newspapermen—there were plenty who liked and respected him—but enough. Terry didn't get along too well with certain sportswriters for the simple reason that he was a strong man who intended to live his own life on a fairly reasonable schedule. He would not make himself available twenty-four hours a day to newspapermen. Shortly after Terry was named manager of the Giants an important sportswriter said, "I want your home phone number." Terry said, "Why?" The newspaperman said, "If something comes up at an odd hour and I have to reach you, I'll be able to phone you and get your reaction." Terry said, "No, sir. You cannot have my home phone number. I will be here at the ball park every day in plenty of time before the ball game, and I'll stay here after it as late as you fellows want. But when I go home, I go home. That's my private life."

They tell me the newspaperman gasped. Boy, you know that's like withdrawing from the union. The idea of withholding your home phone number from a reporter or a columnist. The effrontery. What a stinker this Terry was.

It's a fairly tight little fraternity, sportswriting, and they pass the word around. That was the start of the disillusionment of the New York press with Terry, and the beginning of his reputation as a sour, uncooperative misanthrope. But I had met Terry when I was broadcasting in Cincinnati, and I had found him to be courteous, pleasant, cooperative, intelligent, anything you want. A fine man. I asked him to come on this broadcast on Opening Day in 1939, and he agreed at once. He talked about his club and the season ahead, and he was excellent.

Then Durocher came on. Remember, this was not only Opening Day, not only the first regular-season broadcast of a Brooklyn game. This was also Leo Durocher's first day as a manager. It was the first regular-season big-league game he had ever managed in. And he couldn't have been better. Leo knew the score. He knew that there were millions of people listening to this broadcast, and he talked to *them*. He talked about his batting order, and about his pitching, and how he was going to run his club, and what sort of a year he hoped to have. He really shone.

That pregame show was important. People *heard* Bill Terry and Leo Durocher. It was something special. It was a rare event. People who heard the pregame broadcast talked about it and they told other people. It got us off to a great start in Brooklyn, and we kept right on going. Any time I got a little tired, I'd think of Arch McDonald and *Time* magazine and I'd say, "Well, now, let's see about that. Let's see which ball club and which broadcast has the public fancy now." And I'd get going again.

When I took the job I knew nothing about Brooklyn. I didn't know where it was. I didn't know that it was a borough, or even that New York City had such things as boroughs. I knew nothing —and that turned out to be a blessing, because I decided I had better start to learn something about the place. Eventually, I made it a point to find out everything I could about it. Whenever we had an off day, Lylah and I would take the baby and jump in the car and drive aimlessly through Brooklyn. We didn't take a map. We just drove, in and out and all around, and I learned about Brooklyn. I got to know it far better than I did any other part of town. When I went to Ebbets Field each day to broadcast, I'd ride the subway and then I'd walk from my subway stop to the ball park. I loved to walk along the streets. I think I really got the feeling of Brooklyn by walking along and talking to the people who stood in front of the stores. I'd stop and visit with them as I made my way to Ebbets Field. I'd go in a delicatessen for a sandwich and a bottle of pop, and I'd talk with the people there as I ate. I began to *know* Brooklyn, the sense of it, the feeling of it, the tempo of it. Later on, when World War II came along and I began to work for the Brooklyn Red Cross, I became totally involved. In time, despite my southern accent, and maybe even because of it, I felt that I was as much a part of Brooklyn as the fellow who had been born there. I didn't broadcast with a Brooklyn accent, but I did broadcast with a Brooklyn heart. I believe this was reflected in the broadcasts, and it may have been one of the reasons why they went over while the Giant-Yankee broadcasts of Arch McDonald did not.

There was another important factor. When the broadcasts began, a lot of the smart fellows on Madison Avenue were arguing that baseball broadcasting could not succeed in a city like New York. They said baseball was basically a small town enterprise, and that it was successful in those cities where the people could associate themselves with the ball clubs and get involved with them, where everybody could develop a home-town rooter feeling for the team. But New York City was much too big and much too important to pay a lot of attention to baseball; it wasn't going to stop its afternoon business to listen to a broadcast. They said there was a certain basic number of fans who went out to the ball park, and that was it. For the rest, there was too much going on in New York. There were too many demands on the people's time. There were radio stations all up and down the dial in New York. A baseball broadcast would be lost, swallowed up. They argued that when people in New York did listen to the radio in the afternoon—there were comparatively few night games then, and television was nonexistent, in a practical sense—it was mostly women who listened, and they listened to the soap operas.

People who are too young to remember that era can't appreciate the hold that the radio soap opera had. Descendants of those early shows live on in television, but they are a comparative handful and whatever their current popularity is, it cannot compare with the impact of the old radio soap operas. The big secret of radio was imagination. It's not stretching things too much to compare it to Shakespeare, who would ask his audience to imagine that the little stage was a vast battlefield in France. His audience would put its imagination to work, and Shakespeare would wow them with his words. In radio, all they had was words, and sound effects. The listener had to supply the rest. You were told that the scene was a living room. *You* had to supply the living room. You knew that this particular actor was the husband; *you* had to imagine what he looked like. As a result, the soap opera was all things to all people—nobody could quibble that an actor didn't look right in the part, or that the stage settings were unreal. It was all in your own mind. Talk about identifying with something; millions and millions of people identified with the soap operas. They were called that because most of them seemed to be sponsored by one or another soap product from Procter & Gamble and the other big companies. There was one fifteen-minute soap opera after another; they came along as though they were being turned out on a production line in a factory. People by the millions listened to them. It was a form of addiction, like taking dope. Housewives arranged their household duties so that they could listen to soap operas as they worked. They got all tangled up with these fictional people and their problems.

So, we were warned that soap operas would be our Waterloo. We were going to find our radio baseball sound waves bouncing into nothingness and back. But it didn't happen that way, and the reason it didn't is because baseball is played by human beings. It is real-life drama. Sometimes it's melodrama. But it's real. Lincoln talked about fooling some of the people all of the time, and all of the people some of the time, but not being able to fool all of the people all of the time. People en masse, without knowing how they know it, know what is true and what is phony. They know what they want, and they know what they don't want. As long as the soap operas were grinding along and there wasn't anything to compete with them, they did fine in their make-believe continuity and agony. The people listened to them and enjoyed them, but down underneath they knew this was just a bunch of actors and actresses and scriptwriters, and a fellow sitting over in the corner of a studio at an electric organ, and another fellow with dulcet, pear-shaped tones selling various soaps and liquids. (I almost said detergents, but this was before anybody ever heard of detergents.)

Then baseball on radio came along, bringing with it not a contrived drama, but actuality. Suddenly—even in the broadcasting booth—you found yourself wondering what was going to happen next. Nobody knew. Nobody knew what was going to happen. This was not made up. This hadn't been ground out in some mill. The emotion was reflected not by an electric organ but by a real, live crowd, yelling and cheering and groaning. It was like magic. It was exhilarating.

They said baseball broadcasts could not compete with soap operas, but they did, right from the first day, and they captured a substantial part of the daytime audience. And the broadcasts from Brooklyn had something beyond the drama of the ball games. They reflected the working, striving, hopeful, fearful, anguished *human* quality that was in the borough. Human beings lived in Brooklyn and came to Ebbets Field. Human beings played in the uniform of the Dodgers, and terrible human things happened to them. The people listening could understand this because, in a sense, it had happened to them. There was a famous expression that Joe Jacobs, the fight manager, came up with one time when he went to a football game. Everything had gone wrong that day, and it wasn't much of a game and, to top it off, it was bitter cold. Jacobs, shivering, said to a sportswriter, "I shoulda stood in bed." Any human being who has tried to make a living in this world knows what he meant. What does the poet say? "Lives there the man with soul so dead, who never to himself has said, 'I shoulda stood in bed.'"

The Dodgers were human. They shoulda stood in bed. They could figure out a new way to lose a ball game better than anyone. That's where they got their famous nickname, "The Bums." No sportswriter hung that one on them. It came from thousands of loving, frustrated fans rising to their feet in disgust and shouting, "You bums!" because the Dodgers had done it again. But the Dodgers could figure out ways to win ball games better than anybody, too. They would lose ball games they weren't supposed to lose, and then beat the tar out of a pitcher that nobody was supposed to beat. Carl Hubbell of the Giants was the great pitcher in the National League in the 1930s—when you came right to it, down to the game you had to win, he was better than Dizzy Dean—but the Dodgers beat him time and time again. Hubbell won twenty-four straight games over two seasons—sixteen at the end of 1937 and eight more at the beginning of 1938, the longest winning streak by any pitcher in the history of baseball— and who do you think beat him in Ebbets Field on Memorial Day to snap that streak? This was a human ball team. They were better than any soap opera.

Everything seemed to happen. In the first year I was there, the Dodgers and the Cubs got locked in an extra-inning game in the middle of May, and it went on and on and on. It went nineteen innings before it ended in a 9–9 tie. It is amazing how a long extra-inning game can hook an audience. Not always in the ball park—there comes a point where a fan *has* to go home, and you usually end up with only a fraction of the original crowd. But on radio—or TV—the audience keeps growing inning by inning. By the time this game ended everybody in New York knew about it. Then, barely a month later, in June, it happened again, only more so. The Dodgers and the Braves played a 2–2 tie that went twenty-three innings. Here was an afternoon game that ended after dinner, if anybody had left the radio long enough to eat dinner. It was typical of what always seemed to happen to the Dodgers in that era. What we were broadcasting was crazy, colorful, stimulating, continually uproarious.

That atmosphere was not reflected in the Giant-Yankee broadcasts. That was partly because the broadcast was divided between two teams and two leagues, which meant that neither Giant fans nor Yankee fans could really feel that this was *their* broadcast. But it was also because the Giants and Yankees weren't the Dodgers. They weren't Brooklyn. They didn't have the human quality that made the Dodgers so universally appealing, and especially when Brooklyn finally started winning. The Dodgers were third in 1939, second in 1940, first in 1941. Here was the poor boy making good. People loved it, from the guy in the candy store on Flatbush Avenue all the way up to world-famous figures like Raymond Gram Swing. Raymond Gram Swing, who was a famous war correspondent for WOR and the Mutual network, flew back from Europe one day in 1941. He had been over there covering World War II. I would say that Mr. Swing was a man devoid of humor, devoid of any penchant for the flip remark. His was an analytical mind always searching for news, for information. He stepped off the plane in New York, just back from Europe and the war, and the first thing he said was, "How did the Dodgers do?" He meant it. He wanted to know. That's how people felt all over the country. They were for Brooklyn. They went to Ebbets Field to see it, and they listened to the broadcasts to hear all of it they could. You could sense it right from the beginning. I can't read the future, but I knew after Opening Day in Brooklyn that we were on our way. We had a Giant-Dodger ball game that day, Ebbets Field, Durocher, Terry. That was drama. The impact of our Opening Day broadcast was such that I was known in that town in twenty-four hours. People were excited. They were interested. They stayed interested.

I must admit, in all candor and despite my personal regard for him, that I felt a great deal of satisfaction when Arch McDonald left New York and went back to Washington after that season. I had shown them. I had shown *Time* magazine. Most of all, I had shown New York.

That was how you got to feel when you became part of Brooklyn.

Between Innings: NATHAN MILSTEIN

My father taught me a regard for self-respect. He would say that he didn't know and couldn't know what I would be when I grew up, or what work I would do, or what people I would be with, or where in the world I would go. But, no matter what I did or who I knew or where I was, every night as long as I lived I would wind up sleeping with myself. In other words, I had to be with *me* all the time, and I'd better be somebody I wanted to be with.

Self-respect is not pride. Pride in the Biblical sense, in the Seven Deadly Sins sense, is an ignorant, overweening, unrealistic evaluation of yourself. You can say, I am proud that I am better than you because my skin is a different color than yours, and right now mine is a more fashionable color. I'm proud that I'm better than you because my name has a simple Anglo-Saxon spelling, whereas your name has a lot of iskis or ettis in it. I'm proud because, as we used to say down south, I wasn't born on the wrong side of the railroad tracks and you were. I'm proud because I am rich, even though I didn't earn a nickel of it and had it left to me, and you're poor and have to wear overalls and live in a cheap shack. Pride, in this Biblical sense, leads you into man's great sin—man thinking he is better than God, that he doesn't need God. That was the sin of Lucifer. It's not just a Christian concept. You find this idea of pride as a sin all through Greek mythology. If mortals put themselves—or even tried to put themselves—equal with, say, Apollo or Diana, terrible things would happen to them.

That's pride. Self-respect is—well, the Greeks taught that you are to see life as it is. That is one of the bases of Socratic philosophy: the ability to see things as they are. Self-respect is simply that you see yourself as you are, and in the Biblical or Christian concept it goes beyond that to not only seeing things as they are but seeing things as they ought to be. Honesty is spiritual.

Now, to be honest about it, I have done some excellent work in my career. I have intended to do excellent work. I don't believe

I have ever done poor work. I have done good work because I have worked hard. I have put in hours. I have gotten to the ball park early. I have done research. I have prepared myself.

In other words, I have done good work by design. I remember meeting Nathan Milstein, the concert violinist, whose daughter was a classmate of our daughter Sarah at the Spence School in Manhattan. I went over to the Milstein apartment one day to pick up Sarah, who was there visiting. Milstein was in another room practicing, but he finished before we left and came out to say hello. In chatting with him I said, "I heard you playing inside. Do you do a great deal of preparation like that before a concert?"

"Oh, yes," he said. "Yes, indeed."

I knew he was about to perform at Carnegie Hall, and I said, "I was just wondering. Are you ever apprehensive as you get ready for a concert? Is there ever a haunting fear in the back of your mind that you might give a bad performance?"

He looked at me coldly and said, "I cannot give a bad performance. I practice sufficiently. I may give a better performance on some occasions than on others, but I *cannot* give a bad performance."

That was not pride. That was not an ignorant evaluation of himself. That was self-respect—earned self-respect. Milstein was assaying the facts. He knew the fingering. He knew the notes. He knew the score. And come what may, he would be ready.

As he said, he might be more inspired on certain occasions, spiritually lifted—though I don't know what goes into giving a more superb performance on the violin at one time than at others. I do know that in my work I could never be a bit better than the ball game. I could go to a ball park completely prepared, and then the pitcher could go three-two on every hitter and walk eight or nine of them and I'd have a dreary 12–1 game on my hands. After a broadcast like that, nobody was going to say, "Gee, what a marvelous announcer Barber is." But you have to be as fully prepared for the dull game as you are for the great one. Or else you won't be prepared for the great one.

A lot of people remember that I broadcast the fourth game of the 1947 World Series when Bill Bevens of the Yankees had a no-hitter with two out in the ninth inning. Then Cookie Lavagetto got the first and only base hit, a double off the right-field wall that drove in two men who had reached base on walks, and just like that Bevens lost not only his no-hitter but the ball game, too. That was a tremendous game, one of the truly unforgettable ones, and it was a game that challenged the worth of a broadcaster. I was able to handle it. It was my work. It was what I prepared for, just as Nathan Milstein prepared for his work.

RED	1	③							
BARBER	2								

Wonderful things kept happening in Brooklyn because Mac-Phail took a very sick ball club, a second-division ball club, and rebuilt it loudly and publicly, as though everybody should be in on the details of the club operation. You picked up the paper or tuned in the radio every day to find out who was still on the club and who had just left. Players kept coming and going, except that now and then one would stick, like Dixie Walker. MacPhail was picking up anybody who breathed, anybody who moved. Dixie had been a promising rookie with the Yankees years before but broke his shoulder. He had had one good year with the White Sox, but then he had moved on to Detroit and failed to impress them there. He was on the bonepile, but he stirred and MacPhail pounced on him. Dixie turned into a great clutch hitter, and he became the most popular player that ever was in Brooklyn. He was just right for Ebbets Field because he was a castoff, a retread, human. It's an interesting thing that Pete Reiser, who won the batting championship in his rookie year in 1941 and who probably was the most gifted ballplayer Brooklyn ever had, never really achieved great popularity. The crowds liked him and appreciated his skills, but I think he was too perfect for them. He didn't catch the crowd's imagination and affection. Later on, of course, Pete kept running into outfield walls and ruined himself as a player, but that only made people feel sad. Walker was more their type. Dixie was a fellow down-and-outer who had made good. He had some sharp, outspoken, public differences of opinion with MacPhail, too, and Brooklyn loved that. Of course, that was characteristic of Mac-Phail—he not only had good fights, he had them publicly.

I know that the only run-in I ever had with Larry was about as public as you could get. He ordered me not to broadcast one day, and he said that if I did he would have me thrown out of the radio booth. I think that's when MacPhail began to have the respect for me that I had always had for him. I don't believe two people can have a deep friendship unless it's based on respect, and I don't believe two people can have real respect for one another until they test each other—get on the opposite sides of the line and look each other in the face, nose to nose. I know that's a basic factor in marriage. Married people can't really get along until they've had some pretty severe, honest disagreements, because that is how you find out who each of you is. You don't find out who a man is if he's always agreeable.

I can say, without fear of contradiction, that MacPhail was not always agreeable, and I can also say that there is nothing in the world that I would not do for him. That big disagreement of ours came the first year I was at Brooklyn. WOR, which was broadcasting the games, had a firm contract that they would not start the Dodger broadcasts before a specific time in the afternoon. They had certain programs scheduled for early afternoon that were extremely valuable. They had big advertisers, lots of money. I can't remember now the exact time specified in the contract, but it's not important. Let's say it was two-thirty. WOR was not to go on the air at Brooklyn before two-thirty, even if a doubleheader started at one o'clock.

All right. That was in the contract, and MacPhail knew it. He didn't like it, but he accepted it, grumbling probably, because he wanted to be on the air all the time. This particular day there was a doubleheader at Ebbets Field—the Giants against the Dodgers, who else?—and it was going to start, let's say, at one-thirty. We would not go on the air until two-thirty, which would be about the fourth or fifth inning of the first game. But about noontime MacPhail learned that WOR was going to cancel the soap opera that was scheduled to go on from two-fifteen to two-thirty in order to present a broadcast by Herbert Hoover, the former President of the United States.

That set MacPhail off. He began roaring that he wanted this entire doubleheader broadcast, or none of it. He told somebody at WOR that he wanted them to come on the air at one-thirty, and whoever it was at WOR said no, they couldn't. They would come on at two-thirty, as scheduled.

Now MacPhail had the bone in his teeth. When he makes up his mind that he wants something, he wants it and he goes after it. He kept hollering that he wanted the air at the beginning of the first game. Contractually, he was dead wrong, but that didn't faze MacPhail. He wasn't listening to anybody. He insisted the whole doubleheader was going to be broadcast. WOR said, "Two-thirty."

I didn't know anything about all this. I was sitting down in the radio booth, going over my notes and my score book. About half an hour before the game was to start somebody came in and said MacPhail wanted to see me in the press room. That was odd. He had never sent for me before. I walked back to the press room, and there was Larry, leaning on the bar.

He started in on me, and he told me in quite a few words that he wanted *both* games broadcast in full, and that WOR said they would *not* come on until two-thirty, but that they were putting on a special *Hoover* broadcast at two-fifteen! It was the Hoover thing that touched him off. If WOR had done nothing different and had gone ahead with the regular schedule, there would have been no reaction.

But when they canceled a soap opera for a special broadcast, MacPhail got sore. If they could cancel a soap opera for a broadcast by Hoover—whether he used to be President or not—why couldn't they cancel soap operas and get on the air over at Brooklyn for his ball games?

He went through all this with me in the press room, how WOR isn't going to come on until two-thirty, and so on, and how he's put out about it, and how he's demanded that they start earlier, and on and on. I listened, but I didn't say a word. It was no battle of mine. I went on the air when the engineer raised his hand and pointed. Until he gave me the signal, I didn't go on. It was as simple as that. I had nothing to do with *when* we went on. I was a broadcaster. My problems started after I got that signal.

MacPhail said, "Now, listen. I'm going to tell you something. If that radio station doesn't come over here for the first batter, you are *not* to broadcast. You are not to go on the air at all today."

"I can't do that, Larry," I said. I was under contract to General Mills and their advertising agency, Knox Reeves. Any orders not to broadcast had to come from them.

"Listen to me. If they put that Hoover broadcast on and then they try to come over here and start at two-thirty, and you *dare* try to broadcast, I'll have you thrown out of that booth."

"Larry," I said, "I'm sorry, but I don't work for you." And I turned and went back to the booth. Five minutes later in came the ball park electrician and another big, hulking fellow who was one of his assistants. They were both very nice fellows. They said hello and I said hello. Then the electrician said, "Mr. MacPhail sent us in here, Red."

"Fine. Make yourself at home."

"No, it isn't that, Red. Mr. MacPhail said if you try to talk into that microphone, we have to pick you up and take you out of the booth."

"All right. You do it."

"Now, Red," they said. "You're making it hard on us."

"I'm not making it hard on you," I said. "Who do you work for?"

"We work for Mr. MacPhail."

"What did Mr. MacPhail tell you to do?"

"He said to pick you up and carry you out if you talk on that microphone."

"Then do it," I said. "Do your work." It was still a long way from two-thirty, but this kept up.

"Red," they said. "You're just making it hard on everybody. All you have to do is not go on the microphone. Then we won't have to carry you out, and everybody will be happy."

I said, "You've told me who you work for—MacPhail. I don't work for him. I work for somebody else. My job is to broadcast when they turn this microphone on, and I'm going to broadcast. That's *my* work. Now, isn't that fair? Isn't that what *I'm* supposed to do? I'll do my work, you do yours. In the meantime, nothing is going to happen around here for at least an hour, so let's watch the start of the ball game. Sit down. Have a cigarette."

The WOR engineer over in the corner had heard all this and, without my knowing it, had phoned master control back at WOR and apprised them of what was going on. It was a holiday and all the big WOR executives were off one place or another, but master control immediately made the decision that until they got further instructions they would not put me on at two-thirty. They didn't want to risk throwing the air to me, and then have me taken forcibly away from the microphone. That would be *heard* over the radio, and they didn't want that. That was the worst sin of all in those days.

I didn't know the engineer had phoned, and I really didn't care. I sat there watching the ball game, and the first half of that doubleheader turned out to be one of the most memorable baseball games I ever saw. Carl Hubbell, beating Brooklyn for a change, faced only twenty-seven batters and gave up just one hit. Johnny Hudson hit a single, the next fellow hit into a double play, and not another Dodger reached first base. Hubbell missed a perfect game by that much. To my recollection, it was the only game I ever broadcast—ever sat in a broadcasting booth and watched, I should say—in which the pitcher faced only twenty-seven men. I didn't broadcast the World Series in which Don Larsen pitched his perfect game.

I sat there, and my electrician friend sat there, and his big burly assistant sat there. I wasn't fooling with that electrician. When the time came I would go on the air, and we'd just have to see what would happen. But as it got close to two-thirty the WOR engineer said to me, "I don't think they're going to switch out to us." Master control was still chasing around, looking for an executive. Finally they found Ted Stribert, the general manager of the station, playing golf someplace over in New Jersey. He got off the course fast, put a phone call through to MacPhail, and quickly smoothed things out. That was all MacPhail really wanted, that extra attention. He wound up with the station begging him to let them come back on the air and broadcast the second game—which they had every contractual right to do. Larry very graciously let them.

That was the end of that. Once it was apparent that WOR wasn't coming on at all for the first game, the electrician and his helper left and I sat back and watched Hubbell pitch to his twenty-seven men. I died all the way through it, too, because I wanted to detail that great game over the air, and I couldn't. Hubbell was something to see that day. He was a masterful pitcher any time, but that day he was at his very best. It wasn't that the Dodgers were hitting an occasional line drive and the Giant fielders were catching them. Except for Hudson's little hit, Hubbell didn't let anybody do anything. It was an absolutely beautiful game, the most impeccable pitching job I ever saw.

During it, I was duly informed that the thing with MacPhail had been straightened out and that we would go on the air with the second game. It was routine. We broadcast, and I didn't say anything to Larry afterward and he didn't say anything to me. Our relationship went on just as warmly as ever.

But just about a year or two ago, Larry and I were at a cocktail party down on Key Biscayne. Larry was renting a house there, and we were around together a lot, playing golf and so forth. He is an amazing man. He had an operation for cancer of the throat and beat it: he had an operation for cancer of the intestines twice and beat it: he had open heart surgery and beat that. I don't know what else he has had. He's up in his late seventies, and we played eighteen holes of golf and I swear he is younger than I am. His voice is strong, and he's still on his way. He's up at four or five in the morning to go see about his horses. He's here, he's there. He has a great deal of strength left and I think it's because he never wasted any of it looking back.

That's why that don't-you-broadcast-today thing in Brooklyn never caused any strain between us—Larry never bothered to go back to it. You didn't have go-backs with MacPhail. You kept going on. As far as he was concerned, we went on the air and broadcast the second game, and that was that. But down at Key Biscayne at this cocktail party, a group of us were sitting around talking and suddenly Larry laughed and said, "Do you know what this man did to me once? He almost made me throw him out of a broadcasting booth." He laughed again and said, "I really hadn't noticed him very much until then. But all of a sudden he bowed his neck at me."

In other words, while I had always had great respect for him, that's when he finally realized that maybe I was old enough to shave and vote, too.

That same year, 1939, here and there you would hear somebody talk about television. Television then was on about the same level of speculation as a trip to the moon is now. It was feasible, within reach, about to happen, actually happening, but, even so, it was still away out in the future. People would say, "Boy, this television, that's going to be something. Pictures on the air! Pictures on your radio!"

I didn't know anything about television, and I didn't even think anything about it. But there was a man in Manhattan named Alfred H. Morton. Doc Morton, everybody called him. He was a vice president at NBC, and I had met him when I had come to New York a year or so earlier to talk about going to work for NBC. That didn't work out, but Morton wrote me a very nice letter after my visit and he and I became good friends. Now he was in charge of NBC's infant television operations, and I mean infant. This was a little tiny baby that was cute, but nobody took its gurgling very seriously.

Doc Morton phoned me in July, or it might have been the beginning of August. This is really a laugh when you think of the way television, more than any other factor, now controls baseball and football and everything in sports; television is *it*; you cannot begin to talk about sports today unless you start with television. But Alfred H. "Doc" Morton, vice president of the National Broadcasting Company in charge of television, phoned me in the summer of 1939 and in a hopeful voice, yet a voice that really did not have too much hope in it, asked, "Red, do you think there is any chance at all that Larry MacPhail *might* let us do a television broadcast of a ball game from Ebbets Field?"

Isn't that a beginning for the story of television in major league baseball? Or for professional sports? "Do you think he *might . . . ?"

"Doc," I said, "I don't know, but I'll find out."

"Would you, Red? Would you undertake this for me?"

"Why, Doc," I said, "for you I will."

And for him I went to see MacPhail. I was curious anyway. I have always tried to study people that I have been associated with, not to learn coldly how to motivate them, but because I feel that the way to get along with people, from your wife on down, is to understand them. You have to know what they are like so that you won't step on their particular corns. You give them the courtesy of thinking about them, rather than just thinking about yourself. In being around Larry MacPhail, it became rapidly apparent to me that one of the things he dearly loved was to be first. He particularly loved to be first in something new and constructive, the way he was first with a season-ticket plan, first with night ball, first with a radio broadcast in New York. He had a lot of firsts. He liked that; he still likes it. And I think it's great. It's the mark of a man who is alert and alive, willing to get up and do something, a man who moves. You lose once in a while, but that's okay. If the percentage is right, make the move.

That was MacPhail. So it was obvious to me that if you wanted to get him to do something, all you had to do was show him how he could be first in it. I dropped by to see him at the Dodger offices at 215 Montague Street. He looked up at me when I walked into his office. He studied me. Right away, it was a contest.

"You've put in a few months here," he said, "and the only time I've seen you is when I've run into you at the ball park. What are you doing over here? What do you want?"

I sat down and said, "I don't want anything, Larry."

"What did you come here for?"

"I wanted to know if you wanted something."

"What are you talking about?"

I said, "Larry, would you like to be the first man ever—ever in history—to put on a television broadcast of a major league baseball game?"

He said, "Yes."

That was all. MacPhail didn't believe in beating around the bush.

NBC came in to Ebbets Field and telecast the first game of a doubleheader between the Dodgers and the Reds in August of 1939. The fee that MacPhail demanded for the rights to that historic telecast was that Doc Morton would use his influence and the influence of NBC to arrange for a television receiving set —they were rare items—to be placed in the press room at Ebbets

Field so that while the first telecast of a major league game was going on, MacPhail and the sportswriters and a few other people could watch it.

I didn't see it. I couldn't, because I was doing the telecast. I didn't broadcast from a booth. I sat out in the open in a box in the upper deck in back of third base, right in there with the fans. I had earphones on that were connected with the director down in the truck. The camera—I forget now whether there was one camera or two—was in the upper deck. I do remember that I had to guess which way the camera was pointing, and I never knew for sure what was on the picture. There was no monitor—this was years before anyone ever dreamed of a monitor. Burke Crotty was the director, and every once in a while he would holler at me through the earphones that the camera was on second base now or it was on the pitcher. But only once in a while.

We had commercials, too, and to the best of my knowledge they were the first commercials ever done on television. Nobody paid a fee for them; it was simply that the three sponsors of the Dodger radio broadcast—Wheaties, Mobiloil and Ivory Soap —were given one message apiece over television as a courtesy for letting NBC put the telecast on. I called television an infant earlier. I was wrong. It wasn't an infant. It wasn't even a baby being born. This was a fetus, just beginning to develop. Think of the time and money spent now on preparing TV commercials. Back there in 1939, I did all three commercials on the spur of the moment, off the cuff. They put the camera on me, and I held up a box of Wheaties and poured them in a bowl. I took a banana and a knife, and I sliced the banana onto the Wheaties. Then I poured in some milk and said, "That's the Breakfast of Champions." For Mobiloil, I put on a Mobil service station cap and held up a can of oil. For Ivory Soap, you'll never guess what I held up. Right. A bar of Ivory Soap. All three commercials were done completely ad lib. Not a cue card in sight.

They didn't telecast the second game of the doubleheader, but between games we ran a microphone down on the playing field and put the camera on some of the players while I interviewed them. We had Leo Durocher—naturally—and Dolf Camilli of the Dodgers and Bill McKechnie, manager of the Reds, and Bucky

Walters, his great pitcher. They were the first managers and players to be interviewed on TV, and I suppose you could call it the first postgame show ever on television. I recall very distinctly that I got Dolf Camilli to show his hands on camera. I had always been much impressed with the size, the agility, the dexterity, the grace, the beauty, the strength of Camilli's hands. I remember when we were in spring training in Havana one year they took some of us out to a zoo where there was a big gorilla throwing himself around the cage and cutting up and showing off. He was impressive, but as we stood there I said, "Dolf, that gorilla looks rough, but I bet it would be a pretty good contest between the pair of you if you could get your hands on him." Dolf said, very simply, "Yes. If I could get my hands on him, I think I could hold him." They were magnificent hands.

In 1966, at an Old Timers' Day in Yankee Stadium, Camilli and I were standing there talking when all of a sudden he said, "Red, do you remember in Brooklyn when they had the first telecast, and you asked me to show my hands?" I was very pleased that he remembered.

Between Innings: THE PRECISE MOMENT

If I had to set a precise moment when I knew without question that the Dodger broadcasts were a success and that I was in, it would be a few weeks after Opening Day. General Mills was the key sponsor of the broadcasts, and Cliff Samuelson, who had come from Minnesota, was their big man in New York. Cliff had been the leading figure in working out the broadcasting deal with MacPhail, as well as with the two New York clubs, and he rode herd on the broadcasts at the start. Cliff and Brad Robinson of the Knox Reeves agency had offices in the Chanin Building, across 42nd Street from Grand Central Station. Once the broadcasts got going, Cliff and Brad really didn't have too much to do, but they set up a routine in which they had the broadcasters come into the office every morning. They had Al Helfer and me from Brooklyn. They had Earl Harper, who was broadcasting minor league games from Newark across the river in New Jersey. They had, in effect, two sets of broadcasters from the Yankees and Giants: Arch McDonald and one associate from Yankee Stadium, and Arch and his other associate from the Polo Grounds. They wanted all of us to stop in at the office in the Chanin Building every morning before we went out to the ball park. You'd sit around and wait, and then they'd bring you in and make out like they had something to talk with you about. After the game, in the afternoon, they wanted you to come back by the office again. Usually they'd want you to call your wife and tell her that you wouldn't be home for dinner because you had to stay in town to discuss the broadcasts with Cliff and Brad. So you'd stay in town and have a couple of drinks and eat dinner and talk and get home later.

This went on for a while, and I began to get angry about it. I might add that my better nine-tenths wasn't too happy either, sitting out in Scarsdale with these calls coming at her that I'd be home later on and never mind holding dinner. When I give my word, it's pretty important to me, and the day I gave my word before God and about fifty friends and got married, I swore a very solemn oath and somehow or other it stuck. I've always believed that I should go from my house to my job, and when my work was finished I should go back to my house. I felt I was now being asked to do more than I had a right to be asked. There was no reason for me to come in and sit around that office in the morning before I went to the ball park, and for coming back in the afternoon, and for staying in town for drinks and dinner.

The thing came to a head, and I made up my mind. I went into the office in the Chanin Building one morning, and I said hello to the secretary. She said, "Hello, Red," and indicated with a toss of her head that I was to go over and sit on a chair against the wall and wait until one of the great men decided he wanted to tell me nothing. That was the standard procedure.

I said, "I want to see Cliff."

"He's busy," she said.

"He's not that busy," I said. "I've got to see him now. Right now."

She opened a door and there was Cliff sitting behind a desk, and he wasn't doing nothin'. I walked in and said, "Cliff, I have to get something straightened out. What did you bring me to New York for?"

"Why, to broadcast the Brooklyn games, Red."

"That's what I thought. But I've found out that there is another dimension to this that I never contracted for."

He said, "What do you mean?"

"This thing of coming in to the office every morning and hanging around for an hour, and then coming back to the office again after the ball game, when I've done my day's work and I'm tired. And this other thing of being constantly heckled about staying in town for drinks and dinner with you and Brad. Look, Cliff, I'm perfectly happy to do all the work it takes to do this job right, and if you have something important to tell me about the broadcasting job, I'll come into the office at three-thirty in the morning, if you want. I'll get out of a sickbed, *if* it's something that has some bearing on the job. But if it's this thing we have now, where I come in here for no reason in the morning and again for no reason in the afternoon, then you have the wrong boy. Because I am not going to do it."

Cliff got a little red in the face, and he sent for Brad Robinson. Let me say that I don't know what Cliff is doing right now; I

haven't seen him for a few years. But Brad went into World War
II and I understand he had a very rough time. After it he made
a sizable readjustment—I'd say a complete rearrangement—of his
life. From a fellow who didn't want to go home in the evenings,
he turned into a man who came out of World War II and went
into the ministry. When he was ordained as an Episcopalian
priest, I was invited by Bishop Keller of Minnesota to attend the
ordination, and I wish I could have gone. I was working baseball
and could not. But I was delighted for Brad, and I bring this
in because I think people are usually much nicer and finer than
they sometimes appear to be. Cliff and Brad weren't being
maliciously thoughtless; but they were strangers in New York,
and, after all, there wasn't much they could do about the broadcast of a ball game. Once the thing went on the air the announcer had to do it. I imagine it was a pretty lifeless office, and
having the announcers in a couple of times a day gave Samuelson
and Robinson a feeling of accomplishing something.

But whatever the reason was, it didn't fit in *my* schedule, and
I made my little speech. When Robinson came in, Samuelson
said, "Brad, Red says he isn't going to come in here before the
ball game and after the ball game unless there's something specific
we want to see him about."

Robinson was taken aback and he cried a little about that, but
then he said, "Well, of course, Red, you do have a different job
from the other fellows. You have that long subway ride out to
Brooklyn. And, anyway, the broadcasts are going very well over
there. Larry MacPhail is happy. WOR is happy. We're happy. So
I guess there really isn't any need now for you to be coming in.
If something really important comes up, we'll let you know. We
know you'll come in then, and we'll appreciate it."

I said fine.

"One other thing," he said. "Do me a favor. You don't have
to come in, but don't tell the other fellows. Okay?"

If I needed pinpoint documentation that the broadcasts in
Brooklyn were on the main line and breezing along, that did it.
That's when I knew. I walked out and went down the elevator
and got on the subway, and while the subway was taking me out
to Ebbets Field I *knew* I was on my way—and to something more
than just a ball game that day.

RED	1	3							
BARBER	2	(4)							

The first years in Brooklyn culminated in the great Dodger pennant of 1941. I don't wish to go into too much detail about that pennant. For those who were around then, I want to mention only the highlights, which should be sufficient, because when there are still embers alive in the ashes of memory it takes only a few gusts of wind to fan them into a living flame again. For those who were not around then, I would say only that the season of 1941 merits a book all by itself and cannot be treated in sufficient detail here.

Brooklyn had not won a pennant since 1920, and in the World Series that year the Dodgers—or Robins, as they were called— had been humiliated. They lost to Cleveland five games to two (that was in the brief era of best five-out-of-eight Series), and they looked bad doing it. Their great spitball pitcher, Burleigh Grimes, was hit from here to yonder, and later on came the disclosure that one of the Dodger infielders had unconsciously tipped off the Indians whenever Grimes got set to throw his spitter. The shortstop would see the catcher's sign, know that a spitball had been called for, and would reach down for a handful of dirt so that he'd have no trouble handling the slippery ball if it was hit to him. If the catcher did not sign for the spitball, the infielder wouldn't bother about the dirt. The Cleveland club quickly picked this up, and it was an important reason why Grimes had such a terrible time.

In that Series the Dodgers hit into the only triple play ever made in a World Series, and to make it a bit more humiliating it was an unassisted triple play. In the same game, the Dodgers gave up the first grand slam home run in World Series history. All in all, it was an abysmal experience. So in 1941, Brooklyn not only had the bitter realization that it had not won a pennant in 21 years, it had also the embarrassing memory of that World Series.

But now the Dodgers were rising. They had finished an on-rushing third in 1939; they had been a solid second in 1940. MacPhail was building a healthy, growing-ever-stronger, brawling, very human ball club. Most of the players, like Dixie Walker, had come in from other teams via deals and purchases engineered by MacPhail. Some had been rescued from oblivion; others were recognized stars. Mickey Owen, from the Cardinals, was the catcher; Camilli, who had played with the Cubs and the Phillies, was at first base; Billy Herman, late of the Cubs, was at second; Durocher, who had been with the Yankees, the Reds, and the Cardinals, had been both the playing manager and the shortstop, though more and more in 1940 and 1941 he turned the shortstop responsibility over to a youngster named Pee Wee Reese, whom MacPhail had bought from the Red Sox farm system. Cookie Lavagetto, who had played for the Pirates, was at third base. Joe Medwick, from the Cardinals, was in left field; Pete Reiser, winning the batting championship as a rookie, was in center; Walker, the American League discard, was in right. Whitlow Wyatt, the team's big pitcher, a twenty-two-game winner that year, had been with the Tigers, the White Sox, and the Indians. Kirby Higbe, another twenty-two-winner, had followed the Camilli route from the Cubs through the Phils to Brooklyn. Fred Fitzsimmons had come from the Giants a few years earlier. Hugh Casey, a big, rough Southerner who had had a brief trial with the Cubs, was the principal relief pitcher. There were others, many others, who contributed to this colorful team's success.

Cincinnati had won in 1939 and again in 1940. The Dodgers gave them a contest in 1940, not one that too seriously worried the Reds but one that was a very plain straw in the wind. This was a sleeping giant waking up in Ebbets Field, and MacPhail did everything he could to help it flex its muscles. He had made Durocher the manager, and he could not have made a more astute choice. Durocher had the toughness and the ferocity and the pugnacity and the verbal strength to control this gang of hungry old professionals.

It was a rough pennant to win. I haven't dug into any record books to refresh my memory of that season, and I don't want to. I don't want my own memory of what happened to become dusted over with the facts and figures listed in dry columns of type. This is just one man's memory speaking now. It may be quite fallible, but it is a very warm and vibrant memory. I know that Brooklyn went into the season with its mind directed toward beating Cincinnati. But when the reality of the season came into focus, it turned out that the Cardinals were the team to beat. Cincinnati was still strong; any time you had fellows like Paul Derringer and Bucky Walters pitching for you, it took a good deal more than a slap on the wrist to put you out of contention. But, nonetheless, it was the young, rising St. Louis club—which added a kid outfielder named Stan Musial to its roster late that season—that fought the Dodgers to the wire. The Dodgers got the lead, but the Cardinals kept coming, faster and faster.

If anyone becomes at all curious about that season, he ought to go back and look up one game, because the pennant race came to its climax in one series and, finally, in one day, one ball game, the last game of the last series Brooklyn had in St. Louis that year. The Dodgers were being closely pursued and had been fighting off their pursuers, but this is where they stopped and turned and fought it out. This was it. If Brooklyn lost and reeled out of St. Louis, everybody—including the Dodgers—knew that the Cardinals would keep right on coming and trample them. The Cardinals had to be stopped. The Dodgers had to win.

It was a rough, raw showdown from every standpoint. Oh, it was rough. It was in that series in St. Louis that Fred Fitzsimmons, fat and past forty, went to the mound and won a ball game in which he probably had less stuff than he ever had in his pitching career. But Fitzsimmons was a strong man physically, and he was a violent man with a flaming temper. He was old but he was angry, and that great body of his, like a big round bear, was ready.

Fitzsimmons was near the end of his career, and this was deadly serious business to him. He *had* to win. All the Dodgers felt that way. They had been around, most of them. They were tough and hardbitten, and they wanted this pennant. They didn't intend to let it get away. Fitzsimmons, with nothing on the ball, pitched with his mouth and his anger and his spirit. He yelled at the Cardinals from the pitcher's mound. He cursed and threatened and ranted, and on sheer, spiritual, profane, vocal guts he convinced them that they had better not take a toehold and a big swing against him. The Cardinals were a rising club of marvelous players, but they were young, and this cursing, raging, tough old man on the pitcher's mound confused them. Johnny Mize was playing first base for St. Louis, and John was an easygoing, amiable fellow if ever there was one. Fitzsimmons threw at Mize and swore at him and kept it up until Mize finally backed out of the batter's box and called out, "Fred, I'm not mad at you." The Cardinals kept waving flags of truce all afternoon; but the belligerence and hostility of the Dodgers was genuine. They weren't behaving like a bunch of pleasant fellows who, if they happened to win and get into the World Series, would have a little more money in the bank than the fellows who didn't win. This wasn't just another series of games to them. There was nothing of the computer about it—no figuring out the combination of wins and losses needed to clinch the pennant, no counting the number of games left to play, no magic numbers. This was a showdown for the pennant, right now in St. Louis. These were lusty, hungry human beings. That pennant was theirs, and they were going to get it. This was a *fight*. That was the feeling that was transmitted to the country. It was everybody's fight because everybody wanted Brooklyn to win.

Fitzsimmons beat off the Cardinals and stopped them with help from Casey, and now it came to the final game of the series, the big one, the one they both had to win. Just before the Dodgers had left for St. Louis, Bill Corum wrote a column in the New York *Journal-American*. He called it an open letter to Leo Durocher. Leo had decided to put himself in at shortstop and bench Reese. This was partly at MacPhail's urging. Leo was a superb fielder and a magnificent competitor, and MacPhail wanted him in there. Reese was just a slender kid who had showed up in training camp looking so young and blond and skinny that Senator John Griffin, the veteran clubhouse man of the Dodgers, wouldn't let him into the locker room. Griffin thought Reese was a kid trying to get in close to the players, and he chased him away. Pee Wee had to go find a club official to tell Griffin who he was. He was a boy, and he hadn't been in anything like this pennant race before. Leo had been with the Yankees, and he had played shortstop for the Gas House Gang. He didn't know anything but tough, no-holds-barred baseball.

But there comes a time when a man's reflexes are tempered and slowed. The mind is still quick, but the muscles are just a split second late responding to the call. So Bill Corum wrote his open letter to Durocher. This is not exact now, but it is the gist of what Corum said: "Dear Leo, We all want you to win this pennant. It's great, and we're behind you, and so forth. And you've been a great shortstop in your day. But, Leo, you can't win the pennant out there in St. Louis playing shortstop. You've got to let this kid do it. For better or worse, whether you win it or lose it, he is going to have to do it for you."

I can't be positive that Corum's column was the reason, but in St. Louis, Leo did what Corum had suggested. Bless Leo's heart, nobody has ever accused him of being a small man. He may have committed a few sins here and there, but if he did they were big ones, because Leo doesn't do anything in a small way. He is a big man, and if you look it up you will find that Reese played more shortstop out there in St. Louis than Leo did, and when the final, last, showdown game came along, Reese was in the starting lineup.

Billy Southworth of the Cardinals had his big righthander, Mort Cooper, rested and ready. He was tough. Durocher had his man ready: Whitlow Wyatt. Wyatt was just as tough. He was the only fellow I ever heard of who, in full view of the public, deliberately flattened Joe DiMaggio with a pitch in the World Series. DiMaggio was noted for his restraint, his lack of obvious emotion, but he was visibly upset by that one. When he got a hit later, he hollered something at Wyatt from second base and Wyatt hollered back, and but for the intervention of the umpires they would have tangled right there in a World Series between the mound and second base. DiMaggio was a great, revered ballplayer, but Wyatt was great, too, that year. Billy Herman, who played on four pennant winners and in ten All-Star Games, told me that in 1941 Whitlow Wyatt was the best pitcher for one year he ever saw. Wyatt had had a lot of injuries during his career and a lot of problems. He had had a sore arm and had had his knees operated on. He had bounced around the American League for nine years and had a career record of twenty-six wins and forty-three defeats when MacPhail picked him off the bonepile. He was ready to pack it in; he didn't want to pitch any more. But Larry persuaded him to give it one more shot.

Now here he was in this game in St. Louis, his big moment after all the years of frustration. His opponent was bigger, younger, and stronger, but Wyatt was determined not to let the game get away from him. The Dodgers, up first, didn't score. The Cardinals came up, and they didn't score. The Dodgers got up in the second, again no score. The Cardinals came to bat again. Frank Crespi hit a ground ball to shortstop, to Reese, the youngster. Pee Wee threw the ball wild past Camilli at first and Crespi went on down to second. The next batter hit another grounder to Reese, and for some reason Crespi didn't hold at second. He took off for third base and Reese threw to third in an attempt to catch him. But the ball hit Crespi and he was safe, and the batter went all the way to second. Two routine ground balls to the shortstop, but instead of having two men out and nobody on, Wyatt had nobody out and Cardinals on second and third.

He struck out the next two men and got the third on a pop foul. That was Wyatt. He kept the game scoreless, he settled the ball club down and he settled Reese down. And he continued to keep the Cardinals scoreless inning after inning. As for Mort Cooper, he was not only keeping it scoreless, he was keeping it hitless. They went into the eighth inning o–o, and the Dodgers still didn't have a hit. That might have been killing if they had been weaker fellows. Cooper got the first man out in the eighth, but then Dixie Walker—who was called the People's Choice for continually doing precisely what he did now —belted a double to right for the first Dodger hit of the game.

When Dixie got to second base, he didn't stop to pat himself on the back and applaud himself for getting the first hit off Cooper. He didn't prance around off the base to show people what an alert baserunner he was. He was thinking about one thing—winning the ball game and the pennant—and he did all that a runner at second base could possibly do. He took a little lead and looked in at the catcher, who was Mort Cooper's brother Walker, and Dixie stole the sign. You hear a lot about signs being stolen in baseball, though there is not as much of it going on as fellows write about and as people talk about. But right then there was a sign stolen, and nobody can ever accurately appraise how much that stolen sign was worth. A pennant? Sure, and a share in the World Series for all the Dodgers. But how can you measure the gratification, the satisfaction, the thrilling feeling of success that it was to give the three million people living in the borough of Brooklyn? And, for that matter, the countless millions around the country who were rooting their hearts out for the Dodgers?

Walker Cooper, the catching brother, signaled Mort Cooper, the pitching brother, to throw a curve ball, and Dixie got it. Billy Herman was at bat, and he and Dixie had signals worked out between them for a situation like this. Dixie flashed the curve ball sign to Herman, and Billy, who was as sharp and quick as any ballplayer who ever lived, caught it. Billy played the game with his wits; he didn't miss things like that. But he *was* surprised. Billy has big brown eyes, almost pop eyes. Dixie said later, and he put his head back and laughed as he did, "When I gave Herman the curve ball sign, those eyes of his bugged six inches out of his head." Sure enough, Mort Cooper threw the curve, Billy's eyes bugged out a little farther, and he hit the curve ball for a double. Boy, you didn't give Billy Herman a curve ball sign for nothing. Walker scored and the Dodgers won that intensely important ball game, 1–0, because nobody was going to score off Wyatt that day.

That was the pennant. Brooklyn was never headed thereafter. The clinching, which came later on in Boston, was almost an afterthought. They were still fighting, though. They never relaxed. They went into Philadelphia to play the Phillies, who were a terrible last-place ball club, and Durocher was so wrought up that he wouldn't shave. Leo! Old Dapper Dan! He was going around the City of Brotherly Love unshaven. He said he wasn't going to shave until the pennant was clinched. They had a doubleheader in Philadelphia, and the Dodgers won the first game. Luke Hamlin started the second. He was called Hot Potato Luke, and he must have thrown a hot potato that day. In the first inning he got the bases loaded and then somebody hit a grand-slam home run. The Dodgers lost, and Durocher nearly died. Lose to the Phillies? Leo was furious. Hamlin never pitched another game for the Dodgers. He was gone to Pittsburgh the next season, and I don't know where from there. And before the Dodgers could get out of Philadelphia, Leo, still raging, took violent objection to something that a newspaper reporter said, and he hit him.

Those were turbulent days. I remember an incident in Pittsburgh on that last western trip, in which Hugh Casey, the relief pitcher, was involved. Casey was a mean, rough man. It's an old line now in baseball, but I truly believe that if it meant something in a ball game Casey would not only have knocked his own mother down with a pitch, he would have hit her—and in the head. He did not care for man or devil. He didn't even care for himself, as he proved several years later, after he was out of baseball, when he stuck a shotgun in his mouth, pulled the trigger, and blew himself into eternity. In Pittsburgh, Casey and Durocher got in a ferocious argument with George Magerkurth, who was umpiring behind the plate. Magerkurth called a balk on Casey, and Casey said Magerkurth was wrong. Leo joined Hugh in presenting the Dodgers' case, which was not in concord with Magerkurth's opinion. They finally resumed play, but Casey was so mad that he deliberately threw *at the umpire*. He gave his catcher instructions to stay low, and he threw a high pitch right at Magerkurth. He didn't hit him—Magerkurth was too alert—but Casey tried.

Durocher was thrown out of the game, and he had to sweat it out in the clubhouse. They didn't have television in the clubhouse then, they didn't even have a radio, at least not in the visitors' quarters, so Leo had no way of knowing what was happening on the field. Pittsburgh had a little utility infielder named Alf Anderson, who was not the sort of player you would ordinarily remember. He appeared in only a handful of games in 1941 and 1942, but there is no reason at all to remember him as a ballplayer—except for what he did this day. Leo, tossed out of the game, was raging around the clubhouse, furious. The game ended, the Dodgers came filing in and Leo yelled, "What happened?"

Someone said, "The Pirates won."

"*How?*" Leo demanded.

"A triple and then a fly ball."

"A *triple?* Who hit it?"

Whoever it was answered, "Anderson."

When Leo heard that—the idea of *Alf Anderson* hitting a triple to beat the Dodgers—he turned and they tell me he actually, physically, destroyed the interior of that clubhouse, windows, benches, everything. They say that no clubhouse was ever torn up by an angry manager the way Durocher tore that one up that day. All because Alf Anderson hit a triple, maybe the only triple of his major league career.

But that's how important each game was to the Dodgers. This is how they fought and how they felt about every win and every loss. The country watched, fascinated. It was as though there was a free-for-all fight surging up and down the street in front of your house, and you were sitting on the front porch watching it.

The Dodgers won that pennant and went into the World Series against the Yankees. They lost, four games to one, but that had to be the closest four-to-one Series ever played. Brooklyn lost the first game but came back to win the second behind Wyatt. In the third game Fitzsimmons went against Marius Russo, a fine left-hander with the Yankees. With his stuff, Fitz was the equal of anybody, and he had it that day. He and Russo each pitched scoreless ball for seven innings. What happened then was, again, typical of the *human* things that kept occurring to and around this ball club.

In the seventh inning, with two out, Russo came to bat. He was an excellent hitter for a pitcher, and he lashed a hard line drive back at Fitzsimmons. Fred was the best fielding pitcher we had in the league then, but perhaps at his age his reflexes were getting a little slow. The line drive hit him on the knee.

It ricocheted over to Reese at shortstop, who threw to first in time to get Russo for the last out of the inning, but Fitzsimmons' kneecap was broken, and they had to carry him off. Hugh Casey warmed up hurriedly and came in to pitch in the eighth inning, but he couldn't hold the shutout and the Yankees won 2–1.

Then, the next day, came the Mickey Owen game. The Dodgers were ahead 4–3 with two out in the ninth, bases empty, two strikes on Tommy Henrich, and Casey, relieving again, was pitching beautifully. He threw a curve—the best curve Casey ever threw—and struck Henrich out. But Owen missed the ball. It went back to the screen and Henrich got to first base. The Yankees rallied, scored four runs, and won the ball game. And they didn't win just the ball game. That was the whole ball of wax. Instead of the Series being all tied at two games apiece, the Yankees had a three-to-one edge. They wrapped it up the next day, and the great season was over.

I remember, after the Owen game, seeing MacPhail standing in the clubhouse crying unashamedly. It's a terrible thing to see a grown man, a strong man, cry like that. He had worked so hard, he had fought so much, and he had come so far. And then by a quirk of fate, he had had the final victory snatched away from him. Of course he cried. Mickey Owen cried. This wasn't just a game they were playing. This was everything.

As for Durocher, I think he reached his finest moment because of that game. Leo is a much maligned man, and while I do admit he gives them ammunition I happen not to agree with the maligners. In Pittsburgh that time, after Alf Anderson's triple, Leo tore up the clubhouse out of sheer, outraged frustration; he was railing at fate. But that was only one ball game, and as it turned out it didn't cost the Dodgers the pennant. The Mickey Owen game cost them the World Series, yet Leo took that much greater defeat with courage and class, and for the life of me I have never understood why the newspapermen have never written much about it—if they ever wrote about it at all. To me, it is the sort of thing, tied in as it is with one of the memorable moments in baseball history, that should have been written then and rewritten time and time again. A few months after the Owen incident they had a showing in New York of the World Series motion picture that Lew Fonseca puts together. It was shown in the New Yorker Hotel that year, and all the baseball writers in town were there. There are several baseball functions during the winter, where they have free whiskey and free food, and the writers don't miss them. They're always there.

Leo was there, too. He hadn't been around town since the Series, but he came back in for this. So it wasn't that he'd been around and had had people talking to him continually, rehashing the game and the Mickey Owen play. He was fresh copy—as he always is. After the motion picture was over the writers naturally centered in on Leo, who was always quotable, and they got to talking back and forth, and of course they were talking about that third strike. There had been a lot of discussion about the pitch, and it boiled down to a few questions. Did Casey throw a spitter? Did he cross up Owen? Whose fault was it that the Dodgers lost the game and the Series?

Leo said, "I've talked this over with Mickey and I've talked it over with Hugh. From what they tell me, Owen called for a curve ball and that's what Casey threw. Hugh just got a little more on the pitch than Owen expected. It wasn't anything more than a simple mechanical error. It was a tough pitch to handle, a curve breaking low, right down on the ground. Maybe the fault was Henrich's, the fact that he even swung at it. Nobody ever said anything about that. That wasn't a pitch right over the plate. It was a curve down around his shoes. You could see it in the pictures. Owen was down there on the ground, back of Henrich's feet. He was down to his bare right hand grabbing for it, and he just didn't come up with it. There wasn't anything mysterious about it."

Leo lifted his voice and jabbed his finger at the writers and he said, "Now, I'll tell you something. If you fellows really want to get to the reason why we lost that game, you shouldn't be writing about Owen and Casey. That was a physical thing; errors happen. What you should be writing about is me. Look. After Henrich went to first, Joe DiMaggio singled, and then Charlie Keller came up, right?" Only Leo didn't say Joe and Charlie, because when he got in high gear he didn't waste time on first names. Stengel, when he got in high gear, didn't waste time on any names at all. Leo said, "We got two quick strikes on Keller, and that meant we were right there again, only one strike away from winning, right? And then what did Keller do? He hit a ball off the screen for a double, two runs score, and we're behind. *But Casey had two strikes on Keller.* My mistake was, for the first time in my life in a spot like that I didn't get off the bench and go out to the mound and talk to my pitcher. In a spot like that, when my man has two quick strikes on the hitter, I *have* to get off the bench and go out there. I have to slow him down, stop him, talk to him. I have to say 'Look. We got him where we want him. Now that we got him there, we're not going to let him get away. Let's go over what you're going to do on those next couple of pitches. Let's waste a couple. Let's set him up.' I *had* to talk to him because Casey was shell-shocked. Why wouldn't he be, after Henrich gets on and DiMaggio singles? And Owen was shell-shocked, and why wouldn't he be?"

Then Leo said, "The manager was shell-shocked, too. I sat there and I didn't do anything. I let Casey come right back in with the pitch that Keller hit. *That's* where we lost the game. If you want to criticize somebody, criticize the manager. Write about me."

That was Durocher, pointing out something that nobody had noticed and publicly taking the blame for it. That was in 1941, and now it's more than a quarter of a century later. You can go back through all the newspaper and magazine files you want, and if you find anything that anybody ever wrote about Leo saying that, you let me know, hear? Because I don't think you're going to find very much.

One of the things they do write about 1941 is the story about Durocher being fired by MacPhail the very day the pennant was clinched. And that's true. I can tell you about that, because I happened to be part of it, and Leo told me. The Dodgers clinched that pennant up in Boston—the Braves were still in Boston then—and Whitlow Wyatt pitched it. It was the last game of the series there, and after it the Dodgers got on a special train to come back home to New York and Brooklyn.

I wasn't with them in Boston—we didn't travel with the team then—but we made arrangements to have microphones set up in Grand Central Station so that we could interview Durocher and Wyatt and Camilli and Dixie Walker and all the others as they came off the train. We had done a re-creation of the Western Union wire report of the pennant-clinching game, and we had had a pretty big audience. I have mentioned several times the excitement and interest this team generated. Well, during that broadcast, when it was obvious that Brooklyn would win the game and officially clinch the pennant, we announced that the club would be coming into Grand Central and the time the train would arrive. We could have said we were giving money away and there wouldn't have been a greater reaction. Everybody went to Grand Central. Never in the history of that station was there such a gratuitous concentration of people. It was jammed.

MacPhail at the time was still on very good terms with Branch Rickey, then with the Cardinals, and Rickey happened to be in New York. The two of them got in a cab and rode up to 125th Street to the New York Central Station there. MacPhail was going to board the train the ball club was on and make the triumphal entry with them into Grand Central, where the crowd was and where we were with our WOR microphones.

But the players on the train figured that there would be a mob at Grand Central—there was always a mob someplace around the Dodgers—and a few of them got to talking, and they decided that they would hop off the train when it stopped at 125th Street and skip the mob scene. Durocher, who never missed a trick, overheard them. He went to the conductor and told him not to stop at 125th Street but to go right on through to Grand Central. Leo didn't want to lose his ball club. He wanted them to come home in triumph, be greeted by the crowd, be photographed, go on the radio, go through the whole thing.

The conductor said, "I've got orders to stop."

Durocher said, "I don't care if you've got orders from the President. *Don't stop.* Go right on through. This is important."

I don't know whether you ever had Leo Durocher tell you point-blank in that brassy voice of his to do something, but I can assure you that the normal reaction is to do what Leo says. Durocher prevailed, which he often did. And does. And the train didn't stop at 125th Street. It roared right on through, and there stood Larry MacPhail and Branch Rickey on the station platform as it went by.

MacPhail has a low threshold of anger anyhow, and he went off like a rocket going into orbit. All he could do was get in another taxi and go back downtown. And by the time he got downtown, all MacPhail could do was go back to his hotel, because all the festivities at Grand Central were over. The crowd had cheered, the photographers had photographed, we had broadcast. It was done.

MacPhail's hotel was the New Yorker. Durocher was staying there, too. After the triumphal welcome at Grand Central, Leo breezed over to the New Yorker and, boy, he was walking on eggs and not cracking a one. Won the pennant, had the big welcome, the town was his. Nothing would do but he had to put in a call to the boss.

"Larry," he said. "This is Leo."

MacPhail answered, "You're fired!" And he hung up. Larry meant it, too—at the time. The pennant-winning manager of the afternoon slept that night, if he slept at all, fired. They made a rapprochement the next morning, of course, but for the night and a good part of the day, Leo was canned.

The funny thing to me now about this story is MacPhail's recent version of it. The way Larry tells the story now is that the standard version is not true. He says he did not go to 125th Street to get on the train and ride into Grand Central. He says he went to 125th Street because he had learned that Branch Rickey was catching a train out of New York there, and he wanted to see Rickey because he was trying to make a deal with him for a ballplayer. He met Rickey, he says, and they just happened to be there standing on the platform when the train came through. And he swears he never fired Leo that night. But I know that he did.

MacPhail left Brooklyn a year after the pennant, soon after the 1942 season ended. That year the Dodgers had a big lead when they left on their last western trip, and before they left Larry went down to the clubhouse and spoke to them. He warned them. The players were confident that they had a second straight pennant won, but MacPhail said, "The way you're playing and the way you're acting, you're not going to win." He called the turn. They lost a big series in St. Louis, and the Cardinals—who were always a great September team—came on with a magnificent surge under Billy Southworth, caught the Dodgers, and got two games ahead of them. That was all St. Louis needed. Brooklyn won eight in a row as the season ended and didn't gain an inch. The Dodgers won 104 games, but they lost the pennant as MacPhail had warned them they would.

After the season was over, Larry resigned to accept a commission as a colonel in the Army, and Branch Rickey came in from St. Louis that winter to take his place.

Between Innings: THE BLOOD BANK

After Pearl Harbor I got heavily involved in Red Cross work and with the blood donor drive in Brooklyn. I have good memories of the blood donor appeal, partly because we broke an old radio taboo in doing it, but mostly because it was a necessary success.

On Opening Day in Brooklyn in 1942, I was sitting in the radio booth before the game when a man sent word in asking if he could speak to me. His name was Ripperger, and he was a volunteer worker for the Brooklyn Red Cross. I invited him in, we shook hands and he said, "Mr. Barber, I wonder if you can help us. We're having a terrible time at the blood donor center getting people to come in and give blood for the armed forces. People don't know much about giving blood, and they're afraid of the idea. We haven't been able to get much publicity. Yet we simply must get more blood donors, and we'd like your assistance."

"What can I do?"

"We thought perhaps you could make an announcement on the air. Just something about the fact that there is a blood donor center in Brooklyn. You might give the phone number and add that if anybody is at all interested they could telephone and get some information about it, or even make an appointment to come in and give a pint of blood."

I shook my head.

"Mr. Ripperger," I said, "you have asked me to do the one thing I can't do." There was an unwritten law in radio at that time that you could not at any time use the word "blood" on the air. I don't know how it got started, but it was an accepted belief that you would offend and shock your listeners if you used the word. Radio was such an intimate medium, going into people's homes at all hours—at mealtimes, for instance. I suppose the idea was that if people were eating and they heard somebody on the radio say "blood," they would be horrified. They would get sick.

Human beings get strange ideas at times; we accept some

weird beliefs and practices almost without question. This was one of them, but it was a hard and fast rule. You may have heard parodies of old-time radio announcers referring to a boxer who had a cut above the eye as having a "claret optic." Well, the announcer *couldn't* say the fighter's eye was bleeding and he had to say something. I don't know how aware the radio audience was of this rule, but I can tell you that *all* announcers were aware of it. We simply could not say "blood," and I told Mr. Ripperger that.

But as we continued to talk, I got to thinking about the attack on Pearl Harbor, which had stunned the country only four months before, and about the people in Hawaii who had stood in line all night to give blood then. The realization came to me abruptly that the war, as it went on, was directly involving more and more people, and not just those who had been at Pearl Harbor.

I said, "Mr. Ripperger, come along with me." We went back into the press room. There, as I knew he would be, was MacPhail.

"Larry," I said, "this is Mr. Ripperger from the Red Cross blood donor center here in Brooklyn." We explained the problem, Ripperger telling MacPhail what he hoped we would be able to do for him, and me reminding Larry of the radio prohibition against using the word "blood."

MacPhail heard us out, and his response was immediate and direct. "Hell," he said. "There's a war on."

That was all I needed, but when I made the first broadcast for the blood donor center, you could feel WOR shake. Everybody in the radio industry in New York shivered. Oh my, he said "blood," right on the air, run for the storm cellars. But the only reaction from the public was that they jammed the Red Cross switchboard in Brooklyn trying to make appointments to give blood.

From that day on to the end of the war, there was never a broadcast of a Brooklyn Dodger game that did not include a blood-donor appeal. We'd call over an hour before the game to find out their needs for that day. If their schedule was light at a certain hour, we'd suggest that people make their appointments for that time. And so on. We asked the big blood donor center over in Manhattan if they wanted us to include them in our broadcasts, but at first they said no. Then, as the war spread and grew so terribly and the need increased, they phoned us one day and said, "Here's our number."

It was gratifying. I realize—I don't believe in false modesty —that I have had a long and successful career in broadcasting. But if I have to select one thing from that career that I am truly proud of, it is this—the blood donor appeals in World War II.

RED	1	3	⑤						
BARBER	2	4							

MacPhail and Rickey were good friends and very close professional associates. It was Rickey who gave MacPhail his first
minor league job, and it was Rickey who was primarily responsible for MacPhail's first major league job, at Cincinnati. For years,
every time MacPhail needed a player or anything he would almost automatically turn to Rickey. When he was at Brooklyn
and Rickey was still with the Cardinals, they engineered some
big deals. Joe Medwick, who was one of the best ballplayers in
the National League at the time, came from Rickey's Cardinals
to MacPhail's Dodgers in one of those trades.

After the war, when Rickey was with Brooklyn and MacPhail
had taken over the Yankees, they had a terrible falling out over
the Happy Chandler-Leo Durocher thing. To review that case
briefly, Durocher had been in various kinds of trouble. Along
with his constant quarreling with umpires he had fought with
fans, and he had antagonized certain quarters. Part of that antagonism was because Leo had been classified 4-F during the war
because of a perforated ear drum; emotions ride strange and
high during wartime, and the worst thing that can happen to
someone in the public eye is to be deferred from service. Leo
had also come in for criticism because of some of the people
he knew; he was accused of hanging around with unsavory
characters, and Chandler, who had recently become Com-

missioner of Baseball, had warned him to straighten up. Leo did, but he was burning about the criticism because he felt *he* had done nothing wrong and that he had a right to choose his own friends.

In 1947 the Dodgers were training in Havana, Cuba, and one day they played an exhibition with the Yankees. Barney Stein, the photographer, took a picture of the Yankee dugout and the box seats behind it, and the picture stirred up a tremendous hornet's nest. Larry MacPhail was sitting in one box, and across an aisle in the next box were two well-known gamblers, Memphis Engleberg and Connie Immerman. Rickey and Durocher immediately raised their voices in protest, asking whether there was one rule about the company Durocher could keep and another rule for MacPhail. When Larry heard that, he exploded. He demanded that Chandler take some sort of action against Rickey and Durocher for what Larry felt were unjustified insinuations. There were words, accusations, recriminations. It blew up into a very big story, and Chandler held a hearing to look into the matter. Then he stunned the baseball world by announcing that he was suspending Durocher from baseball for the year. There were a few other punishments meted out to the Dodgers and Yankees, but they were nothing compared to the Durocher suspension. Chandler made the announcement only a few days before the season was to open, which meant that not only were the Dodgers losing their manager, they were losing him just before Opening Day. And this was the year that Jackie Robinson was breaking into the major leagues.

It was absolutely staggering news, and many people thought it meant the end of Durocher's career, that he would never get another job after the suspension was up. They didn't know Durocher. Leo was, and is, a flamboyant personality, but he has great strength. He came from a family of, shall we say, modest means, and he had a very limited education. There was no money, no influence; he never had the advantage of college or specialized training or a degree. Leo had to make his way on his own wits and his own ability from a very early age. And he did it quite well. Leo has spent his life learning, and he knows how to use what he has learned. When he was a young ballplayer, they didn't have rookie leagues and batting coaches and early camps. You did it all yourself. When he came up as a young ballplayer, he was a lousy hitter. He couldn't hit a curve ball. But he was a beautiful fielder, one of the best-fielding shortstops you ever saw. He was accepted as a fielder, but he had to sustain himself as a hitter by the intense belief he had in himself. He did all right. He learned to handle a bat well enough to be a major league shortstop for a dozen years. He used his brains. Leo always was a fellow who would beat you playing pool, playing cards, and he'd beat you playing baseball, one way or the other. He never doubted himself. He had a brashness that I think he felt he had to have. When he was a fresh young rookie, he took on fellows like Babe Ruth and Ty Cobb. He didn't pull back from a soul. This is something people don't always remember about Leo. He doesn't give ground. He feels that he *has* to be on the attack, always. And he is.

Leo angers people. He arouses antagonism in some of his ballplayers, but most of them swear by him. He can do foolish things, but he also has a very real sense of pride, of taste. I mean that very seriously. When he was suspended most baseball people thought it was an injustice. I don't think anybody in baseball thought that Leo should have been suspended. Rickey said to Chandler, "Happy, what have you done?" MacPhail, who had blown the whistle on Leo, was shocked. If ever there was a time when a man could not have been blamed for popping off, that was the time and Durocher was the man. But he didn't.

The day after Chandler announced the suspension, Leo came out to the ball park. I was in the clubhouse when he arrived, along with four or five sportswriters. Leo came in through the door and said quietly, "Would everybody who is not a player, please leave. I want to speak to my ball club." We went outside. We stood by the door and waited, and after about twenty minutes the meeting was over. The door opened, Leo came out and he left. He didn't say anything to any of us.

I was curious, of course, about what had gone on in the meeting. I was a reporter, after all, and I wanted to know, generally, what had taken place. I knew Dixie Walker quite well, and I went over to him after Leo had gone. "Dixie," I said, "can you tell me what went on in the meeting?"

"Yes, Red," he said. "I can tell you. Leo was very quiet. He didn't get mad, and he didn't say anything at all about Chandler. He didn't make any alibis, and he didn't sound sorry for himself. He just said, 'Fellows, I'm going. Nobody knows yet who the new manager will be. But trust in Mr. Rickey. He'll get you the right manager.' He said, 'I want you to believe in Mr. Rickey, and I want you to believe in yourselves. You're good enough to win the pennant no matter who Mr. Rickey gets as your manager.'"

And then Dixie said, "Red, you know, I never liked Leo. I never liked him at all, and everybody knows I never liked him. But he showed me something in there. I'll tell you, the way he talked in that meeting, the way he went out of here today—he'll be back."

And he was. And he's still back.

Durocher is about the best manager of a ball club I ever saw from the time a game starts until the time the game ends. He handles a game magnificently, just like a professional riverboat gambler. His problems usually come off the field—an unguarded comment, a too-flamboyant action, not thinking something through before he says it. Or does it. Like in 1941, when he lost his temper in Philadelphia and hit that sportswriter. That is not a good thing to do, and comment on it generates and generates. Leo can be very shortsighted. But there is another side of him, too, which gets almost no attention in the press, and that is his generosity, his good heart, his kindness. It's as much a part of him as his temper and his flamboyance. He goes out of his way to do things for people. I remember a time when there was an illness in my family, and I needed a car. I didn't know that Durocher knew anything about it, but he came to me—he found *me*—and he gave me the keys to his Lincoln. "Here," he said. "Take the keys. Use the car and keep it as long as you need it."

What do you do with a fellow like that?

But, anyway, back there in 1947 Leo was out, and the long friendship between Rickey and MacPhail went out with him. Rickey blamed MacPhail for what had happened, and the thing became bitter. Just as those two men had been very close, now they were far, far apart. It was brutal. They never spoke to each other again. No, they spoke once, exactly once. It was during the World Series of 1947, at the end of that season. The Dodgers and the Yankees were playing each other—as they did so often—and after one of the games at the Stadium, Mac-Phail ran into Rickey as they were coming out of the ball park. Larry stuck out his hand and said, "Hello, Branch." Rickey stopped. He refused to shake hands. He looked at MacPhail and very quietly, but with all the force that a strong man with an undying anger could muster, he said, "Don't you ever speak to me again." He didn't even call MacPhail by name, and he turned and walked away. That was the last word between the two.

Yet in the years Rickey remained at Brooklyn he never objected to *my* friendship with Larry. He brought it up once. He said, "You have an abiding friendship with MacPhail, haven't you?" I said, "Yes, I do." He said, "Good. You keep it. It's all right with me, and it won't come between us. But I will not mention his name again in your presence." He was right on both counts: He never mentioned MacPhail again, and though I maintained my friendship with Larry it never affected my relationship with Rickey.

Shortly before this all happened, MacPhail tried to get me away from the Dodgers. The Yankees and the Giants had continued their combined home-and-home broadcasts until 1946, except for a couple of seasons there when they did not broadcast at all. But after MacPhail took over the Yankees in 1945, he broke loose from that arrangement. He believed in continuity— he wanted his team's games broadcast both home and away, as he had done at Cincinnati and again at Brooklyn. He decided to do it at the Stadium, too, and that forced the Giants to follow suit. So you could say that MacPhail was responsible, all the way, for the pattern of the radio broadcasts of all three New York teams.

That summer, 1946, Larry offered me the Yankee announcing job. He said he would pay me one hundred thousand dollars on a three-year contract—that is, one hundred thousand dollars spread over three years—to leave the Dodgers, join him at the Stadium, and do the Yankee play-by-play. It was a very tempting offer, especially since I had just run into a thing with Ray

Virden at Lennen and Mitchell, the advertising agency for Old
Gold Cigarettes, which then sponsored the Brooklyn broadcasts.
Virden and I had been talking about arrangements for the following season, 1947, and I had mentioned that I wanted more
money. Our contracts were with the sponsors then, and not the
ball clubs, though even now when a broadcaster's contract is
with the club the sponsor has a great deal to say about Who
and How Much. I had a rule of thumb that, any place I
worked, I wanted a raise each time we negotiated a new contract.
I was young—in my thirties—and I felt that I was still on my
way up. I didn't want to level off. You can't level off. If you're
not going up, you start down. But Virden, backed up by Bert
Kent, the president of P. Lorillard, which made Old Golds, told
me that I would not get a raise in 1947 and that I was being
paid all that the job was worth. Mr. Kent is the man they
later named a cigarette for.

I didn't like that at all, and I was beginning to get my neck
bowed about it when MacPhail made me his offer. I thought,
"Gee, this is duck soup. I'm going to get more money, I'll have
it on a three-year contract, and I'll be going to the Yankees,
the big team in the major leagues." But I told MacPhail that
I could not do a thing until I had talked to Rickey. I owed
him that courtesy. MacPhail, an honorable man, said, "Of course.
I wouldn't expect you to do anything else. Tell him everything.
Go into all the details. Tell him what I've offered you."

Even so, when I left MacPhail's office I was ready to take
the job. I went to see Bert Kent and informed him of MacPhail's
offer. Kent said he would not change his position. I told him,
"In that case, I'm going to the Yankees. I'm not going to accept
your statement that I am making all that the broadcast is worth
and that I am not going to get any more money next year."
I walked out.

I still had to pay my courtesy call to Rickey, so I went on
over to Brooklyn. I told Rickey of Virden's refusal to give
me a raise, MacPhail's offer and Kent's reaction, and that I had
told Kent—to whom I was under contract—that I was going to
take the Yankee job the next year.

Rickey said, "Wait a minute. Wait just a minute. We don't
want to lose you here at Brooklyn. Now, you know the Brooklyn

club has never interfered with the contracts between the broadcaster and the sponsor. That has always been alien to the province of the Brooklyn ball club. But with you going to the Yankees, it is no longer alien. It's very much in my province now. I would like you to do something for me. I have to go out of town to attend a meeting, and I'll be gone for three days. Will you give me the courtesy—do you think enough of me personally—do you think enough of your years at Brooklyn— to wait three days until I come back and have a chance to talk this thing over with you?"

"Of course," I said.

Three days later, I was back in his office, and Rickey said, "As far as I know, it has never been the policy of a ball club anywhere to have a contract itself with an announcer. That has always been for the sponsor and the advertising agency. But I am going to make you an offer directly from the Brooklyn club, and from me, that will have nothing to do with Bert Kent, Ray Virden, Lennen and Mitchell, Old Gold Cigarettes, or any other sponsor. *I* am offering you a three-year contract at $105,000 to broadcast our games, and *I* will work out the broadcasting arrangements with the sponsor. What is your answer?"

Bill McCaffrey, my agent, had come with me, and just the three of us were sitting in the room. I had had three days to think about this and to mull over what the Brooklyn job meant to me. I knew that if Rickey asked me to wait three days so that he could talk to me about it, he was going to make me an offer. And it would be an offer that would compare with the Yankee deal—otherwise he would not have asked me to wait three days. I knew that I was going to have to make a choice. The Yankee spot was great—no question about it—but that was quite a job in Brooklyn, too, back there in 1946. I knew that if I went over to the Stadium, I would be competing with what we had built up at Ebbets Field. In a sense, I would be competing with myself. And the truth was, much as I cared for Larry MacPhail, I really didn't want to go to the Stadium. I wanted to stay at Brooklyn.

But I did not want to stay there, even with this impressive three-year contract, if the atmosphere was going to be changed, if Rickey somehow felt he had been coerced into the deal. Not that you could coerce him into anything, but I wanted to know how he felt.

I explained this and I said to Rickey, "At my father's funeral down in North Carolina a few weeks ago, the family was gathered and everybody was standing around out in the yard, visiting together. Two of my distant cousins were talking, and one of them said to the other, 'What did you ever do with that 140 acres you had down on the South Carolina line?' The second one said, 'I had no trouble. I found me a willing buyer.'"

Rickey didn't hesitate. He slapped his hand down on the desk and he roared, "I'm a willing buyer!" And, you know, that's the best way to consummate a deal. It says everything. A willing buyer. That implies a happy relationship; you can work out the details of the contract later.

I have sometimes thought: if I had taken MacPhail's offer and gone over to the Stadium, people might not have heard so much about Mel Allen. Perhaps I would have been known as the Voice of the Yankees. But Mel had worked on the combined Giant-Yankee broadcast, and when I remained with the Brooklyn job the track was clear for him at the Stadium. And, of course, he was a great success there. He had the job for nineteen years.

MacPhail was such an aggressive man that he continually created situations. The things he started caused other things to happen and then other things. He was a prime mover. In 1947, for instance, he came up with another innovation. He sent his Yankee broadcasters out on the road with his ball club. Instead of staying back in New York doing re-created broadcasts from the wire reports, his announcers did live, on-the-spot accounts from the various ball parks around the league. It was the first time that had ever been done on a regular schedule, and, of course, MacPhail had to be the one who started it.

The Giants followed along and began to travel their broadcasts, too, and over in Brooklyn all of a sudden I said to myself, "Oh, oh. Here I am in a radio station doing a Western Union wire report with the dots and dashes sounding all the time, and there are those two other fellows right in the ball park. They're seeing it for themselves. They have the actual sound of the real crowd." I was proud of the way we did the wire reports but there never was any question in my mind but that the best way to broadcast is to broadcast what you can see yourself, instead of taking a skeletonized description from a Western Union man. You had a different Western Union man in every town in the league, and every one of them saw a ball game differently. Each had a different set of experiences, different insight. I began to think I had better get out of the studio and out on the road. I had better start traveling myself.

Now, contrary to a widely held opinion, I have always accepted traveling as a normal and necessary part of my job. I do it only when I have to do it, but I do it. I have always had a strong feeling about not being out of my home any more than was necessary to earn my living. I have to have a reason to leave the house. I don't go off on hunting trips or fishing trips. It's not that I'm not free to, but when I finish my work I am content to be home. I *prefer* to be there. I got this attitude from my father, who was a locomotive engineer. He loved his work, too. He would run those big freight trains up and down the state of Florida, and he enjoyed doing it. He loved railroading. But when he wasn't on the locomotive, he was home. And he was home because that's where he wanted to be. He might not get home until just before daybreak, but he would get up before he had gotten his full sleep to see us children before we went off to school. Then after we had gone to school he would stay up. He would consult my mother and then go off to the grocery store. I'm talking now about the days when you walked to the grocery store—you didn't phone in an order, and you didn't drive an automobile to a supermarket. He'd walk over to the store and come back with a sack or two of groceries and get himself in the kitchen. He wouldn't live in a house that didn't have a kitchen big enough for the stove and a big table and a rocking chair. He wanted plenty of room. If he had a turkey, he'd get the bird ready, make the stuffin', put it in the oven. Or he'd cook country steak, which had to simmer on the back of the stove for hours. Or grits.

The big memory I have of my father is in the kitchen, cooking. Even though he was a locomotive engineer, he had the cleanest hands of any man I've ever known. His work on the locomotives was with grease, and he'd come home in overalls that were so dirty they would stand by themselves. When I was a small boy, my job was to help him get those dirty overalls off so that they could be washed. Oh, they were dirty. This man worked in grease, and you worked long hours in those days. People keep talking about thirty-five-hour work weeks, thirty-hour work weeks, twenty-seven-hour work weeks. His *day* in the busy season was sixteen hours on, eight off. He ran freight trains, passenger trains, whatever had to be run. He retired before diesels. God was merciful when he took my father out of this life while steam was still the dominant force in railroading. It would have broken his heart to have seen the end of steam locomotives. They were his life. After he got his overalls off he would clean his hands, and then before he began to cook he'd give them a final working over in the kitchen sink, with the soap again and a brush, and when he had them right he would shake Arm & Hammer Baking Soda over them and clean them again. Then he would start to cook.

He was a rugged, physical man in a rugged, physical man's world, and you would think that he would be a rough, careless man. But this was what he liked best. He would get the food ready and he'd put it in the oven, and then the enjoyment of his day would close in upon him. He would always have a book—he loved literature—and he would sit there in the rocking chair in the kitchen and read. He would roll a cigarette—he didn't buy tailormades, as he called them—and he would sit in the rocking chair, very gently rocking back and forth, and read and smoke while the food was slowly cooking.

That was my father at home. He loved and respected his home, and I caught that from him. He never gave me any great dissertation about the sanctity of the home and the joys of the fireside. But I learned it. The warmest memory I have of this man, this man of clean hands, was sitting in that rocking chair, rolling his cigarettes, reading a good book and cooking.

So, I have always had a strong feeling about not being away from my home any more than I have had to be to earn a living. Even that last year with the Yankees, when my wife was in Florida and I lived in a small suite by myself in the New York Hilton for the summer. I was never lonely. The little suite was my home, and I have never been lonely in my home. I was content. If I wasn't going to be out with friends, I would cook my own dinner in the little kitchenette in the suite, and then sit there and read. I like to be at home.

And up to this point—1947, when MacPhail set the thing in motion—I had broadcast all my games with the Reds and with the Dodgers right there in town. I did home games from the ball park and away games from the studio, where we had the Western Union ticker, and I went home every night. I traveled only for a World Series or an All-Star game or for football games. But MacPhail had disturbed this pattern, and I began to have some strong feelings. If I had taken MacPhail's offer, I would be the man traveling those broadcasts. I would have been the first man out on the road with live broadcasts.

I watched as the Giants followed along; they didn't like the competition of live broadcasts against their wire reports, and they followed MacPhail onto the road. We didn't over at Brooklyn. We stayed in the studio, and this thing kept eating at me. Every time I went to the studio to do a wire-report game I'd say, "Oh, boy, I ought to be in the ball park like those other fellows."

I didn't want to start traveling, be out of town half the summer. I didn't want it, and my wife didn't want it. It wasn't as though I had started out in baseball and never knowing anything but traveling, or as though my wife had married me knowing that this traveling life was the life she was marrying into. She wasn't used to that, and I wasn't either. But I had to do something. I had lunch one day with Bill McCaffrey at the Lambs Club and afterward, as we stood on the sidewalk outside waiting for a cab, I said, "Bill, I can't stand this any more. We have got to travel. The Brooklyn broadcast has got to go on the road."

He said, "What are you going to do about it?" It was the middle of the season.

I said, "I'm going over and tell Mr. Rickey." I got on a subway and went over to 215 Montague Street and went into his office.

"Branch," I said, "I have got to talk to you about something." Before someone thinks I'm being impudent in so casually referring to the great man by his first name, I must explain something. I had called him Mr. Rickey for years, and when he came to Brooklyn I continued to call him Mr. Rickey. There was never any question in my mind to call him anything but that. After he had been in Brooklyn a few months, going through press conferences and all, he stopped short one day and said, "Why do you call me *Mr.* Rickey?"

I said, "Because my father taught me to call older men 'Mister' until they told me different."

"I'm telling you different," he said. "You call me Branch. It makes me mad that all of these flip newspapermen around here call me Branch when I want them to call me Mister, while a fellow I work with and feel close to calls me Mister when I want him to call me Branch. Now you stop it."

So, I called him Branch.

"Branch," I said, "we have got to travel the Brooklyn broadcasts. The idea of traveling is upsetting to me, but we have to do it."

"Do you really think so?" he said.

"Yes, sir. For years and years now, this Brooklyn broadcast has been first. We can't afford to lose ground now."

"Yes, but all the reports say that everybody is very happy with the broadcasts the way they are. The sponsors are. We certainly are. You're doing an excellent job."

"Branch, I don't care whether they are happy or not. We are not quite major league when we are doing a wire report while the others go out where the ball game is. It's kind of you to say I'm doing a good job, but nobody can do as good a job on a wire report as he can when he looks at the game himself."

"All right," he said. "I'll convey this to Bert Kent." I think he said Bert Kent. I'm pretty sure Old Gold was still sponsoring the Dodger games. In any event, because of costs and things it was essentially the sponsor's decision. Word came back that they were satisfied for that year and didn't want to change things. But the next year they had to. They put it off until the middle of the season—July 1948—but it was inevitable.

So, just for the sake of the record, I want to point out again that it was a full year before the Dodger broadcasts went on the road that I myself suggested that we do it. I stress this because later on, when I left the Dodgers after the 1953 season to go over to Yankee Stadium, the word got around that I had left Brooklyn because I did not want to travel. That was never a factor. That was Walter O'Malley's red herring.

The first trip the broadcasters made with the Dodgers was memorable, which is about as glaring an understatement as you could make. Our first broadcast out of town was in Cincinnati, a night game. Leo Durocher wasn't with the club; ostensibly he had taken a day or two off to go to Montreal to scout some players on the Dodger farm club there. That morning Rickey called a press conference and announced the stunning news that Durocher was leaving Brooklyn. He was going to the Giants to replace Mel Ott as manager, and that Burt Shotton—who had filled in for Leo when he was suspended—was rejoining the Dodgers and would be in Cincinnati later that day to take over the ball club. That was a pretty fair day to start broadcasting out of town. Then we went from Cincinnati to Chicago to Pittsburgh, and I never did get to broadcast in Pittsburgh. The day we arrived there I went out to play golf and collapsed on the course and had to be taken to a hospital. I had ulcers, though I hadn't known it, and they had hemorrhaged. I was pretty sick for a while—they thought that first night that I was going to die—and because we had just two announcers, Connie Desmond and myself, Rickey brought in Ernie Harwell from Atlanta. When I came back nine weeks later in the season, the three of us worked together, and we continued that way in 1949. It was the beginning of three-man broadcasting teams, and with television getting bigger and more important we needed three. We did very few road games on television and only two men went on the road trips, which meant that under the revolving schedule we had, one of us had time off whenever the club was out of town. In those days, the eight teams in the league were divided into "eastern" and "western" groups for scheduling purposes, and along with short trips to Philadelphia and Boston the Dodgers made four major "western" trips a year. In my contract with Rickey I guaranteed to make two of the four western trips, all the games in Philadelphia and Boston and, of course, all the games in Ebbets Field and the Polo Grounds in New York. I *guaranteed* to do that much traveling, but for varying reasons—

one of which was interest—I always made three of the four western trips. I had no complaint. It was fine with me. I never complained to anybody about traveling. When I left the Dodgers, it was for other reasons, which I'll get to later on.

Between Innings: LEO AND CASEY

When Durocher spoke of the mistake he had made in not going out to the mound to talk to Hugh Casey in the 1941 World Series, he was talking of the days when there was no limitation on the number of times a manager could go to the mound during an inning or during a game. Now such visits are restricted, because the rulesmakers decided the managers were delaying the game.

I think it's a lousy rule. Where did the rulesmakers ever get the idea that the fans were sitting there with stopwatches in their hands, hoping the game would get over? If they wanted the game to be over, they wouldn't be watching it in the first place.

And why would the manager going to the mound distress the fans? I think back over all the games I have seen and broadcast and, my goodness, I have such vivid memories of the managers at just such moments. The truculence of Bill Terry slowly walking out to talk to a pitcher in a jam. Billy Southworth, suddenly, in his quick sprinting trot, speeding off the St. Louis bench to go speak to one of his men. Casey Stengel, doing that half hobble of his, swinging his arms as he went out, clapping his hands together. Walter Alston, with his big, calm strength, going out to settle a young pitcher.

I do not understand any legislation that takes the human quality out of baseball. Baseball has nothing but that to sell—*people* doing things, people in situations where they will succeed or fail. That's all that drama is, and baseball is drama.

Durocher had to go to the mound frequently because he was a tactical manager. I said before that he was the best manager I ever saw during a game. I amend that. Make it Durocher and Stengel. I never saw anybody else handle a man as well as these two during the heat, the flow, the fury of the game. A manager's strength—and any manager will tell you this—is not knowing when to use the hit-and-run or the bunt or the take or the intentional walk. It is knowing the strength and the weakness of the player involved at a particular moment. Stengel had that ability to an extraordinary degree. He protected his ballplayer against his weakness, and he had him in there at his strength.

A lot of people call that platooning, and I suppose platooning is a good word for it. But it goes deeper than that. Platooning sounds simple. Platooning sounds as though you always put in lefty batters against righty pitchers, and vice versa. Stengel didn't do that. Stengel would take a right-handed batter *out* of a game against a particular left-handed pitcher and bring a *left*-handed batter in. Why? Because Stengel remembered something about *that* lefty batter and *that* lefty pitcher. He brought in Bob Kuzava, an undistinguished left-handed pitcher, to work against three right-handed batters in the ninth inning of the final game of the 1951 World Series, with the bases loaded and nobody out and the Yankees leading 4–1. Kuzava gave up three outfield flies, and two runs scored while he was doing it, but he preserved the lead and the Yankees won. In the 1952 Series, Casey used Kuzava again in an almost identical situation: the Yankees led 4–2 in the seventh inning of the final game, and the Dodgers had the bases loaded with one out. Kuzava faced one left-handed batter and seven right-handers in 2⅔ innings, got every one of them out, and the Yankees won again. Those were the only times Stengel pitched Kuzava in those two World Series. But do you think old Casey didn't know what he was doing?

Joe McCarthy, the great Yankee manager of the 1930s and 1940s, told me once that managing could be summed up in three words: memory and patience. Stengel didn't always appear patient, but he knew how to wait for the right moment to make his move. And he had a prodigious memory. Sometimes Casey had a little trouble with names, but he knew the people he was talking about. He could remember things that happened on a certain play when he was a young ballplayer in Kankakee, Illinois, in 1910, and how they applied to a situation in Yankee Stadium in 1955. He could remember, on an overcast day, that two years earlier on an overcast day in Chicago, White Sox Pitcher X got Yankee Batter A out with ease but couldn't get Yankee Batter B out. So Casey would remove Batter A, who was hitting .290, and send up Batter B, who was hitting .240. Batter B would get a hit and win the ball game, and people would shake their heads and say, "There's that Stengel

luck again. He went against the book and got away with it."
That wasn't luck. That was design.

Some people thought Stengel was a clown. When George
Weiss brought him in to manage the Yankees in 1949, you'd
have thought Weiss had hired somebody out of the circus. I
never found Stengel a clown except when he wished to be one.
Casey was about the smartest man I ever met. I would say that
he was a deliberate and astute practitioner in the art of mis-
direction. He wanted you to *think* he was a clown. He would
put it on for you as long as he thought it had any validity,
or as long as it served his purpose. He was a master of double-
talk. Years ago, there was a writer whom Stengel did not like.
Casey was sore at him, and he didn't want to say anything to
him. But Stengel knew it was not good practice to deliberately
antagonize a member of the press. I was sitting in the dugout
with him one day, and the writer started toward us from the
other side of the field. As he came around the batting cage,
Stengel said in that growling voice of his, "Here comes so-and-
so. Watch me take care of him." The fellow came in the dugout
and sat down and asked Casey a question, and Stengel answered
him. In his own double-talk. It sounded almost like an answer,
and the fellow was taking notes and thinking he had gotten it
and then he realized he hadn't quite gotten it, so he listened
some more, and Casey kept rambling on and on. The fellow
was hanging on every word, thinking he had it and then not
having it. It went on for about ten or fifteen minutes, and then
practice was over and they had to clear the dugout to start the
game. The writer left the dugout, and he hasn't got a quote
yet. And Casey winked.

The classic example is when Stengel was dragged down to
Washington to testify before a Senate subcommittee that decided
it was going to investigate baseball and the reserve clause and
expansion and get this baseball thing settled and out in the
open once and for all. Casey didn't want to go. It spoiled an
off day for him, and he didn't have anything to testify anyhow. When he got before the subcommittee he threw his double-
talk at the senators. It's a matter of public, written record. He
talked to them for an hour, and they were fascinated, and they
still don't know what he said. At one stage he mentioned a

wooden ball park, and that was the only thing solid the sub-committee had after an hour of testimony.

He never did that to people he liked or trusted, or when he really wanted to tell somebody something. When I reported to my first Yankee spring training camp in 1954, I knew very little about the ball club. I had been around the Yankees in the World Series and I had seen them occasionally during the regular season, but I had no real knowledge of the team. I certainly didn't know it the way a broadcaster should know his ball club. About the second day of training I said to Stengel, "Casey, some day soon when you have an opportunity, I'd like to have you go over your ball club for me." He said, "What are you doing right now?" I said, "Nothing." He said, "Sit down."

We sat in the dugout and he asked the other people there to excuse him. He pulled a copy of his roster out of his pocket, and he went down it man by man, in detail. There was no double-talk, none at all. In thirty minutes he gave me a detailed, analytical report on every last man on his roster. It was remarkable. And all season long, every thing he told me about every man held up.

STATION BREAK

Red Barber broadcast in Brooklyn for fifteen seasons, from 1939 through 1953. Larry MacPhail ran the club Red's first four years, Branch Rickey the next eight, and Walter O'Malley during Barber's final three seasons. Leo Durocher was the manager from 1939 through 1946 and in the first half of 1948. Burt Shotton took Leo's place in 1947 and managed again from the middle of 1948 through 1950. Charlie Dressen was the manager in 1951–52–53.

These were all significant baseball people, and their accomplishments were many. All won pennants at Brooklyn. Indeed, the Dodgers finished first, second, or third in fourteen of the fifteen years that Barber broadcast Dodger games. In ten of those years they were either first or second, and four of the five second-place finishes were by an eyelash (in 1946 and 1951 they tied for first, only to lose the pennant in postseason playoffs; in 1942 they won 104 games behind the racehorse Cardinals; in 1950 they carried the Phillies into extra innings on the last day of the season before settling for second place).

Year in and year out the Dodgers and Brooklyn were big news in baseball while Barber was there (four years after he left Brooklyn the Dodgers did, too). As their chronicler, he achieved a rare pre-eminence among broadcasters. But who was he? Where had he been before? We knew vaguely that he was southern and that he had worked in Cincinnati, but where had he really come from?

RED	1	3	5						
BARBER	2	4	(6)						

When young people ask me how you get to be a sports announcer, if I am completely honest I have to say, "The first thing to do is select your parents carefully." I received a great feeling for language from my mother and father. My mother loved English. She taught it for years and she wrote a textbook on grammar that was used at one time in public schools in the state of Mississippi. She was only sixteen, I believe, when she graduated from Mississippi State College for Women, and she taught school all her life. She gave it up for a while when we children came along—there were three of us—but whenever possible she would do substitute work. When we got old enough to be self-sufficient she went back and taught school full time again until her health failed, and at that point she was principal of a brand, shiny new school in Sanford, Florida. My mother gave me an ear for language. When I was a freshman at the University of Florida they gave us a test in grammar that was four or five pages long in which you pointed out when the verb was wrong or the noun or the adjective. I went through that test swimmingly; I had an almost perfect score. Yet I didn't know many rules of grammar; I just knew how things were supposed to sound. If it didn't sound right, I marked it wrong. If it seemed to fit, I marked it correct. My choices stood up, and that's what I mean when I say my mother gave me my ear. She gave me my interest in religion, too. She had a deep sense of morality, a true feeling for the importance of life.

My father did not have the education my mother had, but he was a wonderful story teller, a natural raconteur. He'd sit out on the front porch and tell stories by the hour. People loved to listen to him. He had some highly perceptive philosophical concepts and the innate ability to sum them up in an earthy way. He said things plainly, and you understood what he said. You not only understood them, you remembered them. When I was a small boy he taught me honesty by telling me simply that as I went through the world and saw things that weren't mine, I was not to touch them. It's a pretty good rule of thumb. Every human being knows whether something is his or not. It goes for money, it goes for jobs, it very definitely goes for women. You know whether something is yours; if it isn't, leave it alone.

My father started out in North Carolina in a little town called Brown's Creek. It's really not much more than a Baptist church with some farms around it in the vicinity of Wadesboro in Anson County, right down close to the South Carolina line. After my father finished high school he started rambling around, working on the railroad. In those days a fellow who went from a railroad job in one place to a railroad job in another was called a "boomer." My father was a boomer. He drifted along as the spirit moved him. I don't know how many different railroads he worked on, but eventually he landed a job as a fireman on a locomotive on the Southern Railway in Mississippi. His headquarters were in Columbus, Mississippi, where he stayed in a boarding house. My mother lived in the same boarding house with two younger sisters and a younger brother. Their parents had died, and my mother was teaching school, and she and her sisters and brother all lived together in this big old family-style boarding house. My mother and father met there and fell in love and got married and started their own home and their own family. And there, in Columbus, Mississippi, my father ended his boomer days.

Jobs on the railroad—firemen, engineers, conductors, brakemen, flagmen—were held by seniority; the older men in service took their choice and the younger men took what was left.

When my father and mother were married the railroad gave them what they called a wedding present. They promoted him from fireman to engineer. Of course, that made him the youngest engineer in point of seniority, and that meant he was at the farthest end of the trough as far as jobs were concerned. Yet they made out, and everything went along fairly well for a while.

But about the time I was ten, the boll weevil had come into the state of Mississippi and was busy eating up the cotton crop. As it ate up the cotton crop, it ate up the Southern Railway in Mississippi, too. My father could see the handwriting on the wall. There got to be less and less work, and times became increasingly harder. He began to think about Florida. As a young man, at the start of his boomer days back about the end of the Spanish-American War, he had drifted through Florida. I believe he was a mule team driver, from what I remember hearing him say, and he covered just about the whole state. He walked where he could and used boats the rest of the way. When he finally left Florida the sand had gotten in his shoes, and he always wanted to go back there again. He detested cold weather anyway, and it could get pretty cold in Mississippi once in a while, especially up there at the head end of a train in the locomotive with the cab wide open to the elements.

So all these things conspired, and he went over to Florida, took an examination, and got himself hired by the Atlantic Coast Line. World War I was going pretty good by now, and railroad work was picking up again. But just when he was moving the family over to Florida, he ran into a snag. Railroading was considered an essential industry during the war, and they had passed a rule against people in railroading changing jobs. My father could accept his new position with the Atlantic Coast Line, but he would have to wait until the end of the war before he could actually start working there. For the duration he was frozen to the job with the Southern Railway in Mississippi. By this time our furniture was all packed and he had rented a house in Fort Meyers, Florida, which was where he was to have begun work. He moved us to Fort Meyers, got us settled, and then went back to Mississippi by himself to the job he was frozen to.

That was a pretty tough winter. We were strangers in Fort

Meyers, in a rented house, and there wasn't much money, and we didn't know when my father was coming back. During the flu epidemic of 1918 he got sick in Columbus, and we couldn't go over to him. That first Christmas in Fort Meyers was a terrible, lonely time. Our first look at Florida in the winter season was not the same one that Thomas Edison and Harvey Firestone and the other rich people who had estates among the tall royal palms along the river at Fort Meyers had. We weren't tourists. We didn't get around to any of the resort places, I promise you.

After my father recovered from the flu and went back to work, he was the engineer one day on a train carrying William Gibbs McAdoo, who was one of Woodrow Wilson's top men. Later on, McAdoo just missed being nominated for the Presidency, and he was married to one of Wilson's daughters. He was a very big man in the country. My father had been trying and trying to get himself released from the Southern Railway so that he could go to his new job in Florida, and there had been tons of paper going back and forth with nothing happening. The hand of officialdom, coupled with a World War, lies very heavy on a person who has no influence.

The locomotive my father was running pulled into a siding to wait for another train to go by, and while it was sidetracked there for a few minutes my father in his desperation walked back through the cars and asked if he could speak to Mr. McAdoo. McAdoo saw him. My father said, "Mr. McAdoo, I know you've got big problems. They're big to you and big to the country. But my problem is big to me." He explained his situation and then he said, "I wish you'd get in touch with somebody and explain to them that they don't *need* me here in Mississippi. They have engineers here *waiting* for work. I have a job and a family over in Florida, and if I'm going to be railroading anyway I don't see why I can't be where my family is."

And, bless Pat, McAdoo sent word to somebody and before you knew it here came my dad to Fort Meyers. He never left Florida again until he was pensioned off by the railroad in his middle sixties. My mother was dead by then, and my father went back to North Carolina to live with his sister in a little town called Lilesville, just outside Wadesboro. He died there and he was buried in the churchyard of that little Baptist church out in Brown's Creek, back where he started from.

Because of the seniority system, my father was a switch engineer at first in Florida and then worked around the roundhouse moving locomotives from one place to another. As his work changed, we moved from Fort Meyers to Sanford and then to Port Tampa and then back to Sanford again. Winter was always the busy time because of the combination of citrus-and-truck farming and the tourist business. There was plenty of work in the winter, but the summers were always long and hot and hungry. My father would go in debt during the summer, and then in the winter he would work as hard as he could to get out of debt again. He did his summer business with the man who would give him credit. The grocery store had to carry him for months, because there simply wasn't any money in the summer time.

As my father's seniority grew and the available work increased, we settled down in Sanford. There I finished grammar school and went through high school and worked for a couple of years before I went to Gainesville to the University of Florida. During my freshman year at the university, the railroad business moved out of Sanford and my father had a choice of going either to Jacksonville or to Tampa. The weather was warmer in Tampa, so he went there. That's where my mother died, and where my father lived until he was pensioned and moved back to his sister's house in North Carolina.

But Sanford is where I grew up, where the things were set in motion that really shaped my life. When I look back at those days, I always think of the phrase from the Book of Common Prayer: "Amid the changes and chances of this mortal life." I think of the people and the incidents coming in and out that profoundly affected my life. I don't mean that I look back from a maudlin, supersentimental viewpoint or in the sense of wishing I had done this or hadn't done that. It's more like looking back over the score sheets of ball games you have seen and recalling who did this in the first inning and who did this in the second, and the effect each of those things had on what eventually happened in the fifth and the sixth and the eighth. You look back and you realize that every person who was in your life had a bearing on it, and if you changed any one person your life would be changed beyond your comprehension.

The things that shape your life. For instance, along with the feeling for language that I received at home I also was given an intense, abiding interest in sports. When I was a boy, my father gave me an all-out official college football every Christmas, which meant that as I grew up I always had a good football to throw and to kick. That meant that the boys in the neighborhood were always around my house, and it meant that we were always fooling with the football. I grew up kicking and throwing a football. I could kick a ball hard and accurately, and even though I have small hands and short fingers I could pass it well. We played all the time. This was before paved roads were so common, and we would play football in the street all day long. And every spring when school finished, my father would give me an official major league baseball, and we'd play with that. If you have the ball you can play the game, so my father really gave me the almost inherent feeling I have for the field in which I have made my living. I was always either kicking and throwing a football or throwing and hitting a baseball. The baseball was precious. If we lost it in the tall grass the game stopped and everybody fell to until we found it. We couldn't afford to lose it. We had to find it, and we always did find it. I had a cigar box in which we kept a ball of bees wax and some heavy thread that we had gotten from the shoe-repair store and a big needle. Whenever we broke the threads on the ball from hitting it too much, we stopped and sewed it back into shape. We sewed it up because we needed it; that was *the* ball in the neighborhood.

I grew up to be a pretty good athlete. I look small around major league baseball and football players, but back there in high school I was big enough. I am 5 feet 8 inches tall and in high school I weighed 165 pounds. I was strong; I was tough. I liked to give a blow and receive a blow. I could run, too. I would say that of the boys I grew up with I was the fastest. One of the games we used to play was called Hare and Hounds. If you were the hare, you started first and then the hounds came after you, and sometimes you would run half a day at a time and think nothing of it. We were always running.

I did pretty well in high school football—I was a good halfback

—and I mention this because it has a significant bearing on later events in my life. I was a successful student, too. I graduated with the highest average in the senior class, and I won a cup for that. I was given another cup for the highest grade in American History. I won a twenty-dollar gold piece for the highest average of any boy in the school. I had good grades; I did good work. But even so, the idea of going on to college did not enter my head then. It was not something that I wanted to do, because when I was in Sanford going to high school I never wanted to be anything else but an end man in a minstrel show. I was very serious about it. Minstrel shows were big business when I was a boy, much the way vaudeville was. There were three major minstrel shows that toured the country, including Florida. There was J. A. Coburn, there was Lasses White, and there was Al G. Field. These shows would come into northern Florida and play Jacksonville and then they would work their way down through St. Augustine, Daytona Beach, De Land, into Sanford, and then on to Orlando, Lakeland, Tampa. They'd make a tour of the state. I used to meet them when they'd come in, and I'd follow them around. I got so I knew the whole show. I could sing anybody's song and tell everybody's jokes. I used to participate in amateur minstrel shows as a blackface comedian, which was an accepted art form in those days. I liked to try the little eccentric dances, the buck and wing, and I loved to tell jokes and sing songs. It became a passion with me.

After I got out of high school I came to know the organist at the Sanford Theatre, a fellow named George Brockhorn. I had gotten a job without much trouble after I graduated from high school. Times were good in central Florida just then—1926—and I went to work for a civil engineering crew. I was paid five dollars a day and worked six days a week, which meant I was earning thirty dollars a week. That was a marvelous salary for a young kid. It is still the most genuine money I have ever earned in my life. I mean that. That was net money. There were no deductions, for taxes or anything else, and there were no expenses. I lived in my father's house and he would never take a cent from me for room and board as long as he had a house and I wanted to stay in it. I was his son and he was my father, and I was welcome, and that was all there was to it. I had no wife, no children, no house to pay off, no rent to pay, no food to buy, and I didn't need any clothes in the job I had. I had thirty dollars net money, every week, with not one cent earmarked ahead of time for anything. I've never had that much since. I don't care how much gross I've made; I've never had thirty dollars net money with nothing calling on it.

So I had a good job, a fine salary, and a consuming interest. I hung around down at the Sanford Theatre with George Brockhorn and talked about minstrel shows. George would play the piano for me, and I'd practice singing and dancing. George knew Hank White, who was the stage manager for J. A. Coburn's show. Brockhorn helped me work out a routine, and when Coburn's minstrels came to town he spoke to Hank White about me. White said, "All right. Bring him around. Let's take a look at him."

I came to see him and Hank White said, in effect, the thing that everybody says in show business: "Make me laugh." In other words, kid, let me see your stuff. Brockhorn played the piano and I sang and did my dance steps and told a few jokes. I did all right. White said, "Well, now. I think you've got a chance. I think you've got a chance to be a black." That was the term they used in minstrel shows for the end men, the blackface comedians. If you were an end man, you were a black. White said, "I think you can make it. Do you play an instrument?"

"No, I don't."

"You'll have to learn one. Only the stars walk in the minstrel show parade without playing an instrument. The rest of the show has to double in brass. You'll have to learn to play something. The simplest one to learn fast—so that you can sort of go along and play a few notes in the parade and *look* as though you're playing something—is a slide trombone. Do you think you could do it?"

"Sure," I said. "I'll learn."

"All right," he said. "Now, I'll tell you what. We're getting toward the end of winter here, and we're about to finish this year's tour. So there's no point in you coming along now to try to break in with the show. We don't tour during the summer. The thing for you to do is to come up to Cincinnati in September and join us then. That will give you the summer to learn the slide trombone. When you join us we'll pay you eighteen dollars and cakes. All right?"

I said, "Fine!"

In those days the minstrel shows—J. A. Coburn's, anyway—traveled in two railroad cars. They slept on them and ate on them, and they used whatever extra space they had to store their equipment. I would get an upper berth and I'd be fed and I'd live off the cars the way the rest of the people did. That was cakes. And I'd get eighteen dollars a week beyond that. I thought that was great: eighteen dollars a week and cakes, and getting a chance with a real minstrel show.

My life was all set. I was on my way. I was going to be an end man. I scoured around town and bought the cheapest slide trombone I could find and looked up the local music teacher and started taking lessons. And I practiced. I sat out on the side porch in the evenings—it was too hot there in central Florida in the summertime to stay inside—and I'd blast away on the trombone. During the day, when the civil engineering crew I was working with stopped for luncheon, I'd get out that old trombone, and while the rest of the crew was sitting under the pine trees eating or trying to catch a quick nap, I'd blast away. I fixed their naps fast. But I practiced, I whaled away at it, and I got to where I could play second trombone on "Swanee River" and stuff like that pretty good. Or at least pretty loud. I wasn't hitting too many clinkers, and I'd reached the stage where I was getting a pretty good lip. When you start playing a brass instrument like a trombone or a cornet you have to get your lip in shape and keep it in shape. It's pretty hard on it.

Everything looked fine, and it was getting close to the time I'd be leaving for Cincinnati. My mother was rather unhappy about the idea, but she fixed up my clothes, put buttons on my shirts and everything. Of course, I didn't have too many shirts. I could take one battered old suitcase and put all my earthly possessions in it.

My father arranged to get me a pass on the railroad—a one-way pass to Cincinnati. I told Mr. Williams, the city and county engineer for whom I was working, that I would be leaving, and I told everybody in town. It was a fact; that was all there was to it. I was going north to Cincinnati to join the minstrel show.

Then, just a few days before I was to leave, I got a special delivery letter from Hank White. He said, don't come. He said, there is no more Coburn's minstrels. The company had folded. Vaudeville was dying, too, but the minstrel shows were beating vaudeville to the grave. Minstrel show days were over and my career as an end man stopped before it began.

Yet that is how close I came to going into the field. I wouldn't have been very good at it. Oh, I would have survived. I would have been good enough. But I would never have set the world on fire as an end man in a minstrel show. I realize now, as I look back on it, that it would have been a tragedy. You were continually on the road when you were a minstrel, and I was never cut out to be a hobo. I would have been very unhappy. When I travel I like to go someplace and come back. I know now that it would have been the worst mistake of my life if that show had not folded and I had become a part of it.

But I didn't go to Cincinnati. (I did some years afterward, and at much better terms, but that comes later in this story.) Back then in 1927, a little more than a year out of high school, I stayed right there in Sanford. I continued in my civil engineering job. I had given notice, but Mr. Williams didn't hold me to it. I kept right on working.

Then the Florida boom burst. The Great Depression that hit the entire country late in 1929 reached Florida a year or two ahead of time. Times got tough, very tough. The civil engineering job at five dollars a day went right down the drain. One day Mr. Williams said, "I'm sorry," and that was all. No job any more. No notice. No severance pay. No nothing. I worked at odd jobs around Sanford at anything I could find, and I had to keep looking harder and harder. I'd no sooner get a job than it would go. The pay scale kept going down, from five dollars a day to three dollars a day and finally to two dollars, when you could find a job. That was two dollars a day for working, as we used to say, from can to can't. From when you can see in the morning to when you can't see at night. Those were just about the hours for a two-dollar-a-day laborer. If you were lucky enough to get six days' work, that was twelve dollars a week.

The last job I managed to find—this was in the summer of 1928, two years after I had graduated from high school—was helping a fellow put on roofing with boiling pitch. Central Florida is, in a word, hot in the middle of summer, and when your job is to stand over a boiling pitch pot and take two buckets of melted, steaming pitch up a ladder onto a hot roof under a broiling sun and then help a man spread that pitch over the roof, you are more than just a little bit warm. I have the sort of skin that never tans. I burn and reburn and reburn. And there I was out in the Florida sun keeping a fire going under the pitch pot and going back and forth from the hot fire to the hot roof. It pained. Oh, it pained.

But the power of pain is an extraordinary thing. I know that it got me to thinking clearly about myself for the first time in my life. I said to myself, "Now, listen. Let's talk about this a little." I knew that I did not know what I wanted to do with my life. I *had* wanted to do one thing—be in a minstrel show—but I couldn't do that. That was finished, gone, up the creek. I didn't know what else I wanted to do. The following February I was going to be twenty-one years old, old enough to vote, and jobs were getting scarcer and scarcer. All you are, I told myself, is a day laborer. That's all you know how to do—just offer your services and a back which right now is pretty strong. But it's not as strong as some other day laborers' backs, and it can't stay strong all your life.

I had quite a few thoughts as I trudged back and forth with that hot pitch. This is no way to live, I told myself. Your father raised a family. How are you ever going to raise a family? You haven't got enough money to buy a wedding license, much less support a wife. You have to do something. I finally said to my-self—I may even have said it out loud, "Well, I may not know what I'm going to do in my life, but I know what I'm *not* going to do. And that's work like this." Then the thought came to me, out of nowhere, maybe I ought to go to college. I had never really thought about college before, but I knew that as a state resident I could go up to the University of Florida tuition-free. I'd have to work my way through to pay for room and board and the various fees, but the idea of working my way meant nothing. I had worked all my life, anyhow, in jobs here and there. I told myself, going to college may not be the right thing, but you can't lose. It's got to be better than this.

I climbed down off the hot-pitch roof when the day was over, and I never climbed back up. "I'm going to college," I said. "I don't know what I'm going to learn. I don't know what I hope to be. But I'm getting out of this place."

Between Innings: MY NAME IS WALTER

My full name is Walter Lanier Barber. My father's name was William Lanier Barber. My father's mother was a Miss Lanier of the Sidney Lanier family, the poet. Her husband, my father's father, was Walter Jones Barber. When I was born, as I was told the story, my mother wanted to name me Cornelius. My father said, "Absolutely no." Then my mother wanted to name me Junior, after him. And my father said, "Absolutely no." It just happened about then that my father's mother came down to see her first grandchild, and in desperation my mother turned to her for guidance. My grandmother suggested that I be named a combination of names after my father and his father, which is how I got Walter Lanier. I got my grandfather's first name, and my father's middle name.

When my brother was born, the pattern being set, he was named William after my father and Martin after my mother's family. My mother's maiden name was Selena Martin. My sister is Effie Virginia, after my father's sister and one of my mother's sisters.

I was always called Walter in the family. My mother called me Walter until she died. My father called me Walter, too, though once in a while, just teasing, he would call me Red. As soon as I started playing with other children and began to go to school, I was called Red, and that stuck. I had real red hair and it was very curly and there was lots of it. It's pretty thin on the infield now, but when I was in my senior year in high school I was voted the student with the most beautiful hair, boy or girl. Honest. I recall all through my earlier years one woman after another would be just furious at me and say, "How in the world can you have such hair? Look at mine."

I didn't care too much about being called Red, though it became universal outside of my family. I preferred Walter. To me, it is still a very warm thing when somebody calls me Walter. Branch Rickey always called me that. So did Bill Stewart, the old National League umpire. Red Smith, the columnist, calls me Walter. That's his first name, too, and we have a little reciprocal deal going; we call each other Walter. *He* likes to be called by his first name, too. That's one of the reasons Red liked Stanley Woodward so much—Woodward was the No. 1 man in the Marching and Chowder Red Smith Society Parade. Woodward used to call him Walter Smith.

We all like our names, but I learned at an early age not to struggle against "Red." It was "Red," and that was that. It was overwhelming, like the tide coming in, and I'm not the guy to stand on the beach and tell the sea to stay back there. When I first met Lylah, she was a nurse at the infirmary at the University of Florida. We met and we fell in love and we agreed to get married. Her mother was living in Jacksonville, and Lylah went over from Gainesville to break the news. She said, "Mother, I'm going to marry Red." Her mother said, "Red. Well. What's his real name?" And Lylah, to her consternation, suddenly realized that she did not know what my first name was. Her mother hit the ceiling. Nowadays you hear about the rockets taking off from Cape Kennedy, but Lylah's mother was the first item that ever took off into outer space from Florida. She said, "Do you mean to tell me that you're going to marry a man, with all that marriage means, you're going to marry him, and you don't even know what his first name is?"

Lylah had to say yes on both counts. But "Red" was that universal, and I had to accept it. Which is just as well. If I tried to coin a radio or television name, I doubt if I could have come up with a better one. I'm happy with it.

RED	1	3	5	(7)					
BARBER	2	4	6						

A day or so after I climbed off the hot roof I ran into a friend of mine named Cloyde Russell, who had been an end on the high school football team. Cloyde had gone right out of high school to Rollins College, which was down the road eighteen miles at Winter Park. It was a private school and an excellent school. My daughter Sarah is a graduate of Rollins, and I'm devoted to the place. Cloyde had put in two years there by the time I made my decision to abandon hot pitch.

I said, "Hey, Cloyde. I've decided to go to college."

"That's great," he said. "Where are you going?"

"Up to Gainesville, I guess."

"Look," he said. "Before you definitely decide, let me speak to Mr. Brown down at Rollins. Maybe he can get you an athletic scholarship. You can play football, and your grades certainly are good enough. I know they can get you a job down there, too."

"Gee," I said. "That would be wonderful."

"Now wait a minute. Let me speak to Mr. Brown first. Let me see if he's interested."

Mr. Brown was the business manager of the school, I believe, though I'm not certain, but in any case Cloyde came back up to Sanford a few days later and told me that Mr. Brown wanted to see me. I went down to Winter Park and I found that Cloyde had told Mr. Brown glowing things about my abilities as a player and as a student and I don't know what else. At this time, Rollins still had an intercollegiate football team. They later matured and became intelligent enough to give it up. Football is certainly not for small, liberal arts colleges.

Brown told me, "I think you would fit in here at Rollins. We can give you a scholarship, which means you will have no tuition to pay, and we'll get you a room and a place to eat. We'll see to it that you'll have a job on campus during the school year and also during the summer. Painting, carpentry, whatever. You'll be able to earn whatever you need to keep yourself going."

I was delighted. Rollins was offering me a guaranteed college education. It was like Christmas being 365 days of the year. Here I was, without a nickel, and here was a four-year college education right in my hands. I went back up to Sanford, floating. I was so pleased.

Then I ran into another fellow I had grown up with. His name was Leonard McLucas, and he was a wonderful fellow, a good friend. This meeting with him turned out to be one of the pivotal moments of my life. It caused me great distress for a time but eventually, as it turned out, great happiness. Leonard, who had been two years ahead of me in high school, had gone right up to the university at Gainesville, which meant that at the time I ran into him he had been up there four years. He was working his way through and it took him about five years in all to finish. Leonard was like that character in South Pacific, Luther Billis, though without the big pot stomach. In other words, Leonard McLucas was a natural-born scrounger with charm. He knew everybody up at Gainesville. He knew Captain Yon, who was the athletic director—he knew everybody.

I saw Leonard and I told him joyfully of my great good fortune. "Leonard," I said, "I'm going to Rollins!"

"Why do you want to go down there for?"

Well, gee. I explained about the scholarship and everything.

"You don't want to go down there with all those rich men's children," he said. "Those fellows down there have raccoon coats and roadsters. You wouldn't be happy there, working your way through. You wouldn't be at home." At that time, Rollins had an unfortunate name as a sort of play school for rich children out of the North. It wasn't true, but it did have the reputation.

"Listen," Leonard said, "don't you go down there and sign up for that scholarship for a few days. Captain Yon and Charlie Bachman are coming to Sanford to see Jim Sternhoff." Bachman was the new football coach at Florida, and Sternhoff was a big strong fullback who had just graduated from high school. "They want Jim to go up to Gainesville. When they come down here, I'll talk with them and see if there's a chance for some kind of an arrangement for you at the big school. If you're going to be working your way at college, you might as well do it at Gainesville. You'll have lots of company there. There's more guys working their way through than not. You just wait a few days and let's see."

I thought, well, maybe I'll wait. That was my first lesson about pride going before a fall. I thought maybe some of those rich kids at Rollins might be a little snotty or something. "All right," I said. "I'll wait."

I sent word to Mr. Brown that I would not be able to come down until the next week to sign with him. It wasn't a grant-in-aid that you had to sign. It was merely a statement of intent that you were going to the school and that they would provide tuition. In effect, you signed for your scholarship. I really didn't know, because I never signed. Yon and Bachman came to Sanford to see Sternhoff, and they talked him into going up to Gainesville all right, but apparently somebody from Georgia talked to him, too, because he stayed in Gainesville only a couple of weeks. Then he jumped campus and went to Georgia and played football there. Those things do go on. But in Sanford that day Yon and Bachman had snared Sternhoff and they were in a happy frame of mind when McLucas brought me over. Leonard had already talked to them about me, and, as I say, he was a very persuasive fellow.

Yon and Bachman said, "Oh, yes. We know all about you. Mac told us. We've heard about that day down at Kissimmee when you gained 270 yards and ran a kickoff back eighty-two yards for a touchdown. We'd love to have you up there at Gainesville."

Then Bachman looked me in the eye and said, "I understand you have a scholarship down at Rollins, and that everything is set there for you if you want to take it."

I said, "That's right."

He said, "I haven't got a scholarship in my pocket to pull out and hand to you. You don't need a scholarship at the university, because in-state boys pay no tuition. I haven't got a job in my pocket for you, either, at least not yet. I'm brand new on campus. I hardly know where my office is. But here's what I want you to do. You come up to Gainesville and register as a student, and then come see me. I don't know what the job will be, but I'll have a job of some kind for you that will keep you in school."

I thought about that for a little bit, and about Rollins, and about the rich boys with their raccoon coats and about working my way through, and then I said, "All right. I'll do it." I sent word to Mr. Brown at Rollins that I thanked him very much, but that I was not going to accept his offer after all. I was going to the University of Florida at Gainesville.

When I went up to Gainesville, I had one hundred dollars, all the money I had saved from the various jobs I had had. I hitchhiked a ride with Andrew Carroway and rode from Sanford to Gainesville in the rumble seat of his Ford. We got there in late afternoon and Andrew found me a place to sleep that night. I think it was in a fraternity house. The next morning I registered. There was a registration fee. I had to buy a pair of shoes for R.O.T.C. (all students had to take R.O.T.C.). I paid for a month's room and board in the dormitory. There were one or two other fees. At the end of that first day, my hundred dollars was shot. I had about three or four dollars left. But I was in school, I had my fees paid, and for one month I knew I could sleep and eat.

The next day I went over to see Bachman about my job, and I couldn't get in to see him. The word came out that the first thing for me to do was go out for the freshman football squad. I did. Later, I tried to see Bachman again, two or three times, but I never could get in to see him. The word would come out, keep going to freshman practice.

The first intrasquad game came along, and I played in about half of it. Two years of athletic inactivity had left its toll. I didn't run as fast. I wasn't as tough. I hadn't kicked a football in a couple of years, and when I tried to I didn't kick too well. On defense, I was playing halfback when a fellow broke loose and came through. I couldn't make the tackle on him, and he went all the way for a touchdown. I looked pretty bad, sprawled there on the ground. In all fairness, I have to admit that I did not impress anybody with my football abilities.

In that game I was kicked in the left shin. I still have the scar; it's as big as a quarter. The kick cut my shin and knocked a piece of bone out of place. I can still feel the spot with my finger; I haven't found that piece of bone yet. When I got in the shower after the game, the water and the sweat and the soap really livened up that cut. It stung like the devil. So here I was. I hadn't played well. I had this leg hurting me and stinging me. Two weeks had gone by with no sign of a job yet, and that was half my month. As I got dressed I was feeling more and more angry and frustrated and apprehensive. No money. No job. No sign of a job. I suddenly felt desperate—something had to give. I went up to Brady Cowell, the freshman coach, a nice man and a completely innocent party to all this, and I cried out, "*Where is my job?*"

He said, "I don't know anything about your job. I don't have a job for you."

I said, "You may not have a job for me, but I have an extra football uniform for you. Here." And I threw my uniform at him. I literally threw it at his feet, and I walked out. That was the end of my football career.

Now I was caught. And I mean caught. I had burned all my bridges. No money, no job. And I was very well aware of the fact that I had left a small town to go up to Gainesville, and I simply could not go back there defeated after one month. I could not stand the prospect of having everyone in Sanford say, "Well, Red's back. He didn't make it. Boy, he went up there with his tailfeathers up, and look at him now."

I could not ask my father for help. His income was limited, my mother was terribly ill, and my younger brother and sister were still at home growing up. I knew that if I wrote home and said, "Dad, I have got to have some money up here to eat on," he would have actually hocked the clothes off his back if he had to, but he would have raised fifty or a hundred dollars somehow and sent it to me. I couldn't do that to him. He had enough of a load. I could not add to it. I never told him about all of this— he's dead now, of course; he won't read this book—and he never knew the trouble I ran into in Gainesville. Nobody knew. I didn't say anything to anybody. What was there to say? Here was my beautiful four-year scholarship at Rollins—complete security for four years, because Mr. Brown had told me the scholarship did not depend on my making the football team—all gone, irrevocably gone. And now, instead of four years of security at Rollins, after only two weeks at Gainesville I had nothing. I was at the end of everything.

Again, Leonard McLucas entered my life, though indirectly. On the first day at registration I had bumped into Leonard, and he said, "What college are you going into?" I didn't understand what he meant. College was the University of Florida. I was there. He said, "I mean, for instance, are you going into the engineering college?" I said, "No, I don't want that." He said, "You can't go into the law college. You have to have a couple of years of undergraduate work first." I said, "Leonard, I was just going to go to college. I guess I'll take liberal arts." I had gone to Gainesville with an open mind. There was nothing particular I wanted to study. They didn't have any courses in minstrel shows there that I knew of. McLucas said, "If you're going to take liberal arts, you ought to go into the School of Education. You'll get your liberal arts there, and you'll also get training in education. Then, when you graduate, if you want to or if you can't find anything else, you'll be qualified to teach school."

That made sense to me, so I entered the School of Education. One of the courses I had was conducted by Dean Talbot, the dean of men, a very pleasant man. In his class I had my first awakening to the realities of college football. Several players were taking that course. There was Royce Bethea, a big halfback, and Carl Brumbaugh, who was a halfback at Florida but who later went to the Chicago Bears and had a great career as a quarterback under George Halas. There was Clyde Crabtree, a quarterback who could pass with either hand and kick with either foot. There was Royce Goodbread, a fullback. These were stars. The Florida team in 1928 lost only one game, the last game of the year. They lost it by one point, and they shouldn't have lost it. They were big time. One day in class, Dean Talbot read off the results of an examination we had had, and he did not read any grades for the football players. Now, Carl Brumbaugh was a devil. He always knew what the score was. After college when they asked him how he liked playing for the Bears, he said, "It's all right, if you want to take a cut in salary." He didn't mince words. He had been brought to the University of Florida to play football, and he was well aware of it. He was a gladiator. But this day when the dean did not read out the football players' grades, Brumbaugh said, "Excuse me, dean. I've got pretty good hearing, and I was listening to you carefully because I was interested. But I didn't hear you give grades for any of us on the team." The dean looked at him and said, "Well, now, Carl. You know how it is with you football fellows. You see me after class, and I'll give you your grades then."

You can add it up from there how they stayed in school. And that was the dean of men. Of course, it wasn't something that Dean Talbot originated or instituted. It was the going operation. The dean was a kind, decent man. I know that in my *extremis* the first thing I did after returning one football suit to the University of Florida was to run right over to his office. I told him I had to have a job. He said, "School has been going on a couple of weeks. All the jobs are gone. There are hundreds and hundreds of boys who want jobs, and there are never as many jobs as boys who want them. This is a small town."

I said, "Look, I have got to have work, any kind of work. If you have something that's worth twenty-five cents, give it to me. I need that quarter."

He sat there thinking for a minute and then he said, "I was talking to a professor the other day—Professor Burritt of the School of Architecture—and he told me he had some fireplace wood out in his yard. He has an apartment up on the second floor of a house and he needs somebody to carry the wood up-stairs and stack it on the back porch. Why don't you go over and see him?" I went to see Professor Burritt and I carried his wood up a flight of outside steps and stacked it on the back porch, and I earned thirty-five cents an hour for that. There was enough wood for a couple of afternoons' work, too, which was important. But even more important, I made a friend. Again, amid the changes and chances of this mortal life. . . . Later in that school year, Professor Burritt kept me in college and changed my life.

In the meantime, I had a few other small jobs. I hoed out a

clay tennis court that was getting overgrown with Bermuda grass, and I grabbed any other job like that I could find. About the time that my paid-up month at the dormitory was to expire, Dean Talbot called me in and said, "I just had a call about a job that might interest you. There's an old lady who has a house across the street from the campus, and she rooms and feeds students. She's pretty old, and she has to have somebody manage the house for her. The fellow she had quit, and she needs a new man."

"What does managing mean?"

"You run the place. Plan the meals, order the groceries, supervise the cook. You have to see that the beds are made and the rooms are cleaned up. If the maid doesn't show up, you have to go get another maid or else make the beds and clean the rooms yourself. You have to collect the board-and-room money from the boys living there, and if there's a vacancy you have to go out and fill it, get some students to come in and live there. You do whatever it takes to run that house. It pays room and board."

Boy, I thought, I can do that. For *room and board?* Gee, that meant I was in. After all, I had the R.O.T.C. uniform, which they gave us—all except the shoes—and which we had to wear to R.O.T.C. drills three days a week. Usually, we didn't have time to change after drill and we wore our uniforms all day, three days a week, and so that took care of three-sevenths of the clothes I needed. I had enough other clothes to get by; I didn't have to buy any. I could go to the library for whatever books I needed. If I had clothes and books and now a place to eat and sleep, how could they ever get me out of school?

I went and talked to the old lady, and I got the job. It worked out fine. My father had taught me how to cook, so planning meals and ordering groceries presented no problem. There were seven or eight boys living there, and the best thing I did for the old lady was to step between her and the boys whenever anything came up, any problem, any dispute. I told the boys, "Talk to me." If she became upset, I'd say, "Don't talk to them. Tell me about it. I'll take care of it."

My life went along evenly for several months. Everything was under control. I had got my world in order. I was enjoying school. I was enjoying my classes. One of them was a freshman

English course in rhetoric, taught by a young instructor named Hampton Jarrell. That class, too, was a key thing in my life. For one thing, I learned from rhetoric something I had never known before—something I had never learned even from my mother—and that was the difference between language that was gramatically correct and language that was rhetorically correct. Knowing that difference helped me to survive and develop in the rather hurly-burly, play-by-play existence around ball parks. I can quote a ballplayer or use a piece of jargon and, even though it may be incorrect gramatically, I *know* I'm on sound rhetorical grounds. If I get pushed on it, I can prove it. Mr. Genung, who wrote the book on rhetoric that we used in that course, helped me make my living. Hampton Jarrell, because he taught the course, helped me, too. He and I began to like each other almost immediately. Remember, I was a couple of years older than most of the other freshmen in the class, and I had a somewhat different point of view. One of the books we had to read for that class—there was a list of required reading issued by the university; it wasn't Hampton's list—was the autobiography of Edward Bok. Bok was an immigrant boy who had made a fortune in the publishing business and he was always being thrown up as a great example of the self-made man. The Bok Singing Tower in Florida, which is a tourist attraction, is one of his monuments. We had to make a report in class on Bok's book, and everybody was saying what an impressive thing it was, how inspiring, how uplifting, and I said I thought it was a bunch of rubbish. It wasn't a dadgummed thing but a rich man with a big ego showing off, and I said I doubted if he had written half of it. He probably got one of his writers to write it. It was just another monument to him while he was alive, like that Singing Tower.

Well, that caused my freshman English professor, Hampton Jarrell, to prick up his ears. At least there was a dissenting voice in the class. I became something more than just a nameless, faceless blur in a sea of students. We didn't become friends on the spot, but Hampton knew who I was.

Things went along smoothly through the winter. Toward the end of it, in March, I had gone home for a few days, and when I came back to the boarding house I started to go into the kitchen to check on the groceries and to see what needed to be ordered.

The old lady called out and said she wanted to speak to me. She said, abruptly, "I'm closing the house. I'm too old to live the way I've been living, and I've decided to go up to Tallahassee and stay with my younger sister. She's been after me a long time to go up there. I don't own this place; I only rent it. I don't have a lease, and I can give it up any time I want. So I'm going tomorrow. You close the house and get everybody out of it to-day."

Boom, just like that. Getting everybody out of the house meant getting me out of it, too. The other fellows were inconvenienced; they had to go scout around and find another place to pay room and board. But there wasn't any point in me scouting around. I didn't have any money to pay room and board. Suddenly, instead of having a secure world, I didn't have nothin'.

I closed up the house. It didn't take long. I got all my things together. I had a duffel bag and I put my shirts and underwear and an extra pair of shoes in that. About four o'clock that afternoon everybody was out of the house, including me. I had gotten to the top of the front step, and that's as far as I had gone. I had not gone any further because I didn't know where to go. I sat on the top step with the duffel bag, and Professor Burritt, the man I had stacked wood for, drove by in a yellow Ford roadster. He waved, and I guess I sort of despondently or dejectedly waved back, and he drove on up University Avenue toward his apartment. I just sat there. I wasn't even thinking. I was too stunned to think. I didn't know what to think. I actually did not have a dollar, not a dollar. When the rooming house closed down, my world had collapsed. I could have walked a block and a half to the so-called Bumming Corner, where the students hitchhiked rides out of Gainesville. You'd put on an orange rat cap, the beanie that freshmen wore, and you'd stand on certain corners in towns around the state, and motorists, recognizing from the rat cap that you were a student, would pick you up and give you a ride. It was easy to bum a ride. The main bumming corner in Gainesville was just a block and a half from where I was sitting, and I suppose my thoughts in the darkness of the moment were, "I can walk a block and a half to the bumming corner and then hitch-hike my way home to my father's house."

But again, that meant that I would go home defeated. I would go back to the small town a failure. Red didn't make it. And after all the trouble I had had, and after coming so close. Only a few more months and I'd have had the first year licked, and I knew I could earn money during the summer for the second year. Everything inside me revolted at the idea of quitting and going home, but I didn't know what else to do, which way to turn. I sat there, sort of licking my wounds before I got up and started moving, and here came that yellow roadster again. This time it pulled up and stopped at the curbing. Professor Burritt got out and came up the walk toward me, and he said, "I had a funny feeling after I drove by before, and I came back to ask: Is anything the matter?"

I was still numb, still sitting there dejectedly. I said, "No, nothing's the matter. Except the boarding house shut down, and I'm out of a job, and I don't have any money, and I'm sitting here wondering where I'm going to sleep tonight and how I'm going to eat."

He said, "Come on, get in the car. We'll go talk about it."

We drove over to his place and went up to his apartment. He made some tea, and we sat there drinking the tea, talking. As I look back, I can see that he had simply appraised my situation and out of the kindness of his heart had asked himself the question, "What can I, Alan Burritt, do this afternoon for this young man, whom I know only slightly, but who is at the moment absolutely destitute?" And the upshot was, he took me in. He said, "It's going to take a few days for you to work things out. While you're doing it—or while we're doing it—you can stay here. Understand, it's just until you get a job and find a place to stay. I'll buy you a card down at Louie's." Louie's was the Greek restaurant down on the square, and you could buy a card there which had twenty-six numbers. Each time you ate a meal—and it was a *meal*—they'd punch out a hole. So if you had an eating card, it meant you could eat. You could eat twenty-six meals.

Burritt not only saw that I was fed and not only took me into his apartment, he shared his bed with me. He had a big double bed, and he shared it with me, a stranger. Nowadays, I suppose, eyebrows would be raised at the idea of grown men sharing a bed, though it was not an uncommon thing at that time. But the remarkable thing was that he did it. He was a man of impeccable, fastidious taste, an architect. He was a New Englander, and he had an abiding interest in antique furniture. His apartment was filled with beautiful furniture, beautiful things, beautiful paintings. He was the first person of genuine artistic taste that I had ever met. My mother had an artistic taste for language, but this man had a taste for other things, things of material texture, things of quality. In his introduction to *Joseph and His Brothers*, Thomas Mann wrote that he thought the book would endure because he felt it was a work of quality. Professor Burritt appreciated things of quality; he kept them. They endured. I am going to some length stressing all this because it was such an extraordinary thing that he did for me. Here was a man in his forties, a bachelor, a very social man but a man who had everything in his life arranged just so, a man who didn't want anyone else in his life to disturb the pleasant pattern that he had established. And yet he took a stranger, a person he barely knew, into his home, into this fastidious, precise life. I don't know what more a man could do.

A day or so after he took me in—I had looked but had not yet been able to find anything on my own—he went off in the evening to play bridge. It happened that he was playing bridge that night with Hampton and Judy Jarrell, who had just recently been married, and with Miss Henry Mae Eddy, a spinster who worked in the school library and who lived in the apartment next to the Jarrells with her aged father. In the course of the evening Professor Burritt, without any rhyme or reason, but just as you make small talk when you're playing cards, said, "I've got a freshman staying at my place for a few days."

"Oh?"

"Yes," he said. "He was earning his bed and board running a rooming house, and they closed the house down on him. He didn't have any place to go, and I happened to come along. I know him slightly because he's done a few odd jobs for me, and he's a nice enough young fellow. So I took him in for a few days until he can find something."

"That's pretty inconvenient for you, isn't it?" Hampton Jarrell asked.

"Yes, it is," Burritt said. "I only have that big double bed. But it's only for a few days."

Somebody asked, "What's his name?"

"Red Barber."

"I know him," said Hampton Jarrell. "He's one of my students." They went on talking, and—I heard this story later from Professor Burritt and from Miss Eddy, so I think I have it right—Hampton said something again about how inconvenient it must be for Burritt, and then he looked at Judy and Judy looked back at him. Hampton said, "Judy, you never met this fellow, but he's a nice young man." Judy said, "I'm sure he is." They exchanged looks again and then Hampton said to Professor Burritt, "Alan, we've got a second bedroom here in this apartment that isn't being used. We thought Judy's mother would come and stay with us, but she can't right now. The room isn't being used, and it's not going to be used for the rest of the school year. Send your visitor over here."

Professor Burritt came home that night and said, "We've got a room for you, Red. At your English professor's." When you're in the fix I was in, you don't argue. I went around to the Jarrells the next day. Mrs. Jarrell couldn't have been nicer, and I got to know Hampton for the first time on a personal basis. I moved in and I lived there with them for three months. And I might as well have been living with Miss Eddy and her father next door, because they could not have been kinder or nicer, either.

We discussed the room and I asked Hampton how much it would cost. He said, "We'll discuss the price later." I said, "I can't do that." He said, "All right. I'll tell you what. The room will be five dollars a month, but you pay us next fall out of whatever money you earn this summer."

"If you'll do it that way," I said, "it will be a godsend to me."

And to keep my sense of pride healthy, Hampton allowed me to pay him that fifteen dollars when I came back to start my second year. I had the money right in my hand; I never felt more satisfaction in my life in paying off a debt than that one.

I moved in. I still had plenty of meals left on the meal ticket that Professor Burritt had bought for me. Also, the Jarrells and the Eddys were always inviting me to have tea and cakes and it seemed that nearly every other day I was invited to dinner in one apartment or the other. I could almost have survived on what I ate there. And I made the fourth at bridge. I don't think

Professor Burritt ever got back to play bridge with them. I moved in, lock, stock, and barrel.

One day Miss Eddy said, "Why don't you apply for a job in the school library? You have to have excellent grades to get a job there, but Hampton says you do have good grades." The quarterly grades had just been released and, by George, mine were high, so I applied to the head librarian, Miss Cora Miltmore—again, someone who changed my life—and I got the job. Now I was not merely secure, I was rich. I was making forty cents an hour working in the school library, and I could put in as many hours as I wanted. That gave me food money after the meal ticket ran out, plus a little extra. I had the room, a lovely room, and friendship with warm, kind people. I was in business again.

I liked that life so much I decided I wanted to become a college professor myself. I liked the Jarrells and Professor Burritt and all their friends—most of whom were professors, too, and their wives. If things had worked out differently and I had become a professor, I think I would have been completely happy.

All this not only gave me the chance to finish my freshman year—and vastly improve my life as I did finish the year—it gave me time to look around and line things up for my sophomore year. I wanted to get a job waiting on tables, which would give me my meals and leave the money from the library to pay for a room. But things didn't quite work out that way.

About the middle of my freshman year I had heard that they were having tryouts for the glee club, and this brought back the obsession I had had of becoming an end man in a minstrel show. I didn't care anything about being a straight singer in the glee club chorus, and I knew I didn't have a good enough voice to be a soloist. But I had heard that the glee club used specialty acts, and that they put on a skit night in which they would present fifteen or sixteen different acts. One boy would sing and another would play the xylophone and a third might do a tap dance. I went down and tried out, and the director of the glee club said, "Fine. We'll put you on skit night." I did my blackface skit and it went over very well. I became a fixture. The glee club used to travel around the state and give concerts in places like Fort Pierce, Orlando, St. Petersburg, and Jacksonville. They would take maybe the three best skits from skit night and bring them along. The glee club would sing the first half of the program, then they'd put on the skits, and then the glee club would come back and finish the evening. It was a good program, and I was good enough in my skit to be invited to be in it. Eventually, I worked into an act with a fellow named Jimmy David, who was a marvelous dancer but sort of limited beyond that. I could sing and tell jokes but wasn't much of a dancer; I could do some of the eccentric steps and make it look as though I was dancing, but I couldn't put the wing on the buck, for example, or anything like that. The director suggested, "Why don't you two get together and work something out?" David taught me a few extra steps, and we split some jokes between us and we worked out a nice little skit. We spent hours working together because we had to put on a new act every time the glee club presented a new show. We did all right. The glee club used to crowd into the wings to watch us when we were on. Oh, that David could dance. He was good.

So now I was doing something I really loved to do, and toward the end of my freshman year, after I had gotten the job at the library, it came time for the glee club to make a four-day trip. I went to Miss Miltmore, the head librarian, to ask for time off. As far as I was concerned, it was a technicality, but Miss Miltmore said, "No." She said I couldn't get off, that I had to stay and work in the library, down in that dusty morgue with all those dry old books. That was a job I didn't much like, though I was happy to do it to earn money to eat.

I said, "Miss Miltmore, really now. This glee club stuff is something I've been doing all year. It's important to me, and for goodness sakes, it's only three or four days. You have plenty of boys around here to work on the stacks." But she was an old maid, and she was stubborn. She had her rules and she put her foot down. She would not give me permission to take the time off.

I said, "Miss Miltmore, you really shouldn't tell me not to go."

She said, "You make the choice if you feel so strongly about it. You go, and there won't be any job in the library when you come back."

I thought it over. The school year was ending in about two weeks, and I had a little extra money saved up by now, and I

130

had the room with the Jarrells. I knew I could get a job home in Sanford for the summer, where I could earn money for the fall. I'd be living in my father's house, with no expenses to speak of. It was one of the few times in my life that I could really be like a hog on ice. I reared up and said, "Well, I'll tell you what, Miss Miltmore. I'm going with the glee club."

She said, "I'll tell *you* what. Don't come back to the library."

And I didn't. I went with the glee club and lost the library job, but that turned out to be a wonderful break because it set so many other things in motion in my second year in school. If I had come back to school with the job in the library for guaranteed cash, my life would have been vastly different. I certainly would not have gotten the job I did get at the University Club. And if I had not gotten that job, I probably never would have become involved with the campus radio station.

I hope I'm not being too prolix on all this, but it fascinates me how much a human being's life is tempered and directed by casual incidents, by people who are little more than strangers or sojourners in your life, people who just happen to come by in a yellow roadster and get four or five blocks on down the street and say to themselves, "There was something strange about the way that boy was sitting there on that front step."

What made him turn around and come back?

Between Innings: MISS HENRY MAE EDDY

Miss Henry Mae Eddy was over fifty when I first met her. Her father was eighty. They were very companionable. They lived together easily and pleasantly. Her father was a fine old man, and Miss Eddy was the only old maid I have ever known who didn't become a bit sour once in a while. I loved to sit and talk with her. We spoke of many things. One day—I don't know how the subject came up—she happened to say that she had never had a sexual experience. But she said it meant nothing to her, that she had never felt that she had missed anything. She had no antagonism toward the idea of sex. It just seemed that she was destined to grow up and live as an old maid who worked in a library and took care of her aged father. You could not imagine a more normal, pleasanter person. She looked the way you might imagine a young grandmother would look in the fullness of her life. She was a lovely woman. I believe she was designed to be just what she was, a beautiful old maid. She had one passion. She wanted to see the harbor of Rio de Janeiro before she died. She dearly wanted to see that, and she spoke of it all the time. Of course, when I knew her, when her father was still alive and in her care, she could not hope to go there.

I never saw Miss Eddy again after I left Gainesville. Years later, around 1940, when I was broadcasting Dodger games, I was sitting at breakfast one morning in our home on Lynwood Road in Scarsdale, New York. I picked up the paper, and the headlines were all about the crash of a Pan American plane in the harbor of Rio de Janeiro. Way down in small type was the list of passengers who had been killed, and the thing that so startled me and startled my wife, who was sitting there at the table with me, was that at the same instant I saw the headline I saw Miss Eddy's name in the passenger list. It jumped out at me.

My mind remembered Robert Browning's line, "A man should die at his pinnacle moment." Miss Eddy had so wanted to see this place, this beautiful harbor. We read the story carefully. It was a mystery crash. It had been a completely beautiful, bright day, with no limit on visibility. So, my wife and I conjectured, Miss Eddy had seen the harbor of Rio de Janeiro. She had lived to see it. Then she died. She didn't live to be disappointed by it, this thing she had wanted so passionately to see.

RED	1	3	5	7				
BARBER	2	4	6	(8)				

I was determined that what had happened my first year at Gainesville was not going to happen again. During the last half of my freshman year I had worked here and there as a substitute table waiter when somebody was sick or wanted to get off for a day. I had got my foot in the door that way at Ma Trumper's, which was an eating place, and I had been promised a full-time job waiting tables in my sophomore year. That meant I'd get my meals. You weren't paid anything and nobody left any tips; you were just waiting on fellow students. But if you could eat, you were in good shape. And I had made an agreement with a boy named Jerry Carter, who was in several of my freshman classes, to share the costs of a room in our second year.

I worked that summer at home in Sanford and I saved every cent. I mean that literally: every cent. I had a government job. There was a great scare that summer about an infestation of the Mediterranean fruit fly, and the Department of Agriculture came in with a bunch of trucks and some money to root them out. I got a job within a week of coming home. I drove a truck five and a half days a week and then I had to come in on Sunday morning for four or five hours to work on the truck—wash it and lubricate it and change the oil. That was done on your own time, but you had to do it if you wanted to keep the job. That was the attitude of the government then. It wasn't too benevolent.

In fact, my experience with the government has been pretty much a one way street toward the government. When I worked for them, they made me work extra time for nothing. Since I've been paying taxes, it seems they stay up late at night to make sure I pay them plenty.

I was paid by government check, and I did not cash one of them. I put them all in the bank. I had some dates that summer but whenever I asked a girl for a date, I'd say, "Can I come over to your house?" I didn't take any girls to the picture shows. I didn't take them down to the drug store for a soda. I was obsessed with the idea of saving every nickel.

About two weeks before I was to go back to school my daddy lent me his car, which had his gasoline in it, and I drove my date around a little bit. We just rode around and rode around and about ten o'clock as we drove through town I saw a bunch of men standing outside the bank. It looked sort of funny. I parked and went over and asked one of the men what was going on. He said, "Go look at the door." I went up to the door and looked, and there was a sign stating that the bank had closed down. It had failed, and when it failed there went the money I had worked all summer for and had refused to spend even one nickel of, the money I knew I'd need so badly at Gainesville. Today, banks and depositors are covered by Federal Deposit Insurance, which came in after so many banks collapsed during the 1930s in the depth of the Depression. But that was a little late for me and my money. I went back to the car, drove the girl home, told her good night in a sort of stunned voice, and went home and got into bed. I was cold all over. I was closer to being a piece of stone than a warm, human body. That was the first time I can recall ever thinking that if I went to sleep, when I woke up it would all be just a dream. But in the morning that bank was still closed. It hit a lot of people hard, and it hit me completely. When I had gone to Gainesville my first year I had one hundred dollars, which wasn't much. When I went up there for my second year I had even less.

But I did have the job waiting tables. And I did go in with Jerry Carter on a room for at least one month. I'm awfully glad I did, and I'll tell you why. Jerry was working his way through school selling cakes and bakery goods. He was provided with an old third- or fourth-hand Chevrolet body truck, and about twice a week he'd drive over to Jacksonville to the bakery and come back with whatever they wanted him to sell to the stores in the Gainesville area. On a Saturday a couple of weeks after school had opened, Jerry had gone over to Jacksonville for a load of bakery goods and he had the truck parked there by our rooming house. I don't know whether he was to deliver the cakes and pies and all on Sunday or wait till Monday, but anyway there they were in the truck. Now, Saturday was a football day, of course, and there had been a student custom at Gainesville that on the evening of a football game the students would gather together and rush the motion picture theater. There was only one movie in town, and on Saturday night, just before the feature was to come on, several hundred students would mill around and by sheer numbers force their way into the theater and see the show for nothing.

They thought it was great fun, but the theater manager, Claude Lee, had different ideas. He didn't think it was funny, but he knew the university couldn't stop it and he knew the police couldn't stop it. There were too many students, and if the university or the police tried to make a case out of it, the students would get a bigger mob together. People had come to accept it as a kind of tradition on football nights, but Claude Lee decided he had to do something about it. He got permission to speak to the students at chapel, which was really like an assembly, and he told them, "Look, I want to work something out with you students. You're ruining my Saturday night business. You make it uncomfortable for the people who come and pay their way in, and you're keeping most people in town from even trying to come. And when you rush the theater, a lot of you can't get in anyway because there are paying customers in there sitting in some of the seats. You have to wander off without seeing the picture. Now, look. I'll make a deal with you. If you'll please not rush the theater during the paying hours, at 11 P.M. every Saturday when there's a football game, the theater will be yours. I'll open it free to students only, and I'll run the feature and two or three short subjects. You'll know it's going to be open, and you can plan for it. You can bring a date."

The students thought that was great. They bought that. That was their show. On this Saturday night, a couple of friends—three, to be exact—came by the room that Jerry and I had, and the five of us were sitting around, killing time, waiting to go to the eleven o'clock free show.

That afternoon maybe a dozen of us had been hanging around out in front of the house and we had gotten into a big bull session on the subject of our lives and the work we were going to do and marriage. It was a regular stump session and when it got around to me, I stood up and I made a beautiful speech. I waxed eloquently and at some length to make the point that I was taking extra hours of classroom work and earning my way through school, that I was past twenty-one, and that this was *my* education, and that I was going to get out of Gainesville in three years and then go on to graduate school to get my masters, and that then I was going to teach. I was going to be a college professor. I was going to make a little money and see how things looked toward studying for a Ph.D. I said there was no room in my plans for a woman. I wasn't about to get married, and I couldn't see marriage for me for at least ten years. The last thing in my future at the moment was marriage. That was my speech, and it was a good speech, a sincere speech, one of the most sincere speeches in the history of mankind. I meant every word.

So that night, there were the five of us sitting around the room waiting for the free show. We started to drink some shine— which is a word contracted from "moonshine," illegal whiskey. This was during prohibition. You couldn't buy whiskey legally. This shine wasn't clear and watery, like white mule. There in north-central Florida they really knew how to make shine. They'd get the clear, white stuff and put it in a charred keg. Then they'd put the keg on the back end of a truck or in a rumble seat, where it would shake pretty good, and they'd drive it around for about a week. And then it would have the loveliest color you ever saw. There's nothing in a liquor store today that has a more beautiful color.

The five of us very quickly disposed of what little shine Jerry and I had, and nothing would do but we had to go out and get some more. The going system was to take a gallon jug and a five-dollar bill. You drove straight west past the country club to some pine woods, and you went into the woods to a particular stump. You put down the five-dollar bill and put the empty gallon jug on top of it, and then you went off. You came back a half hour later and your jug would be full and your five-dollar bill would be gone.

We got five dollars together, which was just about all the ready cash we had, and we piled into Jerry's bakery truck. It had only one seat, the driver's seat, but we all five got in. Jerry was driving, and we headed west out past the country club. There was a slight hill, a downgrade. Memory tricks you. I had always remembered that as a pretty steep, good-sized hill, but I was essentially a pedestrian in those days and hills look bigger when you're on foot. In the spring of 1966 I drove my car from the Yankee training camp in Fort Lauderdale to Atlanta, where the Yankees were playing an exhibition series, and I broke the jump by stopping off in Gainesville to see some friends. When I left, I happened to drive west out of town on the same road to get to the main highway. The big, steep hill turned out to be the gentlest little slope you ever saw.

But that night in 1929 it was steep. And the road was much narrower; two cars had to squeeze to get by each other. And it had sand shoulders. We started barreling down the slope in the bakery truck, and the truck began to wobble and weave and it went off the left-hand side of the road. The left front wheel sank in the soft sand, something snapped in the steering apparatus, and the truck turned over and kept turning over three or four times. As it turned over, it threw us out, one after the other. We must have looked like the succession of clowns in the circus act who keep coming out of a small automobile. When I was thrown out I remember hitting the soft sand and instantly feeling grateful: holy mackerel, I'm out of that. And the next thing I knew was, "Ooomph." I had been thrown ahead of the truck, and after I landed it rolled right over the small of my back.

Nobody was hurt to any extent, except me. I *felt* all right, but I couldn't walk. I was sort of paralyzed from the small of my back down. And I was bloody and covered with dirt and sand spurs and cake dough and icing and commercial pies. I was a mess. There was nothing but calories and cholesterol all over the place, mixed with a little of my blood.

We went back onto the campus—the other fellows carried me —to the university infirmary. It was about midnight by the time we got there, and the nurse on duty who answered the door took one look at the filthy mess that I was and in a tone of utter disgust said, "Take him back and lay him down." As she said it, I noticed that she had the prettiest brown eyes I had ever seen in my life. And that's the woman I'm married to.

She had caught night duty all by herself, and it had been a rough night. There were two or three football players who had gotten hurt that day, including one boy who had sprained both wrists and couldn't do anything for himself. She had to feed him, hold the glass for him when he wanted a drink, everything. There were three boys who had come down to the university from Brooklyn, and some of the Florida boys had told them that the nuts of the tung oil tree were delicious. The boys from Brooklyn had bitten into them and had become violently ill. They were in the infirmary, throwing up all over the place. Then I came in, blood, sand, cake icing, pie filling, and I was the last straw. I was the end of the road. "Take him back and lay him down," she said.

But that's how I met Lylah. The numbness in my back passed very quickly, and in the two or three days I was in the infirmary I became greatly enamored of her. And once I was cleaned up and washed off, I guess I didn't look quite as bad as I had when they carried me in. The day I got out of the infirmary I asked her for a date, and she accepted. On our second date we agreed that we'd marry each other. We didn't set a date. We merely agreed that some day we were going to get married, and we kept steady company after that. It was one week since I had made my reasoned, passionately sincere speech that there would not be a woman in my life for ten years. Lylah always has had to be a little chary of criticizing me if I had a few drinks because I could always point out to her that if I hadn't been drinking I never would have met her.

That was the fall of 1929 and we were married in March of 1931. She had graduated from Florida State College for Women in Tallahassee with a Bachelor of Science degree in nursing in the first college class in the United States to get such a degree. She had a job of instructress of nurses waiting for her at her hospital in Jacksonville, but to qualify completely for it she had to go to Cook County Hospital in Chicago for a post-graduate course. She was working at the university infirmary only until she was to leave for Cook County right after Christmas. She stayed at Chicago for a year and then at the beginning of 1931 came back to Jacksonville and that's when we decided to get married.

But when we met, back there in 1929, marriage was still distinctly in the future. I was at the beginning of my sophomore year, and I was rapidly running out of what little money I had. I had heard of a scholarship loan fund that a Masonic order (Knights Templar) had—I was greatly interested in Masonry—and I had applied for and been granted a two-hundred-dollar loan, which was a lifesaver for me. But, forget marriage, it wasn't enough by itself to get me through the school year. One day, just about the end of the first month of the term, I met one of my professors, a man named Wallace Goebel, on campus and just to make conversation I said, "Whatcha doin'?" He said, "Right now I'm trying to find somebody to be janitor at the University Club."

The University Club was really a rooming house for five or six bachelor professors, but it also served as a meeting place. Professors who belonged to the Club could hold meetings in the big living room and dining room of the house. The Club didn't provide meals, but the half dozen bachelor professors who lived there needed someone to take care of the place. Whoever had been doing it had quit, and when I ran into Wallace Goebel he was beating the bushes to find somebody to take the fellow's place. I was immediately interested, and I asked, "What does the janitor have to do?"

He said, "Make the beds, sweep the place, gather up the laundry and send it out, things like that." I said, "If you give me my room rent, I'll take the job." I was running out of money and I was about to give up the room I had had with Jerry Carter. Goebel thought I was kidding, but I convinced him I wasn't and I got the job. Instead of getting room rent, I was given a room at the Club and it was as nice a room as any other in the house. I enjoyed that job. I did the work—I swept, janitored, made beds, took care of things—but in every other respect I lived with the bachelor professors as an equal. They accepted me as though I was one of them. It was stimulating, being in their company. We always had a table of bridge, and sometimes two, and the conversation was lively. We lived a wonderful life, and the more I saw of it the more I was convinced that this was what I wanted to be, a college professor. As I watched them, there was no doubt in my mind that some day I was going to be one of them.

I had the world by the tail on the downhill pull again. I had my meals; it didn't take me much more time to go up to Ma Trumper's and wait on tables and then eat for free, than it would have if I had just gone up there to eat. There wasn't any choice of menu. You brought out what was in the kitchen and set it down, and after the students finished eating you'd pick up the empty plates and bring them back into the kitchen. They always had mashed potatoes with commercial gravy; my thumb was stained for years from being in that gravy twice a day.

I had my meals. I had my room. In addition I had the companionship of the professors, with their wide interests. Goebel was a sociology teacher. Frank DeGaetani taught Spanish, and he also taught me a great deal about opera. Frank became a very close friend; he was the best man at my wedding. Professor Hauptmann taught German. Ralph Fulghum—he and I shared the same birthday, February 17—was in the Department of Agriculture at the university.

One of Fulghum's assignments was to put on a forty-five-minute farm program over the campus radio station. That was WRUF, for Radio University of Florida. It was owned by the state of Florida and operated by the university. Fulghum's program ran from noon until twelve forty-five, and during it various aspects of farming would be discussed by members of the faculty. They would read ten-minute papers on specific subjects, and in between the readings there might be discussions on raising peanuts, or feeding peanuts to pigs, or what you did about this disease that bothered cows, or ways to prevent erosion.

If a professor was unable to be at the station to read the paper, Fulghum would read it for him.

In the course of the fall term, what with my duties at the University Club and waiting on tables and carrying twenty-one hours of classroom work and dating Lylah before she left for Cook County, I had done a little procrastinating about a term paper on King James I that was due in a course I had in English history. My procrastinating was done subconsciously as much as it was consciously because that class in English history was a bitter disappointment to me. It had been the one course above all others that I had wanted to take. I knew I wanted to be a professor, but I hadn't decided whether to specialize in English literature or English history. I loved both and I don't believe you can separate the two, at least not too much. I could not take the English history course as a freshman, and all through my first year I was looking forward to taking it as a sophomore. I drew as a professor a man whose name I won't mention—because he is still teaching—who was the epitome of the dull, dry, unimaginative college prof. He should have been working behind a counter in a hardware store where they sell different sizes and gradations of nails and screws and nuts and bolts. That's the way he taught English history. His method was to assign certain pages to be read in a textbook, and then, working from index cards, he would lecture, following a careful, precise outline. He would not tolerate questions because a question was an interruption that would throw him off his outline and his time schedule. It was painfully dull. I like to exchange ideas. I like to talk and listen and talk again. I believe the finest teachers operate on that principle—give and take with their students, a mutual stimulation. I wanted to know more than what the textbook said, and more than what the professor told us as he followed his index cards. His lectures were just a rehash of the textbook.

I avoided doing any more work for that class than I had to. I was doing very well in my other courses, and one day this professor called me in and said, "I am aware that you do A work for other professors. Why are you doing D work for me?" I was startled, but I said, "Professor, are you sure you want me to tell you?" He said, "Yes." I said, "Well, I have never been so disappointed in a course in my life. You are the dullest man I have ever met, in or out of a classroom. English history should be the most stimulating course anyone could ever give, but you make it tedious, dry, and boring."

We parted on not completely amicable terms, but a truce existed between us from then on. I did barely enough work to get a passing grade, and he gave me barely a passing grade. I was in no hurry to get that paper done on King James I, but it had to be in at the beginning of school after the Christmas holidays. I came back to Gainesville early, a few days before school reopened, and that was important because the restaurant where I worked wasn't open yet and my source of food wasn't available. I had to spend cash money when I ate, and I didn't have enough to spare on food.

One morning about eleven o'clock I was sitting in the living room at the University Club, working on old James, trying to get that paper finished. My heart wasn't in it, but I was putting down the words. Ralph Fulghum walked in and when he saw me he said, "Red, I'm in a mess."

I barely looked up from the term paper. "That's too bad," I said.

"I've got to read *three* different papers on that farm program today."

"Is that so?" I really wasn't paying too much attention to him.

"Can you imagine that?" he asked. "Three different men, and all three are out of town."

"I expect you'll have to read them all yourself."

"I can't do that. I've got to have a change of voice." He was looking at me. "I wish I could get somebody to read that middle paper for me. It would help a lot."

"I hope you find somebody, Ralph, but look, would you mind leaving me alone? I have to get this term paper finished. I don't have much time."

"That's not that important. Come on. Jump in the car and go out to the station with me and read this paper. Come on, Red."

"Ralph, I haven't got anything to do with the radio station.

There's nothing out there I have to do. You go read that thing yourself. I have to finish this term paper."

"Red, please. Come on. It would be a big help to me, having a change of voice. If I sit there and read all three papers, one after another, it'll be terrible."

I was beginning to get a bit irritated.

I said, "I don't have time to go out there, Ralph. Now, please, leave me alone."

Then came the great turning point in my life. I know that Satan took Christ up on a mountain and showed him the world and said, "If you bow down to me, I'll give it all to you." Christ wasn't tempted, but I was. Fulghum tempted me out of all proportion. He said, "If you come out and read this paper I'll buy you dinner tonight."

I didn't even think about it. I closed the book I was working from and I said, "If you'll buy me dinner I'll read all three papers."

"One will be enough," he said. "Let's go."

We drove out to the station and he handed me the paper. I think the professor who wrote it was out of town by design. It was a very thorough, heavily documented, detailed treatise on "Certain Aspects of Bovine Obstetrics."

I read it. It meant dinner, and I read it. I sat down at a little table in a little room, and a fellow said, "When I point to you you start talking into that," and he indicated the microphone on the table. There was no rehearsal, no voice level tests, nothing. He pointed and I started reading. When I finished, I got up and walked out of the room. I started to leave the station, too, because Fulghum had another half hour to go on the program, and I didn't have another half hour to waste. I was going to walk back across campus to the University Club and King James. As I started to go out the door a man came up to me and said, "Did you just read that paper?"

"Yes, I did."

"I'm Major Powell. I'm director of the station here."

"Yes, sir." I told him my name.

He said, "Your voice registered very well."

"Thank you," I said. And I started to leave again. King James was calling.

"Wait a minute," he said. "What I'm getting at is that we need a part-time student announcer, and I'm wondering if you'd be interested in the job. I'm new here at the station. I've just taken over and I don't know how to go around looking for student help. When I heard your voice, I thought, 'Well, this one will do.' How about it?"

I said, "Thank you very much, but I've got all the jobs I can handle right now."

"What do you mean, all the jobs you can handle?"

I told him about the University Club, and waiting on tables, and taking twenty-one hours in school. I said, "I do thank you, but I don't know how I could take on another job."

And this time I left.

About once each week after that, Ralph Fulghum would come into the University Club and he'd say, "Red, Major Powell wants you to come out to the station and go to work." And every week I'd say, "Ralph, that's the silliest thing I ever heard of. I don't have time. I'm *not* coming out to the station and go to work."

My life was beautifully put together just then. Everything was working smoothly, and I didn't want to change any of it. But Major Powell kept asking, and Fulghum kept bringing me the message, and I kept sending my refusal. Fulghum was getting tired of being in the middle, and I guess I was getting a little sore, too. One day Ralph said, "Red, Major Powell has been giving me such a bad time about you coming to work for him that I hate to go out there and do my own program. It isn't pleasant any more." I said, "It isn't pleasant for me either, having you come in here all the time telling me about Major Powell."

"Well, it has to stop," he said.

I agreed. "It has to stop, and I'm going to stop it. I'll go out and tell Major Powell in person to leave me alone and to leave you alone. Will that suit you?"

"Yes," he said. "Fine. Just so it's settled, once and for all."

I went on out to the station and in to see Major Powell in his office. I said, "Major Powell, you've been very kind and I appreciate your interest in me, but I've come out here to get this matter settled. I want to explain again why I don't have time to work for you." I ran down my schedule and my jobs and my activities, and I said, "Now you show me where I can do all that and still have time left to come work for you."

"On that schedule, I can't," he said. "But how much would I have to guarantee you in salary for you to give up these other jobs and just work here?"

I did some calculating. Let's see. For twenty dollars a month I could have two meals a day, and for another five dollars I could have breakfast, too. Add ten dollars more a month for a room, without any janitoring duties, and that would be thirty-five dollars. Another five dollars for laundry and incidentals makes forty dollars. And—oh, well—add another few dollars for pocket money. This was 1930, and the Depression was really beginning to hit. I told myself, I know how to stop this man from bothering me. I can put a spoke in his wheel right quick. I'll ask him for all the money in the world. He won't be able to pay me, and he'll have to leave me alone. I said, "Major, you'd have to guarantee me fifty dollars a month."

"Okay," he said, "it's a deal."

Holy mackerel, you talk about Mickey Owen wanting to go dig a hole in the ground and jump in when he dropped that strike on Henrich. I had asked this man for a monthly salary that would cover all my room and board expenses, for which I had been working so hard each day, plus an ample amount of extra money for incidentals, plus another amount for spending money, and he had said *yes*. My hard-earned security for which I had struggled so hard—my cheerful, pleasant, well-ordered life which I found so compatible—was washed away. I had told him, "Pay me fifty dollars and I'll come to work." And he had said, "Okay." I couldn't argue any more. I was committed.

I had to tell Ma Trumper that afternoon that I wasn't going to wait tables any more. I had to tell my professor friends that I wasn't going to be janitor any more, though I did arrange to keep my room there for ten dollars a month. On March 4, 1930, I went out to the radio station to start a job that I knew nothing about. I had no comprehension of the work that it would entail, and I didn't have the slightest reason to feel confident I could handle it. I felt I had been boxed in. After half starving and being scared to death my freshman year, after working and saving all my money all summer only to have the bank close on it, after finally getting everything lined up and having it where I could keep on for the next few years as a student, all of a sudden everything was upset again. In that confused, uncertain, uneasy state of mind, I went off to begin broadcasting.

Perhaps people will understand why I have always felt embarrassed when young people ask me, "How did you break into radio?"

Between Innings: THE CARBON MIKE

When I began at WRUF, they had two microphones at the station, two carbon microphones. Every half hour or so the carbon particles would stick together and start to interfere with the sound, and the engineer would have to switch off the microphone and come out and tap the back of the mike with a pocket knife to shake the particles loose.

I visited the university a few years ago to make a talk or some such thing, and I noticed that they had both microphones in the university museum. I did not take a fee for whatever it was I did, but the university insisted that they wanted to give me something. I said, "All right. Give me one of those carbon microphones."

And they did. I have it at home now, the first mike I ever spoke into on radio—or, if it isn't the first, it's the second. Either way, I've got it.

RED	1	3	5	7	(9)				
BARBER	2	4	6	8					

WRUF at the University of Florida was a five-thousand-watt, daylight-only, non-commercial radio station. It was sustained completely by funds from the university's budget, as appropriated by the state legislature. That changed in later years, but that's the way it was when I was there. There were only two jobs of any importance at the station then. One was station director, the position held by Major Powell—Major Garland W. Powell. The other was chief announcer, and that was Ralph Nimmons, who worked full time and was paid $150 a month. Major Powell was a genuine major (he had earned the rank in World War I), and in Washington he had become firm friends with Dr. John J. Tigert. When Dr. Tigert came to the university as its president in the summer of 1928 and found the directorship of the radio station open he gave the job to Major Powell, and it was a wise choice.

Beyond Major Powell and Ralph Nimmons, there was a very small staff. When I joined the station I did odd jobs, anything that came along that they wanted me to do. Nimmons did most of the important announcing, and a fellow named Jack Thompson, who was very good, did whatever ad lib broadcasting that had to be done, particularly sports. Thompson's father was an outstanding attorney in Miami, and that proved to be yet another important factor for me.

I'm getting a bit ahead of my story, but the first sporting event to come along after I joined WRUF was the annual high school basketball tournament. All the high schools in the state came to Gainesville each year for the tournament, and they played basketball all day long and into the night for three consecutive days. Because the tournament was statewide and because the radio station was supported by state funds, the regular broadcasting schedule was thrown out and every last one of those high school basketball games was broadcast in full. Every town wanted to hear the doings of its own team, whatever time of day its game happened to go on. WRUF broadcast every game, starting Friday morning at 8 A.M. and continuing through Sunday night. Games were played consecutively; as soon as one was finished the next one would start. There was supposed to be some intermission between them but games get delayed and, practically speaking, it was an almost continuous operation, with a break only for lunch and supper. One announcer handled the microphone all the way through. Jack Thompson did it the first year I was there, but I did it all myself in 1931, 1932, and 1933. It was the most grueling broadcasting job I have ever had. You sat right next to the official scorer and read off his book. You had no assistant, nobody to spell you, nobody to give the listeners a change of pace. It was terribly demanding and I used to be physically sick by the time the tournament was over. It gave me a complete distaste for basketball; I have never liked the game since. When I finally left Florida for Cincinnati in 1934, I was glad I left at the time I did—at the beginning of March—because I escaped doing the tournament that year.

But in the beginning my job at the station was doing whatever they needed. I read news. I read features. I interviewed professors. I announced singers. I announced piano recitals. I played records. I played all sorts of records—popular music, country music, classical music. I learned a great deal about opera from playing those records and then talking about them with Frank DeGaetani. I came to like opera so much that when Lylah and I moved to New York in 1939 the first evening we had out we went to a performance of *Carmen* at the Metropolitan Opera.

When we played music at WRUF, the announcers put the records on the turntable themselves; the engineers didn't touch them in those years. I played records for four years, so you might say that I was one of the earliest disc jockeys. We made up our own programs and we wrote our own continuity. We just did whatever there was to do. We were the staff. If we came in the studio in wintertime and found it cold, we'd plug in the electric heater. If it was dirty, we got a broom and did a little sweeping. If it had to be done, we did it. If we didn't, it wouldn't get done.

For instance, if you were assigned to handle a half-hour musical program you went back into the record library yourself and dug out the records. We had so few records that they weren't even catalogued. You *knew* where they were. Whenever a record was played on the air, the announcer would write the date on the paper jacket. We had so few records that sometimes we'd play the same one a couple of times a day, though we tried not to. There wasn't much money around in 1930, and you couldn't get extra funds out of the legislators. They met only once every two years, and what they budgeted was all we got. The money had to last. If it ran out, we ran out. Once a month we'd get a half dozen new records, and there'd be a scramble—the announcers would get in a real Kilkenny catfight—to see who would get first shot at playing the new ones on the air.

So I stumbled around doing odds and ends at the station. It felt strange at first, but then I began to get a liking for it. It was a daylight-operated station (we shared the same frequency with KOA in Denver, Colorado, and we had to sign off at the average monthly sundown time in Denver so that we'd be out of their way at night), and that meant my evenings were free. I found myself listening with Lylah and our friends to other stations, and as I began to like the announcing job more and more I found myself becoming more and more interested in broadcasting generally. I'd pick up stations from various parts of the country, and particularly WLW from Cincinnati, which was one of the great radio stations. Unconsciously, I began imitating the announcers I admired. There was a fine announcer at WLW named Robert Brown. I'd hear a show of his at night, and the next morning I'd sound like a thin version of Robert Brown. Another morning I might be a watered-down Milton J. Cross, or an ersatz Kelvin Keech. I was reporting in every morning imitating one established announcer or another. I was so impressed by people like Robert Brown and Milton Cross that whenever I got the chance to give my name over the air, I would say, "This is Walter Barber announcing."

Major Powell called me in his office one day and gave me a little dressing down. He also gave me some advice. I think it's the only advice about broadcasting that anyone ever gave me, and it was the best I could have received. Major Powell said, "Now, listen. Every day when you come in here and get on the air, you're somebody else. And you're not a very good somebody else. Imitations are not your forte. If you were really talented, if you could really imitate these fellows, I probably wouldn't say anything to you. But you're not. I want to tell you something. You go back in there to the studio, and you stop saying 'This is Walter Barber announcing.' You stop being Robert Brown and Milton Cross. Just go in there and be Red Barber. You say 'This is Red Barber announcing,' and talk like Red Barber. Get those other fellows out of your mind."

He shook me up a little. I imagine my feelings were a bit hurt. But I did what he said, and I've never tried to be anybody but Red Barber since. And when you think about it, naturalness is a man's strength. Over the years people have occasionally said to me, "I admire your style" or "You've got a different style" or "You've got a lousy style" or "I wouldn't have your style for love or money." But when I hear the word "style," I always assume that it refers to a person who is consciously creating something. In that context, I don't have a style. I speak on a microphone just the way I speak to somebody I'm standing next to in a hallway or at a party. I know that once in a while an ambitious young announcer or two has paid me the compliment of trying to imitate me a little bit. I wish them well, because I know they are going to be very, very busy. They've got to imitate me, but I'm free of the burden of carrying anybody on my back. I would advise anyone who writes or talks or acts or sings or dances that, while there are certain fundamental preparatory disciplines you must learn, in the long run it pays to be yourself. Be natural. You can't go any farther than your own talents will take you.

About the time that Major Powell straightened me out on

that point, he assigned me to do the announcing for a small hillbilly band they used to put on the air twice a week. I think he assigned me to that program in despair and also because he wanted to save his more established, proficient announcers for more important programs. This little band was unlettered, untrained, and fairly untalented, though it had plenty of enthusiasm. It had a violinist, a couple of guitarists, and a lady banjo player, and that was about it. An Army sergeant named Mack Criswell was the violinist and ringleader; he had put this group together. They came out and played half an hour on Monday nights and a full hour on Saturday nights. They played for nothing; they didn't get a fee. Nobody got a fee. We didn't have any money to pay talent. Mack Criswell had this group and somebody said, "Why don't you go out and play on the radio station?" And they did. It was that simple.

I got the program. Major Powell was putting his worst announcer with his worst program to sink or swim together. And somehow we swam. My early ambition to be in a minstrel show was pretty much dead, though I had done a little of it with the glee club, but one night when I was standing there with that old hillbilly string band playing country music, I just naturally turned to the microphone and sang along with them. And I continued to sing with them. I'd sing "Coming Round the Mountain," and "They Cut Down the Old Pine Tree," and "Casey Jones," and any other songs I could remember the words to. It was fine with the band. They were glad to have a vocalist. It gave them status. My goodness, a hillbilly band with a singer.

When I did my announcements—in that environment of country music and with Major Powell's admonition to be myself still ringing in my ears—I dropped into a folksy, cracker sort of thing of just kind of leaning over the back fence visiting. Without realizing it, I began to refer to the group as the Old Orange Grove String Band. And, in time, the hillbilly show became the best-known program on the station. It was an extremely important step in my development in radio, because it not only made me be myself, it taught me the practical *value* of being myself. I never tried to "announce" the show. I'd simply say, "Well, folks, tonight we got old Uncle Mack Criswell and his fiddle out here, and Mrs. Al Duke and her banjo, and

Joe Williams and his guitar, and Al Parks and his guitar, and if Al can crowd me away from the microphone he may get in a vocal or two later, but now let's just start off with 'Coming Round the Mountain.'" And that's where we went, everybody playing for himself, singing for himself, and we had a very happy time.

Nobody else on the station wanted to announce it, and nobody else really could announce it. I had no competition. It was cracker music and an old cracker boy up there talking. Totally natural. When we got mail, we'd open it and read it on the air. The audience response was impressive. I remember one time I asked Mack Criswell to play something and he didn't want to, so I said over the air, "I'm having trouble with Uncle Mack. He won't play what I want him to. Somebody send me an ax handle, and I'll *make* him play it." By actual count, the station received ninety-seven ax handles within the next week. Another time I got a frog in my throat and I said something about being awful dry because I'd just run out of chew tobacco. I got a ton of chewing tobacco sent to me.

The program caught on with a great many people, and from it I gained strength and assurance. I felt at last that I belonged. When I was doing that program, I knew I was pretty good, and the feeling would carry me through the rest of the week when I was doing other announcing chores that I wasn't so good at.

At the end of the school year, in the late spring of 1930, Jack Thompson's father asked him to leave the station and come back down to Miami and go into his law office with him. Thompson agreed, though he loved radio and would have been an outstanding announcer. Major Powell recognized Jack's talent and ability, and he begged Thompson to stay at WRUF. He wanted Jack to go into broadcasting full time and eventually go on to some other, bigger station. But Thompson listened to his father and went to Miami. He was very successful, too, but I think that all his life he was sorry he didn't stay in radio.

When Jack left, that opened up the ad lib announcing jobs, which were principally sports. You would go over and do a track meet or a boxing match or a baseball game or that basketball tournament. Most notably, you would do football. Football was a big thing. When the University of Florida's Gators were about to open their season in the fall of 1930, Thompson was gone and Major Powell didn't have anybody to take his place. I had played football, so I went to Major Powell and said, "Let me do the broadcast." He said okay, and I went over and did the first game of the season.

Never was there a more unsuspecting greenpea announcer in all the world. Florida Southern from Lakeland had come up to play, and I didn't even have enough sense or knowledge to get a program and some pencils, let alone do any preparation. I thought you just sat down by a microphone and talked about a football game.

That's what I did. I sat by the microphone and talked about the game, and it was undoubtedly the worst broadcast ever perpetrated on an innocent and unsuspecting radio audience. They were not accustomed to much in those days, but they got less. Much less. It was really a fouled-up job. I didn't know the players, I didn't know who was carrying the ball, or who did the tackling. I think I came out with the right score, but I messed up the broadcast. I suffered, and a lot of other people suffered, including the director of the station. When I came off the air, Major Powell said, "Red, I think we'll let Ralph Nimmons do the next game."

I was burning with embarrassment, and it didn't make me feel much better that Nimmons didn't do too well, either. For the third game, Major Powell used a boy who became a very great friend of mine, a fellow named James Leonard Butsch. He later went to work for the Crosley Radio Corporation in Cincinnati, which prevailed upon him to drop the Butsch so that he became known in Ohio as James Leonard. He was a fine executive and a splendid man; he died a few years ago. He did the third game, if my memory is correct, but Major Powell was still not satisfied and he declared that he himself would do the fourth game.

I was still burning. I felt like General Stilwell, old Vinegar Joe of World War II, when he came back to Washington after a terrible defeat in Burma. People were trying to gloss it over and explain it away but Stilwell, tough and honest, would have none of that. He said, "We got the hell beat out of us." Well, I had had the hell beat out of me that Saturday afternoon, and it hurt. When I got up Sunday morning I remembered my father again—his way of saying things. He used to say, "When you go into the world, you're going to make mistakes. That's all right. That's how you learn. But there is no excuse for a man making the same mistake twice. When you make a mistake, don't minimize the fact that you've made it. Go take your shoes off and sit down in a corner and study how you made that mistake, and study even more that you don't make the same mistake again."

I started studying that Sunday morning, after the initial shock, and I started figuring out what I had to do if I ever got to broadcast another football game. Over the next few days, I devised a basic football chart that could be used with a spotter for each team, and it is the same chart that I have used ever since. I haven't had to change any of the basic details to this day. I started going to football practice every afternoon. I got to know Nash Higgins, who was the assistant coach and chief scout, and I studied the detailed information he had on Florida and on the teams Florida was going to play. I found out that it was a demanding business, broadcasting a football game, and that it started many days before you got anywhere near a microphone.

I kept going to football practice and talking to Nash Higgins while first Nimmons and then Butsch did their broadcasts. Now Major Powell was going to try, and I knew he didn't want to. He realized that he wasn't much of a broadcaster. And he had false teeth that would slip on him once in a while. He didn't like to be caught in front of a microphone.

I walked into his office on Friday and said, "Major Powell, when I did that game I learned the hard way that I didn't know the first thing about broadcasting football. But since then I've been watching practice every day and talking to Nash Higgins, and I've picked up all the information I could possibly get on Florida and all its opponents. I think I know better how to broadcast a football game now, and I'm asking you for a second chance."

He gave it to me. And I did that game so well that the

station got a couple of hundred congratulatory telegrams, including one from the governor's mansion in Tallahassee. After that, nobody else did any football games at WRUF while I was there. Except once. Claude Lee, the fellow who ran the movie theater, had done a little work on radio, and he had gotten Major Powell's promise to let him broadcast a game. The major kept his word, and Claude Lee did one game. He didn't do it too well, and if the question of who was going to do the games from then on needed any nailing down, that nailed it. I did them all.

I learned a second fundamental about sports broadcasting that year. Boy, I got both barrels that season. First, I learned the importance of thorough preparation, and then I learned that it was a business and that you had to approach a broadcast in a cold, practical, businesslike manner.

Alabama came down to Gainesville to help Florida dedicate its new stadium, and Alabama had a tremendous team. They went on to the Rose Bowl and beat Washington State 24–0. It was a veteran team of great players, and everybody in the South, where they take their football seriously, knew every one of them.

The day before the game I spoke to Wallace Wade, the famous Alabama coach, and told him I needed a spotter, an observer, to sit with me during the broadcast and pick out the players for me. I knew who the Alabama players were by name and what they could do, but I needed somebody who could identify them instantly for me. I had never seen any of them. Wade was kind of offhand with me—radio announcers were not very popular people—but after a while he gave me a third-string guard who had been hurt and who wasn't going to suit up. He had been brought on the trip as a reward for the way he had been working.

Before the game the next day I explained my spotting chart to the Alabama boy. In that era of limited substitutions, where the same men played on both offense and defense, you wrote down the starting lineup and then simply crossed out one name and wrote in the substitute's name whenever a new man came in. They did not use uniform numbers, and so you had to know the players by sight. But it wasn't too difficult to keep track of things because they used comparatively few substitutes; once a player went out of the game he could not return until the following period. Sometimes a coach would start his second string as shock troops and then after ten minutes or so he would run in his first team, fresh and raring to go.

The Alabama spotter wrote down his starting lineup, with all those famous All America names, and the Florida spotter wrote down his, and the game began. Florida was about a four-touchdown underdog, and four touchdowns then seemed like a lot more points than four touchdowns now. Alabama was supposed to be that much better. Yet when the game began, Florida played inspired football, took the ball, moved it well, got down close to Alabama's goal. I was all excited. I was delighted. I was a Florida boy, and here was my college making this great Alabama team look like nothing. I started saying things like, "Folks, it looks like a great upset in the making here. The Gators are pushing the vaunted Crimson Tide all over the field."

Just about then I happened to glance at the Alabama bench, and there, getting up and putting on their helmets, were eleven of the biggest men I ever saw in my life. I turned to my Alabama observer, and I saw that he was looking at the Alabama bench, too, and I noticed that his face had turned a rather pale shade of green. Always concerned with the welfare of a fellow human being, I leaned over and whispered, "What's the matter? Are you sick?" He nodded and whispered back, "Yes, and you're going to be sicker. *That's* Alabama's first team coming in now."

I had had those great players, that everybody in the South knew, in there from the beginning of the game, and I had been crowing about the fact that the little Gators from Florida had been pushing these supermen around. The hardest thing I ever had to do on the air was to turn back to that microphone and say, "Friends, the Alabama first team is just coming into the game now. Everything I've said about them earlier this afternoon, please forget I said it." I didn't apologize any further than that. I didn't explain it. I merely went on and broadcast.

I was sick with embarrassment because Alabama won that game easily. They were truly a great team, far better than Florida. But the incident taught me something, and I've never forgotten it. This is a business: broadcasting. You don't root. You don't cheer. You don't let your emotions distort the facts. Your job is to report what's happening, and not what you hope is happening. Along with that, going back to my first lesson, it's your job to *know* what is happening. I've never forgotten the Alabama observer, though I don't remember his name. I vowed then that no spotter would ever be able to give me the wrong call again, not for more than one play. I had to know those players. I wanted a spotter for speed, but for positive identification I was going to know the answer myself.

Jack Thompson's decision to go to Miami not only turned me to sports broadcasting, it also opened the way for me to go into radio full time. In my early months, working at WRUF was just another odd job to earn money. My prime interest was studying, taking a full schedule of courses at the university. At the end of my sophomore year, after I had been with the station about three months, Major Powell offered me a summer job working full time as an announcer. I took it, fully intending to go back to part-time announcing when I began my junior year in the fall. But I was seriously ill for a time that summer, which I'll get to a little later, and I ran up a couple of hundred dollars in debts. In the fall, with Major Powell's full approval, I dropped out of school for a semester and continued to work full time at the station to get those debts paid off. I was paid $75 a month.

Early in 1931 I returned to being a full-time student and part-time announcer, but only about ten days later Major Powell called me in and told me that Ralph Nimmons had quit as chief announcer to take a job with WBIG in Greensboro, North Carolina. Powell said, "The job is open. It pays $150 a month. You can have it if you want, but you'll have to quit going to school. It's a full-time job."

I thought about things for just one minute. I knew that if Jack Thompson had still been at the station, he would have been offered the chief announcer's job. I hadn't been there a year yet. But by this time I had fallen completely in love with radio. The charms of being a college professor had paled in contrast to the possibilities in radio. There was the Old Orange Grove String Band. There were the football broadcasts, which had really caught me and which had really given me a taste of what I wanted to do. I knew I was good at them, and I liked the feeling. When a person is doing good work, he *knows* it. If he's doing good work and he doesn't know it, God help him, because all sensitivity is left out of him. And here, suddenly, was the chance to be chief announcer, with all the challenge and responsibility that it meant. Moreover, I had been going with Lylah Murray for more than a year, and I wanted to marry her. Inasmuch as I was twenty-three years old and working my own way through college, the decision that Major Powell had put to me was entirely mine to make. I made it.

"I'll take the job," I said. I never went back to school. I was chief announcer at WRUF for three years, until I left in 1934 to go up to Cincinnati.

Between Innings: A MISTAKE NAMED ANTONELLI

The only other time I made a *complete* mistake on the identity of a player was during a Dodger-Phillie game toward the end of World War II. Fred Fitzsimmons was managing the Phils, and when they came into Ebbets Field they brought with them a new third baseman named Antonelli, just up from the minors. That afternoon I had a dental appointment. I had eight teeth that needed filling, and the dentist planned to fill three or four of them that day and the rest at a later date. While he was working on me the phone rang, and it was the person who was due in the office next calling to cancel his appointment. The dentist said, "I suddenly have an extra hour open. Would you like to get these other teeth filled and get the whole thing finished with? Or do you want to come back another time?" I said, "Let's get it over with," and I sat back, and he filled all eight teeth at one sitting.

When I got out of the chair my teeth were okay, but my head was sore and I felt terrible. I went rather unhappily out to Ebbets Field to do the game that night. My father used to tell me, "The worse thing a man can do is feel sorry for himself," but as I rode the commuting train from Scarsdale into Manhattan and then the subway from Manhattan out to Brooklyn and then walked the few blocks to the ball park, my jaw hurt and my head ached and I felt mighty sorry for myself. I was praying, "Dear Lord, be merciful and get this game over with in a hurry." I wanted to go home and go to bed. I felt very sorry for old Red.

I went through the ritual of preparation, went into the Dodger dugout to get their batting order and then into the Phillie dugout to get their batting order and to say hello to Fitzsimmons, an old friend. I noticed that Antonelli was listed as the third baseman, and I said, "Fred, where is Antonelli? I'd like to take a look at him." Fitzsimmons said, "He's up there hitting now." I took a good look at Antonelli swinging in batting practice. Barrel chest. Hair below the rim of his cap—dark. Swarthy complexion. Slightly bowed at the knees. I fixed the picture of him in my mind. Then I said thanks to Fitzsimmons and went on up to the booth, and I didn't have another thought as I waited for the game to begin except, "Oh, my head hurts. Oh, my mouth hurts. Oh, I hope this is a short ball game." I never even heard the public address announcer giving the batting orders.

When Antonelli came to bat the first time, I checked his appearance, just by reflex, and there were the slightly bowed legs, the barrel chest, the dark hair. He hit two doubles that night and according to my broadcast had a pretty good major league debut for himself.

The next day, feeling much better as I came in again on the commuting train, I read the morning papers and did my statistics —we didn't have statisticians yet to do that chore for us—and I suddenly noticed that Roscoe McGowen's story in the New York *Times* had not Antonelli but Andy Seminick, of all people, playing third base for the Phillies and having two doubles. Poor Roscoe, I thought to myself. He must be slipping to pull a rock like that. Seminick was a catcher, although I remembered that he did occasionally play third. And then a little voice said, yes, and he has a barrel chest, too, and slightly bowed legs, and though he's bald on top the hair that sticks out under his cap is dark. I got a little edgy, and I couldn't wait to get to the ball park. I went right to Fitzsimmons and I said, "Fred, who played third base for you last night?" He said, "Red, it's the funniest thing. After I told you Antonelli was going to play third, you had no more than left the dugout and gone under the stands when he stepped on a ball and turned his ankle. So I put Andy Seminick in."

In other words, it wasn't poor Roscoe who pulled the rock. It was poor Red. I had given Seminick's two doubles to Antonelli, who had yet to play his first major league game. As soon as the microphone opened up, I said, "Friends, they tell me an honest confession is good for the soul, and if that is so I'm going to have the healthiest soul of anybody you ever knew." I explained that it hadn't been Antonelli at third base last night; it had been Seminick. And then I went ahead with the business of broadcasting the game. And do you know, nobody ever phoned or wrote a card or a letter or said anything at all to me about that?

But the point is, when you broadcast you must bring complete concentration to the job. Leave out emotion, leave out your own feelings. Whenever an associate of mine came to a game and complained of a headache or said he felt bad in any way, I always said, "How bad? Can you concentrate on the game? If you can't, go home. Come back tomorrow."

When you can't concentrate, you don't care what you're doing. You get careless. That's all that word means: you care less. If you care less, you let your mind and your body stop working, and you make mistakes. People do terrible things to themselves when they get careless.

RED	1	3	5	7	9			
BARBER	2	4	6	8	(10)			

I believe very firmly that our lives are guided by forces that we are unaware of, and that there is very much a personal, watchful God. Otherwise, I don't think you can account for the dimension or direction of your life. When I try to untangle the wanderings, the meanderings, and the vagaries of my years, I cannot believe that after the miracle of birth it was then all sheer chance—the death of the minstrel shows and the end of that certainly erroneous path of my life, meeting Leonard McLucas and turning down Rollins and accepting the promise of Charley Bachman that he would get me a job at Gainesville, the desperate early stages in Gainesville and the yellow roadster coming by the closed-down rooming house, losing the library job and being forced by circumstances into becoming the janitor at the University Club, the dull professor of English history and the need to return early to Gainesville that his dullness created, being there when Ralph Fulghum was looking for someone to read a paper over WRUF, the persistence of Major Powell, the opportunity to work with the string band, which taught me the invaluable lesson of being natural in front of the microphone, Jack Thompson's decision to leave the station, which left me with the wide-open opportunity to do sports announcing and then become chief announcer. These seemingly haphazard incidents form a straight line. Then,

too, there was the accident with the truck that brought me directly
to the girl who was to become my wife.

But if anything ever set in motion within me an awareness of
a personal God and the way he watches over you personally, it was
the episode of the pain attacks that took me to a major hospital
up North (to which I will give the fictional name Municipal)
and turned my whole life around, physically, emotionally, and
spiritually. None of the things that followed after that, none of
the experiences and successes that I have had in radio and television, nothing, not even my marriage, would have happened
without the providential guidance I received at Municipal. I could
not have stayed in radio. I could not have gone into television
for one second. My whole life would have been so dreadfully
changed that I don't know what I would have become.

In the summer of 1930, between my second and third years at
the university, almost a year after I had met Lylah and several
months after I had gone to work at WRUF, I took a few days
off to go home for a short visit with my parents and my sister
and brother at Sanford. That was the last time I was ever at my
parents' home at Sanford to spend the night because within a
few weeks they moved to Tampa. I was hitchhiking back to
Gainesville after my visit, and I had gotten as far as Palatka. I
was standing on a corner in a residential section of Palatka, waiting hopefully for a free ride on to Gainesville, when I suddenly
had a tremendous pain in the right side of my face and head
that centered in my right eye.

Until that moment I had always been an almost completely
healthy person, with no pains, no aches, no sicknesses. I had
always had robust health, exuberant health. But this was an intense, shocking pain. It was a pain that made me feel as though
someone had gotten his fingers in the socket and had grabbed
my eye and was very slowly and diabolically pulling it out by the
roots. The pain went down my right cheekbone, past my right
ear, into my right temple. It was absolutely agonizing, so much so
that in a few moments, strong as I was at that age, I found that
I had to lie down. I could do nothing else. I lay there completely
alone. It was the middle of the day, but nobody came by. Or,
at any rate, nobody stopped. I don't know how many people

saw me, if any did. I was just a man lying in the grass on a hot summer's day.

The pain lasted almost an hour. When it finally subsided, I stood up, shaken and frightened. Nothing like this had ever happened to me before. You can hear about other people having pain, you can see other people have pain, you can read about pain. But until you yourself have experienced excruciating pain, you can have no comprehension or understanding of what it means. Right now, thinking back to 1930, I can still bring that pain back in my memory. I remember how I felt when I experienced it. Of course, the true pain itself is beyond memory. That's a gift of God; once you have gone through pain, it is past. Otherwise, I doubt that women would ever have a second child. Another great gift of the Almighty is that we cannot foresee the future. If we could see what we have to go into, I doubt that very many of us would have the strength and the courage to go on into it. Only one man knew exactly his future and had the courage to go face it, and that was Christ.

When I finally got back to Gainesville after this pain attack I went directly to the university infirmary. The doctor in charge told me at once that as a general medical man he could not help me with the type of pain that I had experienced. He sent me to an eye, ear, nose, and throat man in Gainesville. I saw the Gainesville doctor, but only two days after the first attack a second one struck that was fully as excruciating, and they continued to come every other day, almost as regularly as clockwork. Sometime during the second day after a pain attack, I would have another one which would last within minutes of an hour. I would have to lie down and, if possible, grab something and hold it. If I were in my room, I'd lie on the bed and hold the headboard with all my strength. Dr. Jones (I have fictionalized the names of all the doctors who come into this chapter) gave me the classic ear-nose-throat treatment of shrinking the tissues and the sinuses, but it did not help. The pain attacks continued. I became increasingly, almost totally, apprehensive. I got so that I was afraid to leave my room because I did not know when I'd have another attack, and I did not want to have one out in public on the street again. I left my room only to go to Dr. Jones. Naturally, I did not go to work at the radio station.

After several visits to Dr. Jones, I had to tell him bluntly that he was not helping me. He said, "You've only said what was on my mind. I was about to tell you that I am unable to help you. I want you to go over to Jacksonville to see Dr. Gray, who is a neurologist. Maybe he can do something for you."

I had no way to get to Jacksonville. Lylah was in Chicago that summer. I had not written her about my difficulty; I had not written her about anything. I had not done anything but have one pain attack and then wait for the next one, and in between them be very moody and depressed. I have never been so depressed.

But Major Powell very kindly drove me from Gainesville to Jacksonville and then waited in Jacksonville until Dr. Gray could see me. When I went in to the doctor, Major Powell went into the office with me and explained to the doctor that I was a student at the University of Florida, that I was in serious trouble, and that I had no money. He waited while Dr. Gray made his examination and after it he drove me back to Gainesville. Major Powell was as kind to me as a man could be.

Dr. Gray said almost immediately, after he began his examination, that there was no doubt in his mind but that I had a classic case of *tic douloureux*. I had never heard of it before, and he explained that it was a French term describing a terrible, twitching pain in the fifth nerve area, and he added something I didn't need to have him tell me—that it was as severe a pain as medical science knew. He said I would have to go North, to Municipal Hospital, to see Dr. Dowd, who had a great reputation as a brain surgeon. Dr. Dowd had very recently developed a brain operation for *tic douloureux* in which he removed the ganglia from the fifth nerve area to relieve the pain. Dr. Dowd, I later learned, also developed an operation to fuse the spine. He was a great surgeon, but he was obsessed with surgery. That was his reputation. When I got to Municipal I found that the nurses, whenever they mentioned his name, always looked around first as though to be certain he could not hear them. They mentioned his name as though he were the devil incarnate.

Dr. Gray got in touch with Municipal. He told them I had no money but he also stressed the seriousness of my condition and he had them make a reservation for me. Municipal could not take me immediately; I had to wait a week. I went home to Tampa, to where my folks had just moved. My father spoke to officials of the Atlantic Coast Line and, though I was not supposed to be given a pass because I was twenty-two years old and no longer a dependent, the railroad, because of the emergency, gave me a round-trip pass on the day coach to Municipal. And so, for the first time in my life, I traveled North.

I had not written to Lylah before from Gainesville, but after the booking had been made at Municipal I wrote and told her what had happened. She was a registered nurse, and she immediately went to specialists there in Cook County Hospital to ask them what *tic douloureux* meant. I had only the very real knowledge of the pain, but she found out a good deal more, and she almost died when she did. The specialists told her, if Dr. Dowd decides your friend has *tic douloureux*, then that's what he has, and if Dr. Dowd decides he's going to operate, then that's what he's going to do. They told her what the operation would mean, which I didn't know then. They explained that the operation, while relieving the pain, would affect my appearance. My face would sag, my mouth would droop, my speech would be affected. I don't believe Lylah ever thought it all the way through on a conscious level—and, thank the Lord, she never had to make a decision about it—but subconsciously she had to be deeply concerned, not only for me, but for her own predicament. I would not look or talk the same. My career would certainly be affected. In other words, after that operation I would not be the same young man she had promised to marry. It was a terrible time for her.

My train got to the city in the middle of the afternoon. I took a streetcar up to Municipal, and when I arrived I found that there had been some confusion, somewhere, as to my economic state. A private room had been held for me. Maybe this accounted for the delay of a week in their being able to accept me as a patient. I had to explain that I had no money, that I could not possibly pay for a private room. They said, "We'll have to put you on the surgical ward. We'll admit you tomorrow morning."

I felt no irritation, no annoyance. I had no feelings at all except complete despair. I was far beyond hope. I was going through the motions, but I really expected no help. The recurring attacks of pain had reduced me to complete bottom. They had come relentlessly, remorselessly, every other day. They had continued in Tampa when I was there at home with my parents for the few days before I left for the hospital. I was totally depressed. I had reached a decision—and I use that word advisedly, because in my despair I made a cold, calculated decision—that if these pain attacks could not be stopped, and I didn't care how they were stopped, I did not intend to live. I could not continue to live with that pain; I could not stand it.

I found a room in the neighborhood where I spent the night, and the next morning I reported in to the hospital. I was sent to see Dr. Dowd, and as I was being brought to his office another pain attack set in. When Dr. Dowd saw me and examined me, I was in the middle of an attack. He saw me having one. Then he sent me back to the bed in the surgical ward.

For a young man, being in the surgical ward at Municipal was a rather interesting experience. There were cases of all kinds, some very serious. Some people died while I was there, and almost everyone was hard up. I found some very kind people in that ward. There was an Italian streetcar motorman several beds from me. They were operating on his sinuses, and he was in a great deal of pain. He seemed very lonely, and after a few days, when I was feeling somewhat better, I said hello to him, and we visited back and forth. He got out of the hospital before I did. I was there for two weeks, and the last four or five days I was allowed to have my clothes and go out during the day. One morning this motorman suddenly showed up at the ward and he invited me to spend the day with him; he took me on the streetcars and showed me the entire city. Then he brought me home to his own house and his own family and gave me dinner and some wine that he had made himself. He was such a warm, decent man; I have always remembered him as being the epitome of kindness, the stranger making you welcome. That was a great day.

But that was a little later on. When I went into the ward the first day, I didn't feel like saying hello to anybody, motorman or not. I lay there in the bed, not moving, except when they took me out for examinations. I was punched and mauled and pulled. I was in the ear clinic for a couple of hours. They ran lights that got hot up into my sinuses, and they took X rays of my head and my skull and my back. All of my reflexes were tested. I went here to this doctor and there to that clinic. My blood was tested. Heaven knows the tests they made. The only thing they didn't check—well, I'll get to that later.

The oddest thing was, I had no more pain attacks. The last one was in Dr. Dowd's office. But I kept waiting for one, and between examinations I simply lay there in bed. I had no interest in life, no interest in people. I had no interest in the nurses. I didn't say anything to anybody. I answered when I was spoken to, and that was all. I wasn't bitter. I simply had no interest. I knew another pain attack was going to come, and then another, and then another, and I didn't care what Dr. Dowd did.

One day, about the fourth day I was there, I guess, a girl on the library service stopped by my bed with a cart of books. She asked if I wanted something to read. I said, "No." She said, "Oh, you want to read something, don't you?" I said, "No." She was very pleasant and she tried very hard to get me to take a book. I told her I wasn't interested and to please leave me alone. She reached down without looking, took a book off the cart, and put it on the foot of my bed. She left it there and went off with the cart.

I don't know, maybe it was a half hour later, an hour later, maybe half a day later, but as much as to get the book out of the way as anything else I picked it up. It was *Fortitude*, by Walpole. I had never heard of the book, and I have never since heard anybody else mention it. I've never read it again. I'm afraid to read it. I do not wish a very beneficial illusion—if it was an illusion—to be destroyed or lost or changed or tampered with. I doubt if the book is very much a piece of literature. But, idly, as I lay there, with time hanging heavy, I began to look through it, and finally I read it. The premise of the book—it wasn't original with Walpole; there is little, if anything, that has ever been said that's completely original—was to the effect that it isn't life itself that matters so much as it is the courage we bring to it. Somehow, into my complete despair and hopelessness, vaguely, vaguely came intimations of the meaning of that. Courage. It isn't life itself that matters so much as it is the courage we bring to it. Tillich wrote a book on courage. It's pretty hard reading, and I wouldn't recommend it to somebody unless they were really serious about it. Tillich discusses all the aspects of courage and finally winds up saying that genuine courage is when an intelligent person well understands the dangers and pains that lie ahead if he pursues the course of action he regards as proper and necessary, and in spite of what he knows will happen he goes ahead and does what he has to do.

At any rate, as I lay there in the bed in the surgery ward, life had lost its meaning for me. Anyone who has experienced *tic douloureux* will know exactly how I felt. But that book started something going in me again. It made more sense to me than I realized at the time. It told me where I was at, and what I needed. In Hamlet's soliloquy, Shakespeare says, "To take arms against a sea of trouble and by opposing end them." Shakespeare doesn't say that you are going to win. But if you merely resist, face the wind, move, do something, you are no longer totally defeated. The saddest thing to me today is seeing so many of our young people looking—well, so utterly beat. They don't wish to be clean. They don't wish to be neat. They don't wish to cut their hair. They don't wish to work. They don't wish to serve their country in the armed forces. They don't wish to be anything. They don't wish to do anything but retreat into the walls in their effort to go back to the womb. To do nothing, to know nothing, to have no responsibility, to have no courage to bring to life. It is very sad. When a person has lost the courage to face things as they are and as they ought to be—and things as they may not be—when a person has lost that, he has lost everything. I think that's the ground root of alcoholism, and it may be the ground root of drug addiction, of all this nihilism.

This book the girl placed on the foot of my bed worked its way into my life, and without realizing it I began to look around. I imagine that's when I spoke to the Italian motorman and began that brief but so rewarding friendship. I think it's when I began to live again.

And, too, the pain attacks did not return. That did not deter Dr. Dowd. One day I looked up and there at the foot of my bed was Dr. Dowd with Dr. Howells, who was chief surgeon of the entire hospital. Dr. Dowd said to Dr. Howells, "Here he is. I've looked through all the medical records, and I haven't found

one recorded instance of anyone under forty with *tic douloureux*.
But he's got it. It's a classic case. He's got it, and we're going to
operate on him." They walked away. So I found that I was a
museum piece. I was a novelty. I was in the surgical ward, but I
was a curiosity. I was to be shown off. The chief surgeon had
to come take a look at me. From one of the nurses I found out
that I was going to be operated on in the amphitheater, so that
everybody could see. I read the chart once that was at the foot of
my bed. The nurse would leave it there only for a little while
when a doctor was making his rounds, but when she turned her
back one day I took a look at it. It said what my name was
and my age, that I was a patient of Dr. Dowd, and that I was
a "brain case—undiagnosed." There were some visitors who would
come by once in a while, who weren't medical people, and they
would glance at the chart and then take a look at me and get out
of there in a hurry. Who could blame them? What does that say
to a lay person—"brain case undiagnosed?" A lot of people who
have listened to my broadcasts said the status never changed.

Despite the impending operation and the attitude of Dr.
Dowd, I began to feel better. I was getting the strength of renewed courage from the Walpole book and from the fact that
the pain attacks did not recur. They had told me that if I had
another one, Dr. Dowd wanted to see me immediately. But as the
days passed and nothing happened, they said I could put my
clothes on and go out for a while if I wanted. They said I could
go anyplace I wanted as long as I didn't get more than fifteen
or twenty minutes away from the hospital. If another attack
started, I should jump in a taxi and beat it back. But nothing
happened.

One night I had come back to the hospital after being out
and around during the day. I was in my pajamas. It was about
eight o'clock. An orderly came in to me and said, quietly, that
Dr. Barnes wanted to see me. He was a resident and he was
Dr. Dowd's first assistant on the brain team. The orderly told me
what room Dr. Barnes was living in, and he added that I was not
to tell anybody where I was going. I put on my robe and slippers
and went around the corridors to Dr. Barnes's room and knocked.
And this young doctor said, "Come in."

I went in and he said hello and told me to sit down. Then,
after one or two preliminaries, he said, "Mr. Barber, I'm going
to tell you something, and when I tell it to you I will be placing
my career in your hands. Dr. Dowd is a man who brooks no
interference. If he ever heard that I was talking like this with one
of his patients, one of his cases, he would be utterly furious. He
could break me, like that. I want you to understand that I have
studied and worked for years to get where I am. I'm very close
to ending my residency here and going on to my own practice.
I am risking all that because I have to tell you something. You
trouble me. I keep worrying about you. There is something about
your case that isn't right.

"Let me tell you something about this operation that Dr. Dowd
has scheduled for you. It's brain surgery, as you know, and perhaps you know that he's going to remove the ganglia from your
fifth nerve area. When he does that you will have no sense of feeling in the right side of your head. That's why the pain attacks
will no longer come back. They may recur, but you won't know
it because you won't be able to feel them. You will have no sense
of feeling in or around your eye. But you will also get a droop
of the eyelid in your right eye. You will get a droop in your face,
in the cheek, in the jowls, at the corner of your mouth. The
entire right side of your face will sag because you will have lost
the nerves there. The chances are very real that you will eventually lose your right eye. If you get something in it you won't feel
it, and it will be easy for your eye to become badly infected, so
much so that it would have to be removed.

"I am telling you all this, Mr. Barber, because I want you to
understand that this is a maiming operation, with no recourse, no
reverse. Once that ganglia is out, it's out forever. You're a young
man, and a fine-looking young man. Your whole life is ahead
of you. If you have this operation, the pain will not come back,
but your life will be vastly affected. Your appearance, your speech,
everything. Now, I have gone over your case very carefully. I
have read the reports. No one can find any reason why you
should have these attacks. You have probably been told that no
one under forty has ever had a true *tic douloureux*. But they say
you have one at the age of twenty-two. That is the thing that is

bothering me so much, that and the fact that your pains have not recurred now for almost two weeks.

"You are scheduled to be operated on in a few days in the main amphitheater. You're a piece of medical history. A lot of people want to see what's inside your skull, one person in particular. And he is going to see. *If* you stay at Municipal.

"My advice is this. If I were you, tomorrow morning I would say nothing to anybody. But I would get my clothes and get dressed and walk out of the hospital, and go back to Florida. If, when you're back there, the pain attacks return, then you come back up here. We'll know then what we *have* to do, and we'll do it with a better conscience.

"But please remember, if Dr. Dowd hears that I have told you to leave this hospital, my career might very well be terminated."

I got my clothes the next morning and did as Dr. Barnes said. I walked out, and I went home to Florida. And I've never had a pain attack since.

A year and a half later—almost two years later—in the spring of 1932, after Lylah and I had married, we were living in Gainesville and one night she became ill. I got up to get her a glass of ice water, and after giving it to her, I got a glass for myself. I tipped my head back to drink it and when the water hit my front teeth it was like the top of my head flew off. *Whooomp!* It felt as though my front teeth had exploded. The next morning I went to a dentist in Gainesville—I'll call him Dr. Reed—who became a warm, close, personal friend of ours. Again, how life moves in cycles. The office nurse for Dr. Jones, the ear, eye, nose, and throat man back at the beginning of all this, later married Dr. Reed, and they were both close friends of Lylah's and mine through the years. You keep meeting people, and you never know who you meet, who they are going to be, what they are going to be to you.

I went in to see Dr. Reed with this awful pain in my front teeth, and he said, "You've got abscessed teeth, but I'm going to X-ray them just to be doubly certain." He took the X rays and showed them to me. There were abscesses in two of my upper front teeth, and they were tremendous. He didn't have to wait for the X-ray plates to dry to see them. He pulled the teeth right then and there, and they were beautiful big abscesses, oh, terrible-looking things, sitting up there in the right side of my face, directly under my right eye.

And then I remembered something. For all the tests and examinations and pushing and pulling they did to me at Municipal, they never X-rayed my teeth. They X-rayed everything else, but not the teeth. I remembered that one of the interns, in taking my medical history in the early stages when I first got there, had looked into my mouth and asked, "Ever have any tooth trouble?" I answered, "I've had a few teeth filled, but that's all." He said, "Okay," and wrote something down, and apparently he must have written down the definitive passing mark for teeth, and everyone respected it. Municipal never X-rayed my teeth. I had had without any doubt the classic pain of *tic douloureux*, but what was obviously causing it was this abscess as it ate into the nerve. I had *tic douloureux* because of the nerve involvement, and the rhythmical every-other-day pattern was probably caused by the particular behavior of that abscess and the nerve it was attacking. The pain attacks apparently stopped when the abscess ultimately ate right through the nerve. It cut the nerve.

Dr. Reed and practically everyone I have ever talked to about this find it incomprehensible that my teeth were not X-rayed at the hospital, but it is in the nature of man to overlook the obvious while he searches for the obscure. X-raying my teeth was the obvious thing to do, but somewhere in the mechanism of the great hospital one human being stubbed his toe. And because he did, I would have had at the age of twenty-two this terrible maiming operation. But for Dr. Barnes and the provenience of the Lord, I would have had brain surgery at the hands of the great Dr. Dowd—for abscessed teeth.

Christ said you must love your fellow man, have concern for him. He told the Pharisees, "I was in prison and you didn't come to see me. I was thirsty and you didn't give me anything to drink. I was hungry and you didn't give me anything to eat. I was naked and you didn't clothe me." They were indignant and they said, "Why, lord, when did we see you naked and hungry and thirsty and in prison?" He said, "Whenever you saw any of your fellow men in that predicament and did nothing about it."

Dr. Barnes saw me, and at great risk to what later proved to be an eminent medical career, he showed concern—for a boy he had never met before and would never see again, a boy who did not have money or family or influence. All he had was youth, and a still small voice inside Dr. Barnes saying, "There is something about this case that is not right."

Between Innings: DR. BOWMAN

When Dr. Reed pulled my abscessed teeth in the spring of 1932, I had two front teeth missing for several weeks. The area had to heal, first of all, and it took a little while to make the bridge and fit it properly and put it in there permanently. When Reed did put it in, he said, "That's the best I can do. It'll probably stay in there for five or six years, but that's all I can guarantee you." That was in 1932, and as I say these words it is thirty-five years later, and that bridge is still sitting there, sound as a rock. I have very warm feelings toward that bridge. It has had a great deal to do with how I have made my living. I remember very well that, while I was waiting that spring for my poor gums to heal and the bridge to be put in place, it was baseball season and I had to do play-by-play with a gap in my mouth where my two front teeth used to be. I learned the hard way that when you say anything beginning with the letter F, a pocket of air has to form behind your front teeth for an instant. If you have a couple of teeth missing, you can't form the pocket of air and it becomes almost impossible to say words like "foul" or "first base" or "fast ball" or "fielder." There I was, a kid announcer trying to broadcast some ball games, and here was an entire body of words that I could not use. I had never realized before how many cussed words begin with the letter F. I kept trying to avoid them, to figure out some way to keep from saying them. I learned. I would use a player's name instead of his position to avoid "first base" and "fielder." Instead of trying to pronounce "foul ball," I would say, "That's out of play, back in the stands." I guess that may be how I started developing an announcing vocabulary, how I began looking for and using different words and phrases in my broadcasts.

RED	1	3	5	7	9	(11)			
BARBER	2	4	6	8	10				

I joined the campus radio station in March 1930, did football games that fall, and was made chief announcer early in 1931. In other words, after stumbling painfully in the beginning and again when I began the football broadcasts, I developed quickly. Two announcers ahead of me—Nimmons and Thompson—left the station and opened up the opportunity for me, and I was able to take advantage of it. Much of the credit for that goes to Major Powell, who was always in my corner. He dragged me into radio, gave me the best advice I ever received, and he put me on the shows where I developed whatever talent I had. And as I developed and began to chafe under the limitations of this small, non-commercial, daylight station, he understood perfectly. I wanted to move on. I heard Graham McNamee on the World Series. I heard Bill Mundy, out of Atlanta, doing football games. I heard Ted Husing. I used to grind my teeth and say to myself, "I'll be up there." I meant the top, the major leagues, the big football games. I wanted to go up, and Major Powell was behind me all the way.

But moving out of that station was not a simple thing to do. Nothing seemed simple in those days, not even marriage. Early in 1931 Lylah had come back from Chicago, but because she had an obligation to put in a full year at Riverside Hospital, she was living over in Jacksonville. I was eighty-five miles away in Gainesville, at the radio station. We weren't seeing too much of each other, but we decided to get married. Our friends were astounded. Why were we getting married? She was going to be in Jacksonville, I was going to be in Gainesville. We didn't have an automobile. She had only every other weekend off, and I had only one day a week off. People said to us, "What sort of marriage is this, that starts off with a separation?"

Those details didn't bother us. We wanted to marry each other, and we felt it would be better to get married and work out the mechanics of seeing each other as we went along, rather than not be married and still try to work out the details of seeing each other. You don't use a slide rule when you want to get married; you listen to your heart.

Lylah had four days in a row off from the hospital late in March, and that's when we decided we would be married. Major Powell gave me a week off; he was more liberal about things like days off than the hospital was. Of course, maybe playing records on the university radio station wasn't as important as taking care of sick people in a hospital. And I must admit that the best wedding present we received was from Dr. T. Z. Cason, one of the doctors who founded the Riverside Hospital. He loaned us a Franklin automobile to use during our four-day honeymoon, and in it we drove to Charleston, South Carolina, and back. It was wonderful, the best honeymoon anyone ever had, and the loan of the Franklin was a perfect wedding present. Otherwise, I don't know where we could have gone. Things work out. People are very nice. People have been very nice to me all my life. Most people.

As far as money was concerned, I married a rich woman. I was making $150 a month as the full-time chief announcer for WRUF, but she was making close to $200. This was 1931; you have no idea how tight money was. As a matter of fact, I wasn't making $150. Just before we were to be married there was a 10 per cent wage cut right across the board at WRUF because of the Depression. My salary was reduced from $150 to $135 a month. Lylah's salary was unchanged, and she had complete maintenance on top of it. She had her room and her meals and her laundry taken care of. She didn't have to spend one red cent. When I say I married a rich woman, I mean it. And what happened? Nine months after she married me, she quit her job, came to Gainesville, and said, "Okay, son. Here I am." I'll never marry for money again.

My first commercial fee for broadcasting came about because of our divided marriage. I had to figure out a way to get up to Jacksonville to see her, and I worked out a deal with Edgar Jones, who had been a great football player at Florida and was then athletic director. I told him I had talked to WJAX in Jacksonville and they said they would give me fifteen minutes once a week to talk football over the radio on evenings before University of Florida games. I told Edgar that if he thought it would be good publicity for the school, I would go up to Jacksonville and do these broadcasts, providing he gave me bus fare up and back. Edgar was a big dealer—he became a Cadillac executive later on in Miami—and he made an immediate decision. He said "Okay." So that was my first fee for broadcasting on a commercial station —bus fare over and back.

Those broadcasts were fun. They had to be thorough and detailed, yet concise; I enjoyed the discipline of doing them. They whetted my appetite for bigger things. I was continually listening to Graham McNamee and the others, and I was burning to go where they were. McNamee is a dim, faded name now, but he was about the biggest figure in broadcasting then. He had a marvelous, magnetic voice, and when he came on with his characteristic introduction, "Good evening, ladies and gentlemen of the radio audience, this is *Graham* McNamee," you *knew* something great was going to happen. He made errors, lots of errors; he wasn't a baseball expert or a football expert or a political expert. But when there was a World Series or a big football game or a political convention, he was on it because he was Graham McNamee. He was truly great. He was exciting. He created an audience. He was the first important sports broadcaster and the best. There were cynics who laughed at his mistakes. Some sportswriter—it may have been Ring Lardner—wrote once that he didn't know whether he should do his story of a World Series on the game he saw or the game McNamee broadcast. Once McNamee said, "There's a high pop fly down by third base and Lou Gehrig catches it." It was a slip of the tongue; McNamee knew Gehrig played first base. But his critics pounced on that, and that silly unimportant little mistake is still dragged out and run up and down. It didn't matter. McNamee was what mattered. Things passed him by eventually, but when he was the king, he was the *king*. He was the best. I hero-worshiped him, so much so that when Lylah and I were married the campus newspaper ran the story under the headline: WRUF'S GRAHAM McNAMEE WED."

Lylah knew of my ambitions, and she was very understanding. It was not always easy for her to be that way because as the years went by, and I was still there at WRUF broadcasting for a trivial salary, our friends in Gainesville became increasingly critical. They didn't say much to me, but to Lylah they would ask, "When is Red going to quit playing around that radio station and get a real job?" She would say, "When he gets ready to."

I didn't sit there and wait for opportunity. With Major Powell's blessing I went out and hunted it. I had a month's vacation coming, but I would not take it in a lump. I would take several days off, borrow money against our savings, and go off job-hunting. I worked out a route that went from Gainesville to Atlanta to Charlotte to Louisville to Cincinnati—and once all the way to Chicago. I'd ride the bus, and I'd ride it at night in order to eliminate a hotel bill. I'd get in those towns in the morning and go look for a barber shop. In those days you could find barber shops with bathrooms that you could rent. I'd go in the barber shop and rent their bathroom and take a bath. I'd come out and get a shave and a shoe shine and then go down to the radio station and importune an audience. I'd take an audition, meet people, talk with them, do everything I could to impress myself on them favorably, and then I'd get on the bus and go on to the next town. When I got to the end of the road, which was usually Cincinnati, I would take a hotel room for one night, or maybe two, and I would wash out my underwear and socks in the hotel bathroom. There was no extra money to spare on valet service or anything else. I never took a taxi. If I couldn't find a streetcar to take me where I wanted to go, I walked.

But in radio station after radio station, in every one I visited, the story was the same. They would say, "We'll give you an audition if that's what you want, but there is no job here. We have just laid off several people, people who had been with us for years." Times were desperate; they were hard. I would insist, politely but firmly, on having an audition. After the audition they would say that was fine and good bye. I made a point to get names, and when I returned to Gainesville I would write the people I had met to keep my name fresh in their minds. I would write a letter once a month and remind them that I was available and ready to come to work. I would try to make the letters lively and even funny; I'd tell them a little story about something that had happened in Gainesville.

The receptionists were the toughest people I had to cope with. I don't know why it is, but secretaries and receptionists almost always react negatively when a stranger walks in without an appointment. Their every instinct is to repel him. The time I went all the way to Chicago, I never did get in to take an audition at WGN because the receptionist would not contact anybody for me. She kept saying no, we're not hiring, no, you can't see anybody, no, you can't have an audition, no, no, no. In effect she was saying, leave. I left.

That was a brutal two days in Chicago. I was never so pushed around by strangers in my life. Coming from central Florida, I wasn't used to a big, vigorous, driving place like Chicago. And it was cold, one of those summer cold snaps. From that time on, when anybody made a reference to the Windy City, I knew exactly what he meant. I had linen clothes on that were all right for Florida, but in Chicago my teeth actually rattled, I was so cold. One day I walked across a bridge over the Chicago River to go to the Merchandise Mart, the biggest building I had ever seen in my life. I wanted to take an audition at NBC. I had been totally rebuffed at WGN, and I might as well have been rebuffed at CBS for all that it mattered. Somebody did come out of an office and say, "It's too late in the day. We're not geared to set up an audition. It would be a waste of time, anyway. We've just let people off. Maybe if you came back next week." And so on. I finally said, "No, thanks. I have to be on my way."

I had lost the battle of Chicago completely, but I thought I might as well give NBC a stab as long as I was there. NBC was on two floors of the Merchandise Mart, and I didn't know which was which, so I got off at the first one. The receptionist gave me a bad time, fully as bad as the one had at WGN. She wouldn't phone anybody, she wouldn't even take my name, and she had me back on that elevator before I knew what had happened. I got sore. I said to myself, "I'm going to see *somebody* in this building before I leave," and I went to the other NBC floor. The receptionist there looked up as I came off the elevator, and a name jumped into my mind. I remembered hearing Robert Brown, that favorite of mine, announcing on WLW a few months earlier and saying, "This is my last program from WLW, because I am going to NBC in Chicago." I thought, "He's here. He's right in this building. At least, I hope he's here." I had never met Robert Brown, had never talked to him, had never written to him, but I walked up to the receptionist, smiled sweetly and said, "I'd like to see Mr. Robert Brown, please. I'm Red Barber, a broadcasting friend of his from down South."

She was as nice as pie, and in a few minutes here came Mr. Brown. I knew it was he because he walked into the reception room and looked around inquiringly, as if to see who had come to see him. Before the receptionist could say a word, I walked over and asked, "Robert Brown?" He looked puzzled and said, "Yes." I said, "I'm this broadcasting friend of yours from down South. Let's get out of here for a minute and talk." And before he knew it, I had gotten him off in a corner. I explained my dilemma. He laughed and said, "Let's have a cup of coffee and then go meet some people." He was great. He took me in to see Clarence Menzer, the program chief, and said, "Mr. Menzer, here's a young broadcaster from down in Florida." Menzer said, "Sit down, sit down." We all sat down and Menzer let me tell him my story. It made me feel good just to be able to talk to someone. He and Brown made me feel like a human being again.

Menzer said, "We're in the same position everyone else is, you know. We've had to let fifty or sixty people go lately, and we haven't hired anyone in months. I tell you that quite plainly so that you won't raise any false hopes. There is no job for you, and there's not going to be any job in the foreseeable future. However . . ." He looked at his watch. "I have a luncheon appointment, so I don't have time for you now, but if you'll come back at two o'clock I'd be glad to give you the full NBC announcer's audition. If you want to take it."

I had heard of the full NBC announcer's audition. It was a beauty or a brute, depending on how you did. I wanted the experience of taking it, so I came back promptly at two that afternoon and Menzer put me through it. It was intensive. After it, Menzer took me back in his office and said, "What I told you before about no job, now or in the foreseeable future, still holds. But I want you to know that your audition was fine. I don't know where you're going to end up. I know that you're ambitious and impatient and burning to get someplace, and you may have to wait a long time. But I want to tell you this. You go back to Florida and keep working at that station and keep job-hunting, and don't let anybody discourage you. You are not only going to *be* an announcer. You *are* an announcer right now."

I couldn't have felt better if he had given me a job. If I needed anything to cement my determination, he gave it to me, he and Robert Brown, despite all the receptionists. I left Chicago, got on the bus, rode back to Gainesville, and kept on working. Some months later I heard from WLW in Cincinnati, which I had visited a couple of times, that a job had opened up on their staff and that they were holding competitive auditions to fill it. If I wanted to come back again at my own expense and compete for the job, I was welcome. I wanted to, and I began to make plans.

I went down to the L&L Men's Shop in Gainesville and spoke to Herman Liebowitz, the manager. This was August of 1933. I said, "Herman, I'm going up to WLW in Cincinnati for an audition, and I want to look my best. I not only want to look my best, I want to *feel* my best. I want a new linen suit of clothes and some brown-and-white sport shoes and a couple of new neckties and a new shirt, new underwear, everything. When I take this audition, I want to know that I've got on all new clothes."

"That's fine," Herman said. "We've got the clothes."

"Yeah," I said, "but I haven't got the money."

"You've got the credit," he said.

"I don't know when I can pay you."

"Don't worry about it. When you take that audition, I want to be in there with you. Let's get the clothes. When you come back from Cincinnati, we'll worry about the money."

So I picked out my new suit, new shoes, new shirt, new tie,

new underwear, and rode the bus to Cincinnati. When I got there in the afternoon—the audition was to be held the next day—I went over to the best hotel in town, the Netherlands Plaza, and got a room. That evening I came down to the main dining room, where they had a twelve-piece orchestra playing during dinner, and sat at a ringside table close to the band. I ordered the most expensive meal on the menu—filet mignon. I had never had one in my life before. It nearly killed me to think of the price, but I was going to be in a major league frame of mind the next day if it broke me. I had a very leisurely, pleasant dinner, with a lot of attention from the waiter, and I listened to the band. During its performance it went on the air for a half hour broadcast over WLW. I thoroughly enjoyed watching the engineer and the announcer and everything about it. I drooled. It was a rewarding evening.

I went to bed and got a good night's sleep. I wasn't so excited that I couldn't sleep. The next morning I put on my new clothes and my new brown-and-white shoes and came down and had a good breakfast. Then I got my hair cut, and when it came time to go over to WLW I didn't take a streetcar. I took a taxi. I rode up to the front door in style and walked in.

About thirty fellows from different stations around the country were there for the audition. It was a meatgrinder. You were like a number in a bowl. They'd call your name, and you went on. They had fellows sitting in the control room with the lights off, watching you. You knew they were there, but you couldn't see their faces. They could see you out in the bright studio. The audition was held in Studio A, a big studio where they had a huge Wurlitzer pipe organ. It was the cathedral studio where WLW put on all its important shows, and when you took an audition there you felt very small. In the audition, we did some straight studio announcements, the sort you would do for a musical show or a dramatic show—whatever would ordinarily be done in the studio—and then we read a page of names, on which were cities and people and composers and operas, names that you would be likely to run into as an announcer. We read three or four commercials, things that they dug out of their files and handed to you. It was up to you to figure out the interpretation and where you put the emphasis.

They listened for vocal timbre, how your voice registered on a microphone. They listened to your diction, your pronunciation, the speed with which you spoke. Essentially they judged you emotionally. You can't measure something like announcing. It comes down to a personal reaction: do *I* like the way this man talks?

After it was over, the chief announcer for WLW, a man named Chet Thomas, called me into his office. "I have news for you," he said. "You won the audition." Before I could even feel elated, he went on, "I have some more news. We don't have one job open, we have two. One job is open right now. I don't suppose you could start immediately, could you? I mean today?"

I said, "No, I can't. I have to go back to Florida and give notice to the people at the station there. I have to give them *some* notice."

"Well, that's what I thought," he said. "Now there's a boy from a station up in Dayton who can start tonight, if we wanted to put him on. With two jobs available, I thought what I'd do is hire this fellow from Dayton and put him on the payroll right now, and then bring you back up from Florida in a couple of weeks. Would that be enough time to give notice?"

"Yes," I said. "Two weeks is customary, I believe."

"All right. Two weeks from today I'll confirm all this by wire."

"Fine," I said, and I left. I rode the bus back home to Gainesville feeling very happy, but in the back of my mind a little nagging doubt kept itching at me. Why would he have to confirm it in two weeks? When I got home I told Lylah all that had happened and, of course, she was as pleased as I was, but the two of us kept it to ourselves. I didn't give notice at the radio station. I didn't say a cussed word to anybody.

Two weeks later, to the day, I was scheduled to work late in the afternoon at WRUF, and in the early afternoon I was taking a nap when a telegram came to the door. My wife accepted it eagerly; this was what we had been waiting for. She came in and woke me up and handed me the wire. Lying there in bed, I tore it open and read: REGRET DUE TO CHANGE IN CONDITIONS JOB NO LONGER OPEN. CHET THOMAS.

I rolled over on the bed and cried. I just cried.

I had been listening to WLW right along, and I had heard the fellow from Dayton, the new voice. I listened to that station so religiously that I knew every announcer on it by voice and by name. Two nights after I received the telegram, I heard *another* new voice, and I knew that *this* new voice had the job I was supposed to have. Right then, I sat down and did something you would advise a young man never to do. I wrote an angry letter to Chet Thomas. I don't have a carbon of that letter but, as I remember, I wrote, "Dear Chet: You told me I had a job and to come down here and give notice and you would confirm it. Then you wired and said that due to a change in conditions there was no job. I have just heard your new broadcaster on the air. Chet, you lied to me. I am glad, painful though it is, to find out the type of person you are and the type of organization you represent and to learn that I don't want to work for either one of you. Yours truly, Red Barber."

I didn't hear from him, and the months went by. I put in my winter's work with a bitter taste in my mouth. Through that period I really needed Menzer's encouraging statement: "Don't be discouraged. You *will* be an announcer. You *are* an announcer."

Living next door to us in Gainesville was an elderly man named Professor June, a lovely old man. Mrs. June was dying very painfully and very slowly from cancer. She never complained, never cried out. She was a courageous woman, but her illness was killing him as much as it was her. The houses in that neighborhood were small and there was no more than fifteen feet of space between our house and the June house. One day some friends of ours brought around a bunch of poinsettia clippings and gave them to us. In Florida you don't go to nurseries to buy poinsettias unless you are careless or rich or don't know any better. Poinsettias grow like weeds, and people are always pruning them and throwing away the branches—or sticks; sticks is the proper word. You take the sticks, poke them in the ground, and nine out of ten will take root and grow.

Well, somebody had brought us an armful of poinsettia sticks, and I was standing out in the side yard one day looking at them. I was mad. I was mad at Chet Thomas. I was mad at WLW. I was mad at my wife. I was mad at myself. And I was mad at those poinsettia sticks, in the rented yard of this rented house. I wasn't of a mind to plant them. I was belligerent. I was standing there being mad where Professor June came out on the side porch of his house.

"You going to plant those poinsettias?"

"Nope."

"You're not?"

"No, sir. Not a one of them."

"Why not?"

"I don't want to. Why should I? Why should I beautify this place? I don't own it."

Professor June said, "You're still mad because you can't find a job and get out of that radio station, aren't you?"

I said, "Yes, I *am*." He didn't know about the disappointment in Cincinnati, but he did know generally about my hopes and ambitions. Everybody in town knew that I had been taking those job-hunting trips. It wasn't any secret.

Professor June said, "I'm an old man, boy, but I'm going to tell you something. You want to find that job you're looking for?"

"Yes, sir."

"Then go plant those poinsettia sticks. You plant them, and you may not be here when they bloom."

What Professor June was saying was a variation of what Judge Landis, the first Commissioner of Baseball, told another impatient and impetuous young man one time. The young man was pressing the judge about something and trying to make time run faster than it would, and Landis finally interrupted him. "Do you have a garden?" he asked. The young man, surprised, said, "Yes." The judge said, "I have some advice for you. Whether you like onions or not, go out and plant two or three rows of them, right now." The judge and the professor were both saying, "Instead of standing around being mad and impatient, go do something constructive. Go on living, for the hour, for the day. Let the future come to you."

I planted the poinsettias and before they bloomed I received a telegram, on March 4, 1934, from the last man in the world I expected to hear from—Chet Thomas. I still have that wire.

It said: WILL YOU DO CINCINNATI REDS GAMES TWENTY FIVE DOL-
LARS A WEEK. CHET THOMAS.

I forgot all about being mad. I jumped at it. I sent him a
telegram: YES. WIRE INSTRUCTIONS. RED BARBER. And in a couple
of hours he wired again, saying: REPORT TOMORROW SCOTTY RUSTON
TAMPA FLORIDA. I was to stay with the Reds in Tampa for a week
and then go up to Cincinnati to WLW and wait there—working
at the station—until the ball club came north for Opening
Day.

This happened in the middle of the morning after Lylah had
gone off to the university to do some laboratory work. I went
out to the radio station and told Major Powell what had happened. He was delighted. The break had finally come. He told
me there was no need to give notice to the station. I could
leave right away. Russell McCaughan, who later became a very
successful lawyer in Fort Lauderdale, was running the business
affairs of the station and he immediately began figuring out
how much vacation time I had coming. Then he translated that
into dollars and cents so that the station could give me a check
in that amount and let me walk out of there with a little extra
cash.

I went downtown and bought a cheap trunk, took it back
to our bungalow, and began to pack. I hadn't been able to reach
Lylah by phone at the laboratory and the first she knew about
what had happened was when she came home at noon and saw
the trunk in the living room. She was great. I couldn't take
her with me to Tampa and then to Cincinnati on twenty-five
dollars a week; she was going to have to wait there in Gainesville
until I could send for her. But she didn't fuss a bit; she was as
happy as I was. Because of her I know the joy that can come into
a person's life when someone else rejoices with you.

After I got things packed and had arranged to have Lylah
send the trunk on to Cincinnati, I went to Tampa. My mother
had died some years before and my sister had married, so my
father and my younger brother were living there by themselves.
My father was taking a nap when I arrived, but I woke him up
to tell him the news. He was pleased. He said it was grand, it
was wonderful. I mentioned that I was going on ahead and that
I'd be sending for Lylah later. Out of his practical experience

as a working man, a husband, and a father, he said, "How much are they going to pay you?"

I said, "Twenty-five dollars a week."

He had been sitting on the side of the bed, still waking up from his nap, but now he straightened up and got to his feet and said, "What? That's less than you're making in Gainesville, isn't it?"

I said, "Yes, sir."

He said, "Do you have any idea how much more it's going to cost you to live in a city like Cincinnati than in a small town like Gainesville?"

I said, "No, sir."

He said, "Do you realize that you are leaving a secure job in your home state to go to an insecure job in a distant place?"

I said, "Yes, sir."

He said, "You don't know whether you can broadcast major league baseball or not. You've never done it."

I said, "No sir."

He said, "I am aghast. You have no sense. Have I raised a son who is going to an uncertain job in a strange part of the country, an expensive part of the country, and leaving his wife home alone, *for twenty-five dollars a week?* Have I done that? Has it come to this pass?"

I didn't say anything.

He said, "Can you tell me *why?*"

I said, "Because I want the chance." I was not prepared for his outraged reaction, and I had no way of anticipating his question. I answered it instinctively, and when I did I guess I said it all. I wanted the chance. This was my career and my profession and I had worked hard and long and I had prepared myself, and this was the chance I had been waiting for. I had to take it.

The next morning I went over to the Fair Grounds in Tampa, where the Cincinnati team was training. It was a huge place, with two baseball diamonds and a great deal of activity. I had never met a major league ballplayer in my life, and I didn't have the slightest idea who Scotty Ruston was. Nobody was there when I got to the Fair Grounds, but after a while two or three people happened by and I asked each of them where

Mr. Ruston was. None had ever heard of him. Finally, two men came walking in toward the Cincinnati clubhouse and I said, "Would either of you know where I could find Mr. Scotty Ruston?"

The younger of the two looked at me and his face clouded very slightly, and he said, "Ruston? Why do you want to see Scotty Ruston?" I fished the telegram out and showed it to him. He read it and then he said, "I'm Scotty Reston, not Ruston, and I'm the road secretary of the ball club. I guess I'm the man you're supposed to see."

You might be familiar with this fellow today if you read the New York *Times*. He is James Reston, the political writer who does columns telling Presidents what they're doing wrong. He wasn't with the Reds very long—he left later that year to join the Associated Press in New York—but he and I, as young men in Cincinnati together, became the best of friends. He was a bachelor, and after Lylah came up to join me, Scotty would come over to the small apartment we had and Lylah would cook dinner for the three of us.

Naturally, I didn't know a soul on the Reds, and I told Reston that. He took me around to meet a few people, and he introduced me to Bob O'Farrell, the manager. O'Farrell was an outstanding figure in baseball. He had been the Most Valuable Player in the National League in 1926 when he was catching for the world champion St. Louis Cardinals, and he had managed the Cardinals in 1927. O'Farrell took me in tow and brought me around the ball park. "This is Red Barber," he would tell everyone I met. "He's going to broadcast our games when we get up to Cincinnati." O'Farrell gave me status. He made me feel that I belonged. At the end of the first morning of practice I was walking back toward the hotel with them all—I wasn't going to let those people out of my life for a second—and O'Farrell asked me to join them for lunch. He didn't have much choice; I was fastened to him like a leech. But he was gracious about it, and I tagged along. There I was, on my *first* day, sitting at a table having lunch with the manager of a major league club. I was somebody. To heck with the twenty-five dollars a week. I was richer than that.

O'Farrell told me, "You're just starting out, and there will be a lot of things that you won't know. Anything I can tell you or anything I can do for you, you come to me and ask. Don't hesitate." Later that season Larry MacPhail dismissed O'Farrell as manager. I can't quarrel with the validity of MacPhail's judgment. After all, that was his job. But when he fired O'Farrell, he fired one of the best and most valuable friends I ever had.

I hung around the training camp for seven days, and they were seven precious days. I was at the park in the morning before anybody else, and I stayed later than anybody else at night. It was a new world for me. I knew how Columbus had felt. This was the big league, and I was in it.

Between Innings: SCOTTY RESTON

In 1934 they renamed the ball park in Cincinnati Crosley Field. It had been called Redlands Field. When they renamed it, they put a model of a great big Crosley Shelvador refrigerator on top of the scoreboard in left, and that had something to do with Scotty Reston becoming Mr. James Reston of the New York *Times*. Scotty had been a crack young amateur golfer in Ohio. That's how he met MacPhail—they were both interested in golf—and when Larry came down from Columbus to run the Reds, he brought Reston with him. Scotty told Larry that he would not play golf in Cincinnati because it took up too much time, and he would be too busy learning his job. Scotty held to that resolve, too, and he did not play any golf, but then they had some tournament at one of the clubs around Cincinnati and a lot of pressure was put on Reston to play in it. He went to MacPhail, and Larry said he thought Scotty should play—this one time at least. So he did. It was a one-day tournament and Reston, who had not had a club in his hand for months, won it. He was truly an outstanding player. Afterward, sitting in the locker room surrounded by quite a few people, Reston got in a discussion about the Shelvador refrigerator on top of the scoreboard. Scotty, who still states his opinions loudly and clearly, no matter whose toes he might be stepping on, said he thought it was a terrible thing. He said he felt that Powell Crosley should not have changed the name of Redlands Field in the first place, and that he certainly should not have stuck that oversized refrigerator on top of the historic old scoreboard. Of course, one of Reston's listeners trotted right back to Crosley and told him what Scotty had said, and Crosley immediately voiced his displeasure to MacPhail. Crosley wanted Reston dismissed, but MacPhail said, "If he goes, I go with him." The situation became quite strained.

But everything was satisfactorily resolved not much later when Alan Gould of the Associated Press, whom Reston had met on one of the trips the Reds made to New York, invited him to come to work for the AP. Scotty jumped at the chance, partly to get away from the awkward spot he was in at Cincinnati, and thus began his distinguished career in journalism. That took MacPhail off the hook and it satisfied Powell Crosley, and I gather that Scotty Reston was not too unhappy about the way things turned out, either.

Reston has met a lot of big people all over the world, and they have not impressed him unduly, but he told me once that MacPhail was the only man he was ever afraid of.

RED	1	3	5	7	9	11			
BARBER	2	4	6	8	10	(12)			

Larry MacPhail was running the Reds when I got to Cincinnati and he became a monumental force in my life, yet the first time I saw him he was totally unaware of my presence in the room and he couldn't have cared less. I doubt if he even knew my name. After my week in Tampa, Chet Thomas brought me up to Cincinnati to join the announcing staff at WLW and do routine studio work until the baseball season began. One day MacPhail called a press conference, and because I was going to do the broadcasts the station sent me around to sit in on it. MacPhail was announcing a season-ticket plan he had devised. It was the first such plan that ever was in baseball, but it meant nothing to me. I was unaware of what MacPhail was talking about, let alone the historical significance of what he was introducing. Today, season-ticket plans are the backbone of a ball club's paid admissions, but I didn't even know that there had never been such a plan before.

I sat in the back of the room, not paying much attention. It was not that I was bored; I was merely uninterested. I remember that MacPhail was a strong-looking man, a sandy, red-faced blond. He had on a beautiful tweed suit; I learned later that you never caught MacPhail when he wasn't very well dressed. It was one of his trademarks, an evidence of his appreciation of quality. A thing had to be first class or MacPhail wanted no part of it. I remember only one thing that he said that day. One of the reporters asked him why he had held the general admission price to an even dollar. This was still the depth of the Depression, and Larry replied, "Because it is important for a man to know, when he is buying something, that he doesn't have to break into his next dollar."

It was MacPhail's first year at Cincinnati, too. He had been brought in by the bank that held the mortgage on the ball club after the previous owner, Sidney Weil, had gone broke. MacPhail had been running the Columbus farm team in the St. Louis Cardinals' minor-league chain, and his boss was Branch Rickey. The bank had asked Rickey for advice, and Rickey said, "I hate to do it, because he's a valuable man and there's no way to replace him, but the fellow you want is Larry MacPhail." Larry had graduated from Michigan and had studied law, but he didn't practice it. Instead, he had a penchant for healing sick cats. As a young man he went to Nashville and straightened out a department store (during World War I, in which he was a major, he and a couple of his friends from Nashville tried to kidnap Kaiser Wilhelm of Germany, and they nearly did it, too). Later on he took over an ailing automobile franchise in Columbus, Ohio, and fixed that up, and then Rickey got him to put his healing hand on the Columbus ball team. From there he received his call to the Reds.

In Cincinnati the first thing he did was persuade Powell Crosley, Jr., who owned two radio stations and manufactured radios and refrigerators and automobiles and lord knows what else, to take over majority ownership of the Reds and become president of the ball club. Unlike most baseball executives of the day, MacPhail liked the idea of radio and he later became its stanch advocate, but the decision to bring me in as announcer was not his doing. Someone in the Crosley Radio Corporation said, "As long as we have the ball club, we might as well broadcast its games." Crosley had two stations—WLW, the big one, whose air time was far too valuable, they felt, for baseball games, and WSAI, a little five-thousand-watt station that was just right for the job since its coverage was basically local, whereas WLW reached large areas of the country.

Once they decided to do the games, they had to find someone

on the staff to announce them. They couldn't find anybody. They had a fine sports broadcaster named Colonel Bob Newhall, who was in his sixties then and who did a regular fifteen-minute sports show every evening, but Chet Thomas said, "No, Bob doesn't do play-by-play. He has always said that he won't do ad-lib work. He writes his show at home, and he likes the regular pattern that he works in. There's no reason to even call him. He's not our man, great as he is and great as his name is." Somebody said, "Well, who can we get?" Thomas said, "Do you remember the young fellow who won the competitive audition we had last summer?" Louis Crosley, Powell's brother and chief executive officer and the dominant day-by-day force of the radio corporation, said, "You mean the boy who wore that beautiful white linen suit?" Thomas said, "That's the one. He told me he did sports. He's done football, baseball." Louis Crosley said, "Send for him."

They did and I came, for the twenty-five dollars a week that so distressed my father. When I tell young people today that I went to Cincinnati to broadcast big league baseball for twenty-five dollars a week, they cannot believe it. Of course, they're thinking in terms of money values today and, in particular, the very high fees that prevail in radio and television. But in 1934 baseball broadcasting was quite casual. For one thing, I was not hired as a specialist to do nothing but baseball. I was a salaried employee of the station, and when I wasn't doing baseball or football games I did straight announcing in the studio. Moreover, we did not do an entire season of broadcasts that first year. We were scheduled to do no more than fourteen or fifteen home games. Once in a while, if MacPhail thought he had about as many people in the ball park as he was going to get, he'd let us come on the air at the last minute and do an extra game. Even so, I don't believe we did more than eighteen ball games in 1934. We didn't have the sponsorship. And I'm fairly certain that WSAI did not pay MacPhail one nickel for radio rights, even in a bookkeeping sense from one Crosley enterprise to another.

So the Crosley people weren't quite as penny-pinching as they sound. That twenty-five dollars was a beginner's pay. Before the season began I got up nerve enough to ask Chet Thomas for a small raise so that I could bring my young wife to Cincinnati, and I got it. So I did not start broadcasting major league games for twenty-five dollars a week. It was thirty dollars. And I might add that when I had told Chet Thomas back when I was looking for a job that I had broadcast play-by-play baseball, he did not ask me if they were professional games that I had done and I did not bother to tell him. The only baseball I had done was college and American Legion and semipro. I never had broadcast a professional baseball game before I went on the air Opening Day, 1934, in Cincinnati. I had never even seen a major league game before. I broadcast the first major league game I ever saw.

That does not mean I wasn't ready for it. When I was doing football in Florida I used to subscribe to seven different southern newspapers, from Atlanta, Birmingham, Nashville, places like that, and I read everything I could find on every team in the South. I clipped and filed items. In Cincinnati, I did much the same thing for baseball at the beginning. When I was there doing routine studio announcing waiting for the season to open, I asked the station to get me newspapers from every one of the National League cities. I'd sit in the studio by the hour, waiting to say, "This is WSAI, the Crosley Radio Corporation, in Cincinnati" every fifteen minutes, and for fourteen minutes between each of those station breaks I'd have my nose in the newspapers, reading about major league baseball. When I saw the Chicago Cubs play the Reds on Opening Day I knew every player. I didn't know them by sight, but I knew them.

I knew them better than MacPhail knew me. MacPhail didn't know about me, and I didn't know about him. The ball club had nothing to do with announcers in those days. It made arrangements with the station for a broadcast, and the station assigned a man to do it.

Except for that one press conference I never even saw MacPhail. I saw the ball park only once before the season began. One day I took a streetcar out to take a look at it. I did it as much to have something to do that day as to see the place where I was going to work. I was saving to bring Lylah up—I got her there before Opening Day—and I didn't have much spending money. I was living in the YMCA and eating in the cheapest places I could find. It was a dreary, dull way to live. I realize that the YMCA does good work and I hate to say anything against it, but I never was more lonely in my life than when I was living there.

So I got on a streetcar and rode out and looked at Crosley Field. It is the smallest ball park in the major leagues—it doesn't seat 30,000—but it looked tremendous to me. It was by far the biggest ball park I had ever seen. I had just come from down South in the pea patches. You would have to expand Yankee Stadium ten times to even approach the magnitude of Crosley Field when I first looked at it. For the first time, I realized what I had gotten myself into, and I had to keep reassuring myself that I could do it, that I could broadcast there. It took a lot of strength for me to walk in that ball park on Opening Day. I knew what I didn't know, the experience I didn't have, the things I hadn't done.

The day before Opening Day MacPhail got another idea. He decided that he wanted a fifteen-minute interview to be broadcast every day from the ball park whether we did a play-by-play that day or not. He wanted players and managers interviewed about the game that was coming up that afternoon. (We didn't have night ball in the majors yet; MacPhail didn't put that in until the next year.) The radio station liked the idea. It gave them an interesting new program and it meant nothing more than sending an engineer down to the ball park at eleven forty-five to turn the amplifier on, and sending an announcer—meaning me—out there at that time to do the interview.

The program wasn't planned or projected or tested. MacPhail simply said, "Put it on," and it was up to me to find a major leaguer and interview him live—no tape recorders then—for fifteen minutes. There was no sponsor, no fee, no gift for the player, and starting time for the ball game was three o'clock. I had to have my man on the air three hours before the game. MacPhail was smart. He wanted the interview on the air in plenty of time so that if any people in Cincinnati became interested in the idea that there was going to be a ball game that day, they would have time to get out to the ball park. It happened, too.

But it was up to me to put it on. It was too much of a

production problem to stretch lines and microphones down to the dugout. I had to do my interview upstairs in the broadcasting booth. And the "broadcasting booth" was nothing more than a microphone set up in front of some box seats in the upper stands. When I snared my ballplayer I had to parade him up through the stands to the top deck and down to this exposed box seat right there with the early-bird spectators.

The Cubs were in for Opening Day that year. They were a top-flight team of outstanding players. The Reds were a last-place club. They had finished last three years in a row, and they were going to finish last again that season. I decided to interview Charlie Grimm, the famous manager of the Cubs. I had read about him. He not only had been an outstanding ballplayer and a pennant-winning manager, he was a very talkative man—Jolly Cholly, everybody called him, the best left-handed banjo player in baseball.

About eleven-thirty I wandered up to the visiting clubhouse and knocked on the door. Nobody came. I tried the door and it was locked. I knocked again, loudly. This time I heard a noise and the door opened. It was the Chicago trainer, the veteran Andy Lotshaw, a sloppy, loudmouthed fellow, belligerent and bellicose by nature, who satisfied his ego by hollering at people. We got to be fairly good friends later, but I didn't care much for him that day. He said, "What the hell do you want? Get away from here." I explained that I had to speak to Mr. Grimm. I wasn't on a first-name basis with ballplayers in those days, not to mention managers, and especially not managers I had never met. Lotshaw gave me some more profanity and said I couldn't see Mr. Grimm. Didn't I know Mr. Grimm was holding a meeting with his ballplayers?

I didn't know that. I didn't even know there was such a thing as meetings held by managers with their ballplayers. I didn't know what ballplayers did other than play, except that I presumed they ate and breathed and slept and procreated.

Lotshaw slammed the door shut. I swallowed hard and knocked again. I didn't have much time, and I knew I couldn't send word back to the station that I would not be on the air because I couldn't get anybody to interview. It was too late to go over to the Cincinnati clubhouse and try to rouse up somebody. Besides, I had planned on Grimm, and I wanted Grimm.

I beat on the door again. I hammered on it. Lotshaw came out a second time, and he was just as loud and twice as abusive and three times as profane. But I would not leave. Finally, a great big hulking fellow in a baseball uniform with a loud voice himself came to the door and said, "What in the hell is going on out here? I can't hold my meeting with all this racket."

Lotshaw said, "This fellow says he wants to see *Mr.* Grimm, and I keep telling him he can't see *Mr.* Grimm, because you're holding a meeting."

The fellow in the uniform said to me, "What do you want to see Mr. Grimm about? I'm Mr. Grimm."

I blurted out that I wanted him to go on the radio.

He said, "I'm holding a meeting."

I said, "This is very important. I've just got to have you."

I don't know what went over Charlie Grimm, but he said, "Okay, what time do you *got* to have me?"

"We have to leave here at five minutes to twelve at the latest to get up to the microphone on time."

"All right," he said. "Let me finish my meeting, and I'll come out."

I have learned since that a club meeting such as the one he was holding on Opening Day is inviolate. The President of the United States had better not try to interrupt one. It is the manager's supreme moment of ego and authority. But Charlie Grimm finished his interrupted meeting and came out and met his interrupter in time to walk up the many steps through that old grandstand and down to the microphone in the box seat on the upper level.

I didn't know him. I had never met him before. We didn't have time to visit or get acquainted before we went on the air. But he gave me a wonderful interview. He talked for fifteen minutes about his excellent ball club, and he did it without much help from me. If that interview was a good one, it was good because he made it good. I will go to my grave with a deep appreciation of what many people have done for me, and one of them is Charlie Grimm. What a help it was to have that interview behind me when I returned to the microphone to do the play-by-play that afternoon.

It was a big day in Cincinnati. Opening Day is always big there, much more so than in any other town in the majors—it's a local holiday—and it was especially important that year, 1934. It was Powell Crosley's first year, and Larry MacPhail's. Things had to go right. I had gotten the interview over with, but the play-by-play was another thing. I didn't know how to score a baseball game then. In Florida when I broadcast baseball I always sat next to a fellow named Earl Blue, who was the sports editor of the Gainesville paper, and I would lean over and read off his scorebook. If I couldn't understand something I'd ask him on the air, and he'd tell me. This thing of having a color man working with a play-by-play announcer isn't necessarily a new idea. It's what Earl Blue and I were doing in Florida in the early thirties.

But I still didn't know how to score, and I asked WSAI if they would send somebody out who could score to sit with me during the game. They sent a fellow named Eldon Parks, and he and I sat down together in the front two seats in the box and I read off his sheets. A few minutes before we went on the air, a tall, dark, curly-haired man came quietly into the rear of the box and sat down. It was Peter Grant, the top announcer at WLW. He wasn't a sports broadcaster, but he was WLW's top ad-lib announcer. In other words, he could talk; he was a performer. Nobody had to tell me why he just happened to pop out to the ball park on Opening Day and sit down right behind me. It meant that somebody in authority at the station had said, "We've never heard this kid Barber broadcast a game, and we don't know for sure whether he can do it or not." It was too important an occasion to be messed up by an unknown kid, so they decided to send Peter Grant out as a backstop. Peter didn't know baseball, but he was professional enough to carry it off if he had to. They said, "If the kid goes so bad that we can't tolerate it, we'll take him off and put Grant on. We'll get through the day, anyway, and then we can look around for another baseball announcer."

The game started, and I got busy broadcasting it, and I forgot about Peter Grant. It turned out to be a beautiful ball game.

Lon Warneke was pitching for the Cubs, and he had a no-hitter for eight innings. In the ninth Adam Comorosky got a scratch single, and that was the only hit Warneke allowed. I talked about the no-hitter on the broadcast. I have never believed in the superstition about not mentioning a no-hitter. It's all right down on the bench, where mentioning it could upset a pitcher or distract him, but in a broadcast, which the pitcher cannot hear, the idea of not mentioning it has absolutely no validity. I am a broadcaster, a reporter. I deal in facts. If the big fact of the game is the number of hits a pitcher has allowed, I broadcast it. Years later, when I broadcast that memorable game in the 1947 World Series when Cookie Lavagetto broke up Bill Bevens' no-hitter with two out in the ninth, I came in for a lot of criticism. I was accused of jinxing Bevens' no-hitter by talking about it. That's nonsense. I pay no attention to criticism like that. From the very first, I have felt that my responsibility is to keep my listeners informed. I know I informed them that first day in Cincinnati.

Along about the fifth inning there was a little stir behind me. Eldon Parks leaned over and whispered, "Peter is going back to the station." I knew what that meant, too. It meant that I was doing the game to everyone's satisfaction, and that Mr. Grant had been released from his obligation.

That was a satisfying day. People often ask me what ball game stands out most in my memory, which was the biggest game I ever broadcast. There is never any doubt in my mind: Opening Day, Cincinnati, 1934. It was the biggest challenge, and everything followed from it. I remember so well the feeling of exhilaration I had that evening. It's a rare feeling. It comes only a few times in your life. You've done something well, and you know it, and other people know it, and you know they know it. It's an extraordinary feeling, and I had it. There was Peter Grant leaving, for one thing. There was the perfection of the game that Warneke pitched—and there is no question about it, the game makes the broadcast. You can do a superb job technically in a dragging, dull, sloppy game filled with bases on balls and long flat stretches, and it doesn't mean a thing. But you can do a quick routine job on a great game, and everybody tells you what a fine job you did.

That was the most joyous day of my life, next to my wedding day. Bill Stoess was the musical director at the station, and a big man there. I had to go back down after the game to do a fifteen-minute wrap-up of scores, and when I came into the studio Stoess almost ran over to me. He said, "That was a great job. That was a ball game." I mean, if the Israelites at the beginning of their wanderings were as hungry as the Old Testament makes them out to be, I experienced then the satisfaction of the hunger that the manna from heaven did for them. It was great. People went out of their way to say nice things. WLW was a hard-bitten place. It was loaded with talented people, and they were in competition with each other almost as much as they were with people from other stations. They worked to survive. They didn't throw compliments around freely. And then to go home to Lylah, who had heard the broadcast, and tell *her* of the compliments I had received. It was the hunter come home from the hill, and this hunter was loaded with meat.

Things went along nicely after that, though not all the managers I met were as pleasant as Charlie Grimm. George Gibson of the Pirates, for instance. Look him up and you will find that he was a famous old-time ballplayer, and he was a tough manager of the old school. When I think about him, he still makes me shudder, though the shudder is concomitantly followed by a wave of gratefulness. After that opening series with Chicago, I asked Scotty Reston if he could send a telegram to the managers of the different teams before they came into Cincinnati telling them of the interview program and asking them for their cooperation. Then when I went to speak to them, they would know about it and I wouldn't have to go into a great detailed explanation of what I wanted them to do. It would break the ice for me. It would be a big help.

Reston sent the telegrams, and I felt that a major obstacle had been hurdled. About a week after the season began, I was still floating on the glow from that wonderful beginning. The Ford dealers of Greater Cincinnati were sponsors early in the season, and the sales manager at WSAI had arranged to have a Ford put at my disposal for several weeks. When the Pirates came in to play the Reds, I hopped into my borrowed Ford and drove downtown to the Sinton Hotel, where the Pirates were staying. It tells something about what it was like in 1934 when I say that I drove into the heart of downtown Cincinnati with no trouble or delay and without a second thought parked the car in the street directly outside the hotel. Try that today in any big town.

The Pirates were a team of famous stars—Paul and Lloyd Waner, Pie Traynor, Arky Vaughan, Gus Suhr—and one of their coaches was an almost legendary figure, Honus Wagner. I knew about these men as records, but I had met none of them, and I had never met Gibson. I walked into the lobby, and there in the middle of it was a big red-faced fellow who looked like a baseball man. I went over to him and said, "Excuse me, are you with the Pittsburgh ball club?" He half snarled, "Yes, I am." I asked, "Oh, who are you?" That didn't sit too well, and he snapped, "I'm the manager."

"Mr. Gibson," I said, "I'm Red Barber, the radio announcer for the Reds, and Mr. MacPhail wants me to get some of your ballplayers and interview them over the radio at noon."

That's as far as I got. He lifted his voice so that it was completely audible to everyone in the lobby of the Sinton Hotel and he proceeded to give me a profane diatribe about radio announcers, and what a filthy breed they were, and how he wanted no part of them, and that radio was worse than the serpent in the Garden of Eden, and that it was an upsetting factor to civilization in general and to his ball club in particular, and that radio announcers could not be trusted because they deliberately misstated facts and misquoted people and created controversies, and further that they knew nothing about baseball and were the most ignorant breed of men on the face of the earth—all this interlaced and underlined and emphasized with the profanity that Gibson had learned during his many years in the careless, crude life of the dugout and ball field and locker room.

I was utterly stunned, petrified, struck dumb. The Bible says something about the lamb being dumb before its shearers; I know what that means—I found out then. I couldn't say a word for a few minutes. The world, which had been so bright and cheerful since Opening Day, had exploded. Here was the young announcer who had taken Cincinnati by storm, Charlie

Grimm's pal, and he had been devastated. I could not say to this day just what set Gibson off like that. I don't know if he had a real grievance against radio announcers, or if it was something his wife had written him, or if it was because his ball club was going poorly. I do know he was fired as manager of the club a short time later, so perhaps he knew the handwriting was on the wall. Whatever it was, I had come to him when he was primed and ready to unload his accumulated anger on somebody, and I got it. I was crushed. Gibson finished saying what he wanted to say and walked off to an elevator, stepped in it, and disappeared from sight, leaving me alone in the middle of the lobby, speechless, embarrassed, humiliated.

There were two nice-looking men sitting on a sofa in the lobby, and as I stood there, dismayed and bewildered, the two of them got up and walked over to me. One of them remarked, "We heard everything that Gibson said, and it was very unfair of him. He didn't have any business talking to you that way. My name is Waite Hoyt, and this is Fred Lindstrom. We're with the Pirates. If you don't mind, we'd be glad to go out to the ball park with you and go on the program."

Well, of course, I recognized their names—Hoyt, a pitcher, and Lindstrom, an outfielder. Both had seen starring days earlier, and both were toward the end of their careers now. As suddenly as I had been crushed, I was uplifted again. I ushered them out of the hotel and into my borrowed Ford. I got the car started, began to move, and turned down a one-way street, going the wrong way. I was so excited I never realized it until I almost hit a man who was crossing the street. He jumped back out of the way, and as we went by him both Hoyt and Lindstrom laughed out loud and one of them called out, "Hey, Dolly, you son of a bitch. It's too bad we didn't hit you." It was Dolly Stark, a National League umpire. A policeman came along then and he would have given me a ticket except that Hoyt and Lindstrom explained that they were ballplayers and that I was an announcer and that we were in a terrible sweat to get out to the ball park for a broadcast. With that, the policeman let me go and he even let me drive the rest of the block the wrong way.

It turned out to be one of the best broadcasts I ever had.

Anyone who knows either Hoyt or Lindstrom can tell you that they are both intelligent men. Lindstrom became baseball coach at Northwestern, and Hoyt later was play-by-play announcer at Cincinnati for many years, until his recent retirement. Waite was a distinguished broadcaster and one of the finest raconteurs I have ever listened to. He can tell stories about the Babe Ruth days better than anyone alive.

When I went to Brooklyn in 1939, Hoyt was out of baseball and living in New York. The Dodger games were being broadcast on WOR, and Hoyt was hired to do a feature program before the ball game and another feature program afterwards. He talked about the baseball picture in general and told his wonderful stories and did anything he wanted to do. That's how he began in radio. When I left Cincinnati, Roger Baker succeeded me, and I think it was in my second or third year at Brooklyn that Hoyt said to me, "I've got the job as play-by-play announcer next year at Cincinnati." I said, "Wonderful." He said, "But I don't know how to score. I can't broadcast unless I know how to score, and I want you to teach me."

By that time I had learned how to score myself and ordinarily I would not have hesitated a moment to agree to his request. But I didn't want to teach Hoyt. I didn't want to because I didn't want to be alone with the man. In those days Hoyt was a drinker, and when he drank he was the roughest man physically I have ever been around. His idea of fun was to roughhouse, and he was strong. More than that, he had a temper—he was irascible, unpredictable. He could go into orbit very quickly. I was deeply grateful to him for what he had done for me in 1934, and I felt very ill at ease about the idea of refusing to grant what seemed like a simple request. I was doing a fifteen-minute sport show at nine-fifteen in the evening, right after Gabriel Heatter, and Hoyt had proposed to come to the studio and meet me after the show. I was apprehensive, and I think justifiably, about the condition he might be in by nine-thirty after he'd spent a few hours killing time waiting to meet me. Yet, if anyone ever owned me, he did. I couldn't turn him down.

I finally said, "Waite, I would be glad to teach you how to score on one consideration. I'll teach you. I'll sit with you one night, two nights, three nights, as many nights as you want to come. I'll go over scoring with you. I'll tell you everything I know about Cincinnati. I'll discuss broadcasting techniques. I'll talk about play-by-play. It's another world, doing play-by-play. It's just as if I came to you with a baseball in my hand and said, 'Tell me how to pitch to batters.' I'll do everything I can. But there's one stipulation. When you come to see me you have to bring Mrs. Hoyt with you."

He got red in the face, and I was slightly nervous because of that low boiling point of his, but he said, "All right. I will." And he did. Mrs. Hoyt came along and Waite and I spent a couple of evenings working, and things went very smoothly. And then I told him something else, with Mrs. Hoyt there. I said, "You may not enjoy hearing what I'm going to say, Waite. Cincinnati is a major league city because it has a baseball team in the National League. But it's really not a city at all. It's a small town. It's a conservative town. It is based fundamentally on German people who take pride in owning their homes and in keeping out of debt and in being thrifty. It's a town that goes to bed early at night and gets up early in the morning. They drink a lot of beer in Cincinnati, and you know about that. But you can't go out there and do a lot of drinking the way you do in New York, and get away with it. In New York they don't know or care about you. There are too many people. But in Cincinnati they'll know you, and they'll know what you do." Then I said good night and got out of there.

They say a leopard can't change his spots, and it's true that when Waite first went to Cincinnati he continued to have his problems for a while. He got lost over in Kentucky for three or four days at one point, and everybody in Cincinnati knew about it. When I heard about it, I felt sad. I thought, "Oh, my. Now he's done it." But Waite got himself into Alcoholics Anonymous and he changed completely. I take my hat off to a man who defeats something the way he did, who wins over himself. From a drinking man who was mean and selfish and rough, Hoyt became a leading figure in AA. I have heard so many people tell me stories about Waite Hoyt getting out of bed at four in the morning to answer a phone call and then getting dressed and going out in the night to someone who needed help, someone who wanted somebody to talk to, someone who wanted somebody to pour coffee for him. He made his years in Cincinnati valuable ones. And far from resenting him, the people of Cincinnati came to love him.

So many things started for me in 1934. When Cincinnati lost to the Cubs on Opening Day it was the best possible thing that could have happened to me professionally, because when the Reds lost they fell into a tie for last place with the three other teams that also lost on Opening Day (it was an eight-team league then). Two or three days later, losing consistently, Cincinnati was in last place all by itself, and never once all season did they emerge or even threaten to emerge. My first big-league team was a last-place ball club from the first day of the season to the last. That was important to me professionally because, not breaking in with a winning club, I was not misdirected by the success of the team. That can happen to a broadcaster. The team wins and everybody is happy, and the broadcaster comes in for his share of the praise. But there is a hard core of work that has to be done by a professional broadcaster, and because my first team was a loser all the way I had to learn right from the beginning what that hard core of work was. I had to find out things and do things and broadcast things that were over and above the straight reporting of cheer-inducing victories. Whatever interest the Cincinnati broadcast had in 1934 was not anchored on winning, and there were only a few good ballplayers on that team, so it was not based on the star system either. I had to learn as much about baseball, in every aspect, as I could, and I had to pass on what I learned to the listeners.

By and large, the Reds were an old, used-up team. They did have Paul Derringer, the big pitcher, and they had Ernie Lombardi, who was later to win two batting championships. There were one or two other respectable players, but generally it was a last-place team from top to bottom. MacPhail knew it, I believe the bank knew it, and I'm certain that Bob O'Farrell, the manager, knew it. MacPhail fired O'Farrell late that season, though I doubt if Larry faulted O'Farrell for the team's play. Mac-Phail was a realist; he knew it would take some years to develop a winner and he began by building a farm system. But even in last place MacPhail was deadly earnest about winning and losing, whereas O'Farrell had an easygoing, philosophical attitude. This basic difference in approach came to a head after a series the Reds had with the Boston Braves. Cincinnati blew substantial leads and lost two straight games to the Braves, and an outfielder named Hal Lee drove in the winning run both times. O'Farrell had pitched to Lee in similar situations in both games, and MacPhail thought he should not have pitched to him either time. When Lee broke up the second ball game MacPhail burned, and when MacPhail burned you didn't need a motion picture re-creation of the destruction of Rome to learn what a conflagration is. To add to his exasperation, when he stalked in anger to his office after the game he kicked the door open and broke his toe. He sat there behind his desk burning about the two lost ball games and burning about Hal Lee and burning about this broken toe that was killing him—and he had enough sense to know that he had no business kicking the door in the first place, and that was burning him, too. Then Bob O'Farrell came walking from the clubhouse, along the corridor that passed MacPhail's office. He had a brand new golf club in his hand, a driver. When he saw MacPhail behind his desk, O'Farrell made the great mistake of stepping into the office, waggling the club as though he were on a golf tee, and saying, "Look at this new driver, boss. Isn't it a beauty?"

MacPhail said nothing—except to himself. But to himself he said, This is the last straw. I'm getting me a new manager. He left the ball park, took a taxi, went to the airport, and flew to Nashville. Charlie Dressen was managing the Nashville club, and MacPhail liked what he saw. But Fay Murray, who ran the club, wouldn't let Larry have him. MacPhail flew on out to the Pacific Coast, looked at some more managers there, and then came back to Cincinnati just in time to get a phone call from Fay Murray. Fay said, "Larry, my catcher broke his hand. You get me a decent catcher to take his place, and I'll let you have Dressen." MacPhail found the catcher Murray wanted, sent him to Nashville, and Dressen came up to Cincinnati to replace O'Farrell.

Charlie taught me more about baseball than any other man. I was green, and he'd sit with me by the hour, explaining things and answering my questions. Some of them must have seemed silly and trite to him, but he would go over the same ground with me time and again. He was so patient, so helpful.

Yet he and I had once a very serious falling out, so much so that I did not mention his name on the air for more than half a season. I felt I had no choice. One day the Reds were playing in Pittsburgh, and we were doing a wire-report broadcast from the studio in Cincinnati. The Reds had a good second baseman named Alex Kampouris, and they also had a rookie named Frank McCormick, who was basically a first baseman (he went on to win the Most Valuable Player award as a first baseman with the pennant-winning Cincinnati teams a few years later) but who had played a few games around second. In the ninth inning of this game in Pittsburgh, because of some pinch-hitting maneuvering, Kampouris was out of the game and Dressen put Frank McCormick in to play second base. The Pirates got the bases loaded, and the Western Union wire reported: SINGLE BETWEEN FIRST AND SECOND TO RIGHT, TWO RUNS SCORE, PITTSBURGH WINS 7–6. In my broadcast I announced that the Pittsburg batter had hit the ball sharply to the right side, and I took the liberty of adding that McCormick had made a great effort for the ball but that it had gone through into right field, that the winning runs had scored, and the game was over. That was all.

The Reds came home to Cincinnati, and Charlie Dressen barred the writers and the broadcasters from his dugout. He gave orders to the park police not to let anyone representing the local newspapers or radio stations in there. I was barred, and I didn't like it, but it didn't make too much difference to me at the time. The Reds were playing the Dodgers and of course there was no way Charlie could keep the Brooklyn writers out. They went into the Dodger dugout and then wandered across the field to talk to Charlie. Harold Parrott, who later became an official with the Dodgers, was a sportswriter then, and though Harold and I later became good friends, he set something in motion that day that threatened my job. In the early days of sports broadcasting, announcers were generally disliked intensely by the newspapermen. We were a threat to them, and they wanted no part of us. Alan Gould of the Associated Press told me that spring in Florida, "You should be prepared for some rough years because nobody in the newspaper world is going to like you. Sportswriters have had it easy, but it's not going to be easy any more. If broadcasters are doing a detailed, play-by-play report, that means the newspapermen can't sit back and write what they please. They're going to have to work, go down to the clubhouse, dig out detailed information. You're up-setting a cozy, patterned life, and they're going to blame you for doing it." I found that to be true.

So, in this climate of hostility and suspicion, the Brooklyn writers went over to talk to Dressen, and the first I learned of what they talked about was a couple of days later at breakfast when I picked up the Cincinnati *Enquirer*. There was a box on the front sports page with a headline saying: RADIO AN-NOUNCER HARMFUL INFLUENCE. The *Enquirer* had picked up a story that Harold Parrott had sent back to the Brooklyn *Eagle* in which he quoted Dressen as saying the only reason he had barred everyone from the dugout was because a radio announcer had been picking up tidbits of personal in-formation and putting them on the air to the embarrassment of the players. The *Enquirer*, which did not like radio, made a big thing out of it. It did not mention me by name, but who else could be the radio announcer who was such a harmful influence? I scooted right down and spoke to John Clark, the station manager. I made it clear to him that I was *not* a harmful influence, that I represented the radio station, and that I wanted the station's assurance that it did not feel that I *was* a harmful influence. Clark phoned Powell Crosley and Crosley phoned MacPhail, and they got that straightened out. Mac-Phail also said, "I'll order Dressen to reopen the dugout, but that's all I can do. I can't make him talk to the announcer. I can't tell my manager what to say or what not to say."

It was up to me to confront Dressen, and I did. I said, "Why did you do this to me?" He said, "Because when I got back from that Pittsburgh series some friends of mine told me what you said over the radio. You said that if I had Kampouris in at second in the ninth instead of McCormick, he would have fielded that ball and turned it into a double play and saved the game, instead of it going for a hit and Pittsburgh winning."

I said, "Charlie, I never said anything like that."

"My friends said you did."

"I don't care what your friends said. I did not say it." I turned to John McDonald, who later became secretary of the Reds and then secretary of the Dodgers under MacPhail. I said, "John, you heard that broadcast. Tell Charlie what you heard."

John said, "Charlie, Red never broadcast anything like that. He didn't say anything about you, and he didn't say anything about Kampouris. In fact, he even had McCormick making a great try for the ball."

"My friends said he said it."

Frances Levy, who was MacPhail's secretary, piped up, "Oh, Charlie, he never did."

But Charlie wouldn't change. He reopened the dugout, but beyond that he would not go. I had said something wrong about him. His friends had told him.

I thought, "If that's the way this man is, he is never going to have another opportunity to claim I said anything derogatory about him. I won't mention his name." For the rest of that season, as far as the radio audience was concerned, the Reds had no manager. I never once mentioned Dressen's name, and I never even referred to "the manager." It took a little doing, but I did it. If he came out to argue with an umpire I'd say, "There's a discussion going on down at first base." If he came out to change a pitcher, I'd say, "Relief pitcher so-and-so is coming into the game." The listeners were aware of the moves that Dressen was making, but I made no direct reference to him. And I never went into the dugout.

That fall, after the season, MacPhail called me into his office. He said, "You and Charlie have had a pretty good go at it, and from your standpoint I can't blame you for the way you feel. But from my standpoint, as general manager of the club, the situation is intolerable. I can't have it. Now, I am not going to speak to Dressen about it; I'm just speaking to you. You figure a way to straighten this thing out."

So, at spring training the next year I went up to Dressen and said, "Charlie, let's start all over again." He said, "There's nothing better I'd like to do. We start all over." Neither of us mentioned the Pittsburgh incident, and we remained good friends until he died in the summer of 1966 when he was managing Detroit.

A few days after his death, I was in Detroit with the Yankees to broadcast. I had taken Jerry Coleman's place on that trip with the express idea of getting a chance to do Jerry's fifteen-minute pregame show, just so I could talk a little about Dressen. I told the story about what had happened back in Cincinnati and about the friendship Charlie and I had despite the incident. I talked about Charlie himself, his accomplishments, his great spirit, his tenacity, his ability to come back time and again from setbacks that would crush another man. It was a good broadcast; I was pleased with it. It was what I had gone to Detroit to do. The next morning after breakfast I received a phone call from Charlie's sister, Marge. She had called up merely to say hello, and to talk about Charlie, because we were all old friends. I mentioned the broadcast, and she said, "Oh, I wish I had heard it. I'm so sorry I missed it." I said, "Marge, I have a tape of it right here in my room that the engineer cut for me. Why don't you and your husband come on over? I'd be glad to play it for you." They did, and they listened to it, and when I told the story on tape about Pittsburgh and Kampouris and McCormick and Charlie barring the dugout, Marge looked at me. In the broadcast I emphasized Charlie's undying loyalty to his friends, a loyalty that was both a fault and a strength.

When the tape ended, Marge said, "Red, do you remember that I went to Charlie when this was going on, and I told him that you had not said what he accused you of saying?"

"Yes," I said. "Now I do. I had forgotten."

"I told Charlie he was making a terrible mistake, but he wouldn't give in." And then she added, "Do you know who told him you broadcast that about him? Do you know why he would never back down and admit he was wrong?"

I shook my head.

"It was his wife." Suddenly, after all those years, I understood. The first Mrs. Dressen and I had never gotten along, and she had carried a grudge all those years. For some unknown reason this woman completely misheard the broadcast, and when Charlie came home she gave him her distorted version of it. He believed her at first. And then when he realized that what she had told him wasn't so, he was too proud and too loyal to come out and admit the whole thing was his wife's acrimonious doing. All he could do was say, "My friends say you said it."

Between Innings: JOHNNY VANDER MEER

My phone number is listed under my wife's name and has been ever since John Vander Meer pitched his second successive no-hitter for the Cincinnati Reds in 1938. Before Vander Meer I had my own name listed in the phone book as Walter Red Barber. I had the idea that I should not try to keep away from the listening public. It should be an open matter where I lived and what my phone number was. There were some people who took liberties, of course, some who were irritating and annoying, but that was all right. I felt that was part of the job, and I put up with it.

But then Vander Meer pitched that second no-hitter, at Brooklyn in the first night game ever played at Ebbets Field. I still come across people who tell me about listening to that game on the radio. They tell me they heard me broadcast it. They didn't. First of all, I wasn't broadcasting at Brooklyn then. I was still in Cincinnati. And second, nobody heard Vander Meer's second no-hitter over the radio because *nobody* broadcast it. He pitched it in Brooklyn when the anti-radio ban among the three New York clubs was still in effect. At Cincinnati we usually did wire re-creations of the Reds' out-of-town games, but the New York clubs wouldn't even let Western Union send a report for a re-created broadcast.

So, nobody heard the game. But they heard *about* it. The first intimation in Cincinnati was a news bulletin. The Associated Press sent something over the wire and a radio station slapped it on the air: "FLASH: Johnny Vander Meer has just pitched his second straight no-hitter, something that has never been done before in the history of baseball." I don't remember exactly what time that night the word came through, but I would guess it was between ten and eleven. It set that staid old town right on its ear. Cincinnati went berserk. Those Germans in their beer gardens along the "Rhine," as an old canal near the Ohio River was sometimes poetically called, jumped up and down. They went wild. They got to drinking more beer and talking about Vander Meer and about the Reds and about baseball, and—I don't know how it got started—after a while it seemed that nothing would do but that everybody in Cincinnati had to phone old Red Barber and talk to him about Vander Meer's second no-hitter.

I hadn't seen the no-hitter. I didn't know anything more about it than they did. But they called and they called and they called, and that phone kept ringing until four in the morning. One call after the other, strangers in beer halls, drunks, over and over again. It was a very long night. Every time I'd get my head back on the pillow, *ring*, there went the phone again.

When I finally got up, bleary-eyed, the morning after that spectacular night, there was only one thing to do. After that, our phone was listed under my wife's name. Anyone who looked us up in the phone book who knew us at all could spot it right away. In other words, we didn't hide from the people who had a right and a reason to call us. But for the guy in a beer hall phoning at two in the morning to settle a twenty-five-cent bet on whether Dolf Camilli was five feet eleven or six feet, I was no longer available.

RED	1	3	5	7	9	11	(13)		
BARBER	2	4	6	8	10	12			

When baseball ended at Cincinnati I went right into football broadcasting. I did University of Cincinnati games in 1934 and three or four Ohio State games. In 1935 WLW made arrangements to do the full Ohio State schedule, and I did all those broadcasts. In 1935, too, I broadcast a World Series for the first time. In those days, no one network had exclusive rights to the Series; any of them could get permission from Judge Landis to broadcast. So you would have three or four different accounts of the game going out over the air. There were Mutual and CBS and two NBC networks, the Blue and the Red. Later, the Red network was separated from NBC and became ABC.

Mutual was just being created in 1935, and the Series that year was to be its first really big sports event. They had stations in New York, Detroit, and Chicago, and they hoped to get WLW. Landis said he would recognize Mutual and let it into the Series only if it delivered WLW, because even though it broadcast from a smaller city WLW was one of the two or three most famous stations in the country. WGN in Chicago had joined Mutual for the Series on the condition that two of its announcers, Bob Elson and Quinn Ryan, be on the Series broadcast, and John Clark of WLW said he would not come in unless one of his announcers was included, too. The New York and Detroit stations did not have anybody they particularly wanted to put on, so they agreed to both requests with alacrity. Anything. Let's get the stations and put this network on the air.

When John Clark said a WLW announcer he meant me, and when the 1935 Series went on the air, there I was. I met the other Mutual broadcasters in Detroit. Bob Elson was a professional baseball broadcaster, but Quinn Ryan was just a pleasant fellow with a folksy manner who had more or less fallen into a job in front of a microphone. His basic job at WGN was program director, but his broadcasting style became popular in Chicago in the early days of radio. He used to say, "I talk to the boys in the barbershop back home." That was great back when the boys in the barbershop had never before heard a ball game over the air. They were getting the game as it happened—didn't even have to wait for the evening paper. But by 1935 the novelty had worn off, and they wanted a lot more than the mere fact of a broadcast. I know that I was startled before the first game in Detroit that year. We were about to go on the air, and Ryan, who was to do the opening color broadcast, didn't have a note in his hands. He had done no preparation at all; that wasn't his style. He went on the air and bumbled along for fifteen minutes, and I thought, "Holy mackerel, is this the way they do the World Series?" It was an informal, unorganized presentation, and when he signed the broadcast off after the game, he did it the same way.

I had come into Detroit the night before the first game, and Ryan and Elson told me the broadcasting arrangements: Ryan to do the opening, Elson to do the first three innings, me the middle three innings, Elson the final three innings, and then Ryan the sign-off. That was fine with me. I never questioned the arrangement. I would have been happy to do one inning, even half an inning. If you had scratched me you would have found that I would have been glad to do nothing but the credit lines for the Ford Motor Company, which was sponsoring the broadcasts (and that's all the commercial time they got, as I remember, three announcements). So Elson did his six innings, and I did my three and I thought nothing more about it. That night I went to press headquarters and walked around like a tourist. Here were all the famous sportswriters whose stories I had been reading for years, the men I had read and clipped and studied. There were club officials and old ballplayers and managers and the league presidents. It was my first time in a World Series press headquarters, and I didn't say a word all night. Instead, I sat and listened and drank it all in. I had a wonderful time, and when I went back to my room to go to sleep I had no idea that a storm had been blowing back and forth over my head all evening.

I woke the next morning with the phone ringing at my ear. It was the Mutual Broadcasting people and the people from Ford and they were saying, "Now, Red, don't be angry. Don't get mad and go stomping off to Cincinnati." I didn't know what they were talking about. They said, "Don't be unreasonable. What happened yesterday was a mistake, and it won't happen again." I was still half asleep, but even if I had been wide awake I wouldn't have understood any of this. They said, "You can have anything you want, anything. Do you want to do the whole ball game today?"

What had happened, I discovered later, was that John Clark had heard the broadcast and had noted that Quinn Ryan of WGN had been on both before and after the game and that Bob Elson of WGN had done six innings of play-by-play but that Red Barber of John Clark's own WLW had done only three innings in between all that WGN exposure. He phoned Detroit and raised cain. Here was his little boy that he had sent up there getting only three innings. He told Mutual they had no right to do that to me, and he said if they didn't change things he was going to pull WLW out of the Mutual broadcast and take NBC. Mutual couldn't afford to lose WLW, so they hastened to comply. They thought I had phoned Clark and complained, and now they were trying to smooth things out with me. I told them the truth. I said, "I don't know what you fellows are talking about. I didn't call Mr. Clark, and I didn't make any complaint." I said, "I did notice that he had six innings and I only had three, but I thought that was the way it was supposed to be. I didn't object." They asked if I wanted to do six that day and Elson three to even things up, but I replied, "There's no need for that. But I would like to do half the game." I thought I was going to get kissed over the phone. They thought that was great, and that was the way it was set up. Elson and I split the remaining games.

After the second game, the Series shifted from Detroit to Chicago and there Mutual called me in and told me that along with my four and a half innings I was to do the opening fifteen minutes and the signoff. They were taking Quinn Ryan off. John Clark had nothing to do with that. It was simply that Mutual realized that Ryan's style was outdated, and they felt they had to have a more professional broadcaster in that warmup spot. After all, the other networks had brought their top commentators out. Columbia had Boake Carter; NBC was using Lowell Thomas. Elson and I had no commercials to do during our play-by-play, and in between innings we did our own color and comment. Somebody liked the way I did the between-innings stuff, and when they decided that Ryan wasn't cutting it, they said, "Let's let this kid try it." I wasn't paid anything for it. Heck, I wasn't paid an extra penny for working the entire Series. I was getting my regular salary from the Crosley Radio Corporation, and that was it. I was just happy to be on, very happy. When I got back to Cincinnati after the Series, John Clark said, "You did a good job." I said, "Thank you. And thank you for more than I can say. I wouldn't have been there if it hadn't been for you." He grinned sort of wolfishly and said, "When you sat down to do that second game, were you satisfied with your share of the innings?" I grinned back and said, "Yes, sir!"

Then in 1936, I got on the Series again, though for a time I thought I was going to miss it. John Clark had moved to New York to establish Transamerica Radio and Television, and Don Becker was running WLW. Becker decided to switch from Mutual to NBC, and Mutual protested to the Commissioner. I was waiting there in Cincinnati for something to happen, but nothing did, so I went off to South Bend to do background work for a Notre Dame football game I was scheduled to do the following Saturday. I was hurt that I was not on the Series, and I did not even listen to the first game when it was broadcast. I came into the hotel in South Bend, bought a paper, went to my room, and sat down to read it. Then the phone rang and it was WLW telling me to take the first train to New York—I would be broadcasting the Series, beginning with the second game the next afternoon. I never did find out what settled the dispute, and I didn't really care. I was going to the Series.

I got on the train, went to New York, and reported to John Royal's office at NBC. There was an announcers' meeting and at it I was assigned to work with Tom Manning of Cleveland and Ty Tyson of Detroit (there were no local New York baseball broadcasters then because of the radio ban among the three New York teams). Graham McNamee was at the meeting. I had seen him at the 1935 Series a year earlier, but I had never met him before; he always had an entourage, and I never even got close to him. We were leaving NBC to go up to the Polo Grounds when Tom Manning said, "Come on and ride up with Graham and me. You know Graham, don't you?" I said no, I didn't, and Tom introduced us. McNamee said hello in his big booming voice and we all went down in the elevator together and marched out the front door. Graham had his Cadillac parked right there next to the RCA Building and we got in it and swept up Sixth Avenue and through Central Park. McNamee must have known every cop in town, because if there happened to be a red light that he didn't want to stop for, he didn't stop. It was a great thrill. I had never been to New York before, and here I was riding to the World Series with Graham McNamee.

Tyson did the first three innings of the game, and then I moved in. We had our microphone on a plank in a box in the upper stands behind the press box. The boxes in the Polo Grounds had little iron chairs, and each box was separated from the next by a metal chain. My chair was at the left of our box and next to me, on the other side of the chain, was McNamee. He wasn't doing play-by-play. It was the first time, I am almost certain, that he did not do any broadcast for either of the NBC networks. The parade was beginning to pass him by. The great Graham was sitting only a chair's width away from the microphone, but it might as well have been an eternity.

I was very much aware of his presence, though he sat there quietly. He didn't move around and talk and attract attention to himself, but I knew he was there. I knew who he was. I kept thinking about those days when I first listened to radio and dreamed of being up there with McNamee. And now the dream had come true. I was doing a World Series in New York. I not only was up there with McNamee, I was sitting in McNamee's chair at McNamee's microphone doing McNamee's broadcast.

And he was sitting silent next to me. This isn't an idealized sentiment I suddenly thought up thirty years later for this book. I felt it then. It was an extraordinary sensation. But I had my work to do, and I went at it as best I could. After I had been on without a break for about two innings, there was a fifteen- or twenty-second pause for some short announcement, and I stopped talking and leaned back for a quick breather. In that brief pause I felt a big hand squeeze my left arm and then that wonderful, magnificent voice, the NcNamee voice. He said, "Kid, you've got it."

When you are in the public eye you inevitably receive quite a few compliments over the years. Some are sincere, some are not. Some you treasure, some you don't. I have never had anything that meant more to me than that: Graham McNamee telling me, "Kid, you've got it." That was the accolade.

McNamee, at NBC, was the first and best of all sports broadcasters. Ted Husing, at CBS, was the first great technician. Unlike McNamee, Husing really knew sports. He studied them. He learned them. He knew what was going on. I met him for the first time at the Ohio State-Notre Dame football game in 1935. That was the year John Clark had arranged for WLW to have exclusive rights to broadcast Ohio State's football games. That gave me the chance to broadcast big-time football every week, but there was nothing particularly special about the arrangement—until the Ohio State-Notre Dame football game began to loom ever bigger. Francis Schmidt, the Ohio State coach, had come up with the phrase, "Close the gates of mercy," meaning keep the offense going full speed the entire game and win by all you could. Ohio State was undefeated, and it had ripped its opponents by telephone-book scores. Notre Dame, coached by Elmer Layden, was a decided underdog, but it, too, came to the game undefeated. It had not beaten its opponents overwhelmingly, but it had won steadily, week after week.

So here were two undefeated teams, both at top strength, meeting each other for the first time ever on a football field, the best team in the Big Ten against the famous Fighting Irish. The game aroused tremendous interest, and when it was discovered that WLW had exclusive rights to the broadcast there was an uproar. Everyone wanted to hear the game, and every network wanted to come into Columbus and broadcast it. But WLW's exclusive right to the broadcast was a real and valued thing, and the sponsor, Standard Oil of Ohio, had paid for it. Finally, on the Wednesday before the game, Sohio, realizing that it would be in a dog-in-the-manger position if it continued to hold onto the exclusivity, waived its rights. Immediately, everybody zeroed in on Columbus. Mutual arranged to pick up our WLW broadcast. Bill Slater was there to do the game for NBC. Ted Husing came out for CBS.

Husing did not reach Columbus until Friday evening. As I look back, I realize now that it was a deliberate Husing technique. Let everyone else scramble to get out to Columbus early. He would walk in at the last moment, confident that he would take over and pick up all the marbles. On Friday night the usual smoker was held where the football writers and broadcasters gathered and to which the coaches would come. There was no better way to pick up added bits of information than to attend one of those smokers, and I was there. About nine-thirty an Ohio State official came up to me and asked me if I would go up to Ted Husing's room and talk to him. Ted had just gotten into town and he had not seen football practice or any football films, and it was too late for him to do any real preparation on his own. Inasmuch as I knew Ohio State probably better than anyone but the coaches, would I be good enough to go up and fill him in? I said I'd be glad to.

Husing was in his room with Les Quailey, his associate and good right hand. After I greeted them, Quailey asked me a few questions. Husing was drinking a highball and he seemed not too interested in the questions and answers, but as I answered one of them in detail he lifted his head and said, "Oh, I know all about that." I was somewhat taken aback, but Quailey asked me another question or two and I answered them. Husing did the same thing again. After it happened a third time, I stood up, excused myself, and left. I was trying to be helpful because I had been asked to by Ohio State, but I felt that my cooperation had been rudely rebuffed.

I was halfway down the corridor when Quailey caught up with me. He said, "Red, please excuse Ted's behavior. He's not usually this way. He's a much nicer person than he seems to be tonight."

I didn't say anything, and Quailey went on, "His behavior is inexcusable, I know, but personally I am very grateful to you. I'm the one who has to have all this information tomorrow, about who plays where and who does what, and I would appreciate it— I know this is asking a lot—if you would let me go back to your room with you and finish this thing up."

And I did.

I'm glad I did, too, because that was a marvelous football game, and it would have been a shame if Husing's rudeness or my resentment had affected his broadcast and anyone's enjoyment of it. I have not looked up the details of the game or read anything about it since it was played, but I remember it without question as being the most exciting football game I ever saw. Ohio State ran all over Notre Dame in the first half, scored two touchdowns, and kicked an extra point to take a 13-0 lead. My recollection is that careless, sloppy, overconfident play by Ohio State tossed away two more scoring opportunities and that the margin between the two teams was really four touchdowns to none, Ohio State. But in the second half Notre Dame came back on the field a different team. They hit Ohio State so hard that they stunned and shook them, and Ohio State could never regain control of the game. Notre Dame was in command, and yet it was not able to score until the very end of the third quarter—and then it missed the extra point.

The game battled deep into the last period, with Ohio State leading 13-6. Then, with fifty-five seconds remaining in the game, Notre Dame finally scored a second touchdown. Peters, a substitute end who did the kicking for Notre Dame, went back to try for the extra point. Because the game was to all intents and purposes over, everyone in the stadium knew that he was kicking for a tie or a 13-12 defeat. He missed. Now the name Dick Beltz began to be voiced around the stands. Beltz, a substitute halfback on Ohio State, was the one who had kicked the lone extra point, the margin of imminent victory. The game seemingly lost, Notre Dame kicked off, and Ohio State ran the ball back routinely to about the thirty-yard line, as I remember. Everyone knew that Ohio State would run plays into the line to run out the clock. Dick Beltz carried on first down—and fumbled. The ball was jarred out of his arms and went like a line drive toward the sidelines. The last man to touch it before it went out was the Notre Dame center, so now suddenly it was Notre Dame's ball again, past midfield, but with not much more than half a minute left. Bill Shakespeare, who had been passing beautifully for Notre Dame, faded back to throw again, and he faded and he backed up and he danced around, waiting for a receiver to get loose. When he finally did throw, he threw unintentionally to a man who was completely in the clear—once again, Dick Beltz of Ohio State. But instead of being content merely to intercept and thus regain possession for Ohio, Beltz tried to intercept and run at the same time, and he dropped the ball. Instead of an interception, it was an incomplete pass. Poor Beltz; he kept going from hero to goat, hero to goat. With the game practically over now, Shakespeare went back again to pass. He scrambled around avoiding tacklers and then he threw deep down the field. In the end zone a pair of Irish arms went high in the air and caught the ball, and it was Notre Dame's game, 18–13.

I never encountered anything to match that. It was so unbelievably stunning and exciting that I made one of my greatest broadcasting mistakes and to this day no one has ever said a word to me about it. I don't believe anybody really heard it. When Shakespeare went back to pass I had kept my eyes on him. I was staying with the ball. That's where the game is. I wasn't worried about where the pass receivers were. When Shakespeare threw, I followed the ball and when it came down in the end zone to that Notre Dame player, I yelled, "Touchdown! Notre Dame!" I looked to my right to the Notre Dame spotting board, expecting to see the Notre Dame spotter's finger pointing to the name of the man who had caught the ball. I didn't see any finger, and when I looked a little farther I didn't see any arm. I didn't see any Notre Dame spotter. In the excitement of the moment he lost whatever professional aplomb he had and ran right out of the broadcasting booth into the uproar of the crowd. He never came back. In that wild moment I had to guess who had caught the ball. I knew that Peters was at one end, and Milner at the other, and I figured Shakespeare had taken so long to throw that the ends must have gone down and crossed. On that uncertain logic, I picked Peters, and I signed off my broadcast with Peters the man who had caught the winning touchdown. Of course, it was Wayne Milner. Shakespeare to Milner—one of the famous plays in football history.

I was abashed when I discovered my error, but no one called me on it. Either no one noticed, or no one cared. They tell me that when Notre Dame scored that final touchdown, Notre Dame fans all over the country started jumping up and down and yelling, and running out of their houses into the streets in their exultation. As for the Ohio State fans, such was their disappointment that they didn't give a hoot who caught the ball.

As I broadcast that game there was a man listening to it in New York. I had never met him, and I had never heard of him, but he was to become one of my great friends and a major force in my life. He was Bill McCaffrey, who has been my agent now for more than a quarter of a century. Bill had been a booker in the vaudeville days, and after vaudeville's decline he became associated with the NBC artists bureau. Like so many millions of others, he listened to the Ohio State-Notre Dame game, but instead of staying with one station he switched around from one to the other, and there was something about my broadcast that he liked, and he kept coming back to it. My name stuck in his mind. About a year later when I was in New York for the World Series, a group of us came out of John Royal's office at NBC and McCaffrey was standing there talking to Royal's secretary, Margaret O'Connor, whom Bill later married. There were introductions back and forth and someone said, "Bill McCaffrey, this is Red Barber." Instantly, McCaffrey said, "You're the one who did the Ohio State-Notre Dame game last year." I was pleased that he remembered, and we became immediate friends. When I came east permanently in 1939, Bill and I would meet occasionally and a few years later, after he left NBC, he became my business manager, my agent. We've been in business ever since without a word in writing between us. There is a reciprocal confidence and trust. If a misunderstanding arises, it isn't decided by a legal phrase, with one party standing on his technical rights at the expense of the other fellow's. It's worked out to our mutual satisfaction. I think that's a good way to do business. I'd rather take a man's word than a contract.

McCaffrey has run my business affairs with great skill, and he's helped me in other ways, too. He's done some kind things that

I have gotten credit for. In 1946 I became sports director of CBS after Ted Husing left the job. I was hired by Edward R. Murrow, and I believe I was the first man Murrow hired after CBS brought him back from London following the war and installed him as a vice president in charge of public affairs and news. They made him a deskman, a big shot. I mean that in all kindness. You couldn't prevent Ed Murrow from being a big shot no matter where he was, because he was a genuine big shot. He was a first-rate man, always, in anything he did. I was asked to come in and talk to Murrow, and he didn't waste any words. He said, "Ted Husing has quit. I've been out of the country, so I'm not familiar with your work, but my colleagues tell me you're the man we want to take Ted's place." It was as simple as that. I continued doing the Brooklyn baseball games and I continued doing the New York Giant football games in the fall, but aside from those two big play-by-play jobs, I accepted the CBS job as a full-time proposition. We even sold our house in Scarsdale and moved into an apartment in the city so that I could gain the two or three hours a day I would ordinarily have spent in commuting to and from work. I put in three or four hours a day at CBS during the baseball season, and a lot more than that at other times. I stayed in that job for nine years, and the thing I was proudest of during that time was the CBS Football Roundup, which I conceived and developed. Instead of doing one major college football game on CBS radio, we'd use six or seven different broadcasters at games in different sections of the country and bring them on the air at intervals to report on the game they were watching. If one game was dull or one-sided, we might kiss it off with a very brief summary and stay for a long time with another that was building to an exciting climax. Before television took over so much of the major football coverage, the Football Roundup was extremely effective.

That brings me back to Bill McCaffrey. One day Bill came into my office at CBS and said, "Red, did you ever meet Bill Mundy?" I said, "No." He said, "But you know all about him." I said, "I know a great deal about him. He was a superb broadcaster, colorful, rich in language and description, one of the best. And I know about the tragedy of his drunkenness, too." Mundy had been the first man, to my knowledge, to share a football broadcast with Graham McNamee, and eventually he was on one NBC network every Saturday afternoon and Graham was on the other. Mundy was hugely popular, but he set out to drink up all the whiskey in the world, and though he didn't quite make it, he came close. He lost his job with NBC and his writing job with the Atlanta *Journal*, and then he lost other jobs with stations in Georgia and Alabama, and he kept going down until he was a drunken bum. He hit the absolute bottom. No one would have bet a nickel that he would ever come out of it. Except his wife, who somehow through those years stayed with him and prayed and held on. And he did come out of it. He finally got to that unmeasurable point where he *wanted* to stop drinking, and he did. He got to be a big man with Alcoholics Anonymous.

So my friend McCaffrey said, "You know, Red, Mundy is all right now. It's been a couple of years since he's had a drink. He's all straightened out except for one thing. If he could get to do a football game on a network again, he'd *know* for sure that he had come all the way back."

"I guess that's so, Bill," I said. I was daydreaming along with McCaffrey's philosophizing. Then Bill shook me up.

He said, "Red, you've got a game coming up at Atlanta. Let Mundy do it on the Roundup."

I jumped. I said, "Oh, no. No, sir." I said, "Bill, this isn't *my* network. It's Mr. Paley's. I can't gamble with it. Mundy hasn't been on the air nationally for years. This Roundup thing isn't like straight football broadcasting. There's a technique to it, a demanding technique. It's difficult. Suppose while he's waiting for me to call him in for a quick report, the pressure gets to him and he goes off again. It would hurt the network, and it would destroy him. Paley would run me right out of the building, and he'd have every right to. No, sir, Bill. I'm sorry, but I won't do it."

McCaffrey sat and looked at me. He didn't say a word. I sighed, and I said, "Of course, it would be wonderful, wouldn't it?" McCaffrey just looked at me some more. I said, "Maybe there's a way. Maybe we could do it." Bill gave me Mundy's phone number, and I called him and gave him the assignment. And then I called another announcer—Mundy died a few years ago, and he went to his grave never knowing that I did this. I told the second announcer in absolute confidence that I wanted him to be standing by, no more than ten or fifteen feet away from Mundy. If anyone asked him, he was to say he had no assignment that day and was there simply to watch the game. But if I gave him the signal, or if in his own judgment he felt it was time to move, he was to take the microphone away from Mundy and do the broadcast himself. I owed Mr. Paley that much insurance for his network.

I remember that Saturday switching to Atlanta for the first time. When Mundy came on I thought for a moment that he had blown it. He had a deep southern accent and he spoke in a rapid, slurring drawl, and to me he sounded incoherent. But it was a confused moment in the game and doing the Roundup *was* a difficult technique. The announcer had to be ready any moment for me to say from New York, "Now from Grant Field in Atlanta, Georgia—Bill Mundy." He had to come on and rapidly give the score, say what period it was and who had the ball and where it was and what had happened since the last time he reported in, and he had to capsule all that into one or two minutes at the most, at which point he had to wrap it up and return it to me—unless I suddenly decided to let him keep it and do a few minutes of play-by-play. It was a tough assignment, and when Mundy's first quick report was over I really shook. I thought, "Oh, dear lord. It's happened, and I did it. I pushed him into it. I shouldn't have had him on. Too much was asked of this man, and now he's gone off again." We went to several other games but something inside me kept saying, "Try him one more time. Give him one more chance." We switched back a second time, and there was old Bill Mundy in complete control. The game was going smoothly, and he made a wonderful report in that marvelous style of his. Oh, what a feeling. After that, as long as we were on, Mundy was a star member. Even today, people talking about the old CBS Football Roundup will say, "You remember that fellow from Atlanta?"

You look back and think of the things that have happened. I'm so proud of Bill McCaffrey for coming in that day and telling me I ought to put Mundy on, and I'm glad that after I objected so strenuously he sat there and looked at me until I gave in and did what he wanted.

Of course, none of this would have occurred if I hadn't moved on from Cincinnati to New York. I had gone east several times on broadcasting assignments after the 1936 Series, and when I did I talked to people here and there. Back when I was in Florida I had made no attempt to get in touch with anyone in New York; I knew I wasn't ready. I wanted to wait. I didn't want to hunt a job in New York. I wanted New York to send for me. But the attraction of New York became more real as I went in and out of the city on assignments.

One year I suddenly got a call from NBC, asking me to go from Cincinnati to Philadelphia to do the Army-Navy game. Someone had fallen sick, or something, I forget what. But hurriedly and with almost no preparation I was thrown into the job of broadcasting the most famous of all college football games. I recall it very poignantly because Lylah was pregnant and quite ill with pernicious nausea. I had been refusing to go out of the house for more than fifteen or twenty minutes at a time, except when I actually had a broadcasting assignment, and now I had to leave her and go all the way to Philadelphia. I was uneasy—because of her, because of the importance of the assignment, and because I would be broadcasting without the degree of preparation that I knew was necessary.

It turned out to be a simple game. A skinny little Army back named Monk Meyer took the ball from the twenty-yard line on the first play from scrimmage and ran it eighty yards for a touchdown, an easy play to see and call, and that one explosion was the only shot of the day. This was before multiple substitutions and I had absolutely no problems. I went home happy that I had gotten away with the thing. Shortly afterwards John Royal, who was program chief at NBC, asked me to come in to New York from Cincinnati to see him. He wanted me to fly in in the morning, talk to him, and fly back home at night. He'd pay for my transportation. This was serious. He was an important man. I flew to New York and went to his office. He said, "I want you to come here to NBC and go to work."

"What do you want me to do?"

He said, "Whatever sports this network wants you to do."

"What are you going to pay me?"

He almost climbed over his desk. He was offering me a job

with NBC, the great double-barreled network, and here I was bargaining with him. He said, "I'll pay you what you're worth. You come in here and go to work."

I said, "No, sir. Not until I know what I'll be getting. I don't need to know *exactly*, but I want a pretty good idea." I told him what I was making at WLW and how much extra I was earning from outside broadcasts. I said, "I like doing baseball. I like the satisfaction of it and the continuity. I'm not going to give it up and come to New York unless you can tell me what exactly I'm going to be doing here and what I'm going to be paid."

He said, "I'm not going to do either. You can go back to Cincinnati and sit there by Fountain Square till you die."

So I went back to Cincinnati, but I didn't sit there by Fountain Square very long. And when I did come to New York I got to know John Royal better, and he and I laughed over that conversation many a time.

But I was getting restless in Ohio. I wanted to move. I was becoming increasingly dissatisfied with the way things were going at WLW. John Clark, who had been a splendid boss, had long since gone to New York, and Larry MacPhail had had a dispute with Powell Crosley and left the Reds. The atmosphere at both the station and the ball club had changed.

I was working very hard. By this time, 1938, we were broadcasting nearly every game the Reds played, either directly from the ball park or via Western Union wire. At five forty-five every afternoon I did a fifteen-minute show over WSAI that was basically a rundown of the baseball scores and the results in other sports. I did it alone, and I wrote it all myself. You prepared your own stuff, and if you couldn't do it you weren't worth your salt. And then Colonel Bob Newhall had retired and I succeeded to his fifteen-minute show on WLW that followed Lowell Thomas' nationwide news broadcast at six-thirty. I shared that spot with Nixon Denton, who was sports editor of the Cincinnati *Times-Star*, and a warm friend and a very talented man. I did the straight news and Nixon would follow me with an editorial or a feature or a commentary on something current in the sports news. By the time I finished my play-by-play and my fifteen-minute show on WSAI and my share of the fifteen-minute show on

WLW, I had had a full, busy day. If the Reds were playing at home, I did the WSAI show from the ball park and then drove like mad to the station to get there in time for the WLW show, which started forty-five minutes after the other one ended.

That summer I was called in and told by the latest in the series of station managers who had come along after John Clark that I was slated for one more job. They had sold a sponsor on the idea of a fifteen-minute show at nine-thirty five nights a week in which I would do a sort of historical present, a re-creation of the highlights of the ball game of the afternoon in the play-by-play style that was now so popular.

I was horrified. I said, "No! I can't do it. When I'm finished my day now I'm fatigued. I go home and eat dinner and fall into bed. You want me to come back and write another show and rouse myself to the pitch of doing a dramatic presentation in full voice? It's too much. It's too much to ask. I won't do it."

He said—his name was Bob Dunville—"You will do it. You're under a contract to us. We pay you a salary. When we get a chance to sell a show and make money on you, we're going to do it. You will do this show. And it's going to start tonight."

They had me, and I knew it. Oh, I had a choice. If I did not want to do the program, I could break my contract and walk out, and that would be pretty much the end of my broadcasting career. That's when I realized that there had to be a union of radio people, and one of the first things I did when I got to New York was join the American Federation of Radio Artists. In effect, this fellow at WLW had said to me, "I don't care about your health, or your family or your career or anything. I've sold another program and you're it, and I'm going to deliver you."

I said, "All right. I don't have much choice. But I'll tell you this. When my contract expires, I don't care whether there are no other jobs left on the face of the earth. I won't be back here to work for you next year."

He laughed. And they made me do the program. And it hurt. I mean physically. There is a breaking point. That's why I have such an empathy for people in the theater who have to do a matinee twice a week and then come right back that evening and do another show. I think that's wrong. It's asking too much from the actors. They have to force themselves, they have to drain reserves of energy that should not be touched except in an emergency.

General Mills, which made Wheaties, had become the dominant sponsor at Cincinnati, and they had cornered most of the major league market and a lot of the top minor leagues, too. They wanted to break into New York, and when Larry MacPhail went to Brooklyn they had their chance. I learned that there were to be two broadcasts in New York in 1939—the Dodgers on one, and the Giants and Yankees alternately on the other. In other words, I discovered that there were two jobs open in New York, and I wanted one of them. I was constantly in touch with people at General Mills, but they were elusive. They filled me with stories that there were thirty or forty fellows after the two jobs and that they hadn't made up their mind yet, though they said I was high up on the list. I was so intent on landing one of those spots with General Mills that I kept forgetting I had a very good friend named MacPhail, who was general manager of one of the clubs that would be broadcasting. Forgetting that cost me a good deal of money. When General Mills got to dickering with Larry about broadcasting he said, okay, he would go along with them and break the radio ban, but he wanted three things. He wanted seventy-five thousand dollars for the rights the first year. He wanted a fifty-thousand-watt radio station. And he wanted Red Barber to do the announcing. He told me this several years later. General Mills agreed but they made him promise not to say anything to me about it so that I couldn't hold them up on the price. They kept talking to me about the thirty or forty fellows they were considering, and when they finally said they had decided on me for one of the jobs, I jumped at it, even though they offered me only eight thousand dollars a year.

I remembered we settled things in New York early in December 1938, the day the New York Giants and the Green Bay Packers met at the Polo Grounds for the National Football League championship. I came into New York on an overnight train and arrived on a Sunday morning. I went to the Waldorf, where the General Mills people were staying, and had breakfast in their room. We talked about the broadcasting job, and then we all went up to the Polo Grounds to see the football game. The conversation about the broadcast was brief. They said they still were not positive whether I'd be at New York or Brooklyn, but they said they would pay me eight thousand dollars the first year, ten thousand dollars the second, and twelve thousand dollars the third, though they had the option not to renew. Bill Corum wrote that I came for twenty-five thousand dollars, and he went to his grave swearing that I told him that. It was considerably less, and, as a matter of fact, it cost me money to come to New York. When Powell Crosley heard that I was leaving he called me into his office and told me he wanted me to stay in Cincinnati. He said he would guarantee me sixteen thousand dollars, or twice what I was going to New York for. If I could make more than sixteen thousand dollars with my basic salary at WLW and my outside work, fine. But he'd guarantee that I'd make at least sixteen thousand dollars. And he added, "I'll do something else. I'll create a job for you. I'll make you our sports executive, answerable only to the general manager. You'll be free to select and broadcast any sporting event you want."

I felt like crying. That was a magnificent offer. Crosley was a close-fisted man—the standard joke in Cincinnati was that WLW stood for World's Lowest Wages—and I was flattered and tempted. But I thanked him very much and told him no. He said, "I'm puzzled. I believe I have the right to ask you why you're turning down my offer for a job that will pay you only half as much."

I said, "Mr. Crosley, I'm not turning down your offer. I want to go to New York. I want to go there for the same reason that you went broke six times before you came up with WLW." Which was a fact. In the world of mechanics, inventions, and machines, Crosley had been a Don Quixote tilting at windmills. He kept trying things, and fooling with things, and losing money. And then he finally started messing around with a little radio station in the living room of his house and he kept fooling with it until he turned it into a great, great success.

When I said that to him, he stood up and smiled the most cordial, warm, genuine smile I have ever seen. He came round the desk and shook hands with me vigorously and said, "I completely understand. Good luck!"

Between Innings: THE WIRE IS OUT

Doing re-created broadcasts of ball games from Western Union wire reports was a major part of the play-by-play job in the 1930s and 1940s. The announcers did not travel with the ball club; only home games were done from the ball park, and the rest were broadcast from a studio. Some announcers went to great lengths to build up their reports and dramatize them, back them up with recorded effects of a crowd roaring and simulating the sound of the bat hitting the ball by tapping a pencil against a little wooden box. Some announcers deliberately delayed their broadcasts until they got an inning or so behind the report. Then they knew what was coming, and they would dramatize every play for all it was worth. They turned themselves inside out trying to convince their listeners that they were really and truly at the ball park.

General Mills sponsored the bulk of the baseball broadcasts in the thirties, and they used to bring all us announcers into Chicago once a year for a meeting. One of their broadcasters was Ronald Reagan, the movie actor who became governor of California. He started out as a sports announcer, and he was doing wire re-creations of Chicago White Sox and Chicago Cub games for station WHO in Des Moines, Iowa. Reagan wouldn't know me from Adam's off ox, but I remember him well. Harry Heilmann from Detroit and Jack Graney from Cleveland were there; they were the pioneer ballplayers to go into radio.

We were in the Edgewater Beach Hotel in Chicago—this was in 1938—and a bunch of us were sitting around discussing the way we did the wire reports. I had been listening to all these fellows talking about their sound effects and the things they did to make their broadcasts sound real. I finally asked, "What do you do when the wire goes out?" It seemed in those days that the wire was *always* going out. If you were in Cincinnati doing a report of a game in New York, the wire would go out "east of Pittsburgh"; if you were in New York doing a game in Cincinnati the wire would go out "west of Pittsburgh." I don't know why they always picked on Pittsburgh, but it was always on the far side of Pittsburgh from wherever you happened to be. So I said,

"What happens when the wire goes out after you've convinced your audience that you're right there at the ball park?" A couple of them explained what they did to kill time, and then somebody said, "I had that happen last year. I simply had the batter hit foul balls. I had him foul off thirty-seven straight pitches before they got that wire fixed."

I thought, "I'll be a suck-egg mule. Thirty-seven fouls. That's got to be a record."

I didn't care for that simulated reality. It offended something in me—perhaps a sense of honesty, perhaps just the idea that listeners were a lot brighter than these fellows seemed to think they were. I assumed the audience knew that this was a wire re-creation and I broadcast it that way. I made a point of having the microphone hung directly above the Western Union ticker so that the audience could hear the dots and dashes. Later on, I used to hear all sorts of stories about fellows standing around bars in Brooklyn who were supposed to be able to read the dots and dashes so quickly that they could make a bet on whether a man was going to hit or go out and then win the bet because they had heard it in the dots and dashes before I announced it. In those stories—or legends—it always turned out that the fellow in the bar used to be the champion dot-and-dash man in the entire Western Union enterprise.

Or else people listening to the ticker would say, "That's the sound for a home run!" Once in a while they'd be right—the law of averages—and they'd keep trying to listen for the home run sound again. But it couldn't happen that way. Occasionally, if I was in the middle of a story or an anecdote, I might delay a few seconds in reporting a stray pitch, but not very often. Generally, I put the play on the air as fast as I got it. That meant I was expectant about the next flash. When you did Paragraph One reports, the operator would send a pilot word about the play coming up. If it was a strike or a ball or a foul, there was no delay at all. It would come in STRIKE ONE CALLED, for instance, or FOUL BACK, STRIKE TWO. But if it was an out or a hit, he'd flash that word, to alert you, and then follow with the details, like HIT. LINE DRIVE TRIPLE RIGHT CENTER. That was great. You could build that up, once you knew it was a hit. You had your runners moving and the ball going through. If the fielding or the play was standard, he'd send you the bare bones fast and you'd pick it up from there. You knew the players and the positions. If there was a variance, if the center fielder handled a ball hit to right center or if the shortstop took the relay for some reason instead of the second baseman, he added that.

I remember a wire report I did early in 1940, when the Dodgers tied a National League record by winning their first nine games of the season. The ninth victory was pitched by Tex Carleton against the Reds in Cincinnati, and he had a no-hitter going. He went through the seventh and the eighth and into the ninth. He got one man out in the ninth and then two men out. I was as eager to find out if he was going to get the no-hitter as the listeners were. Then the pilot word came in: OUT. I didn't wait. I yelled, "It's a no-hitter! I don't know what he did yet, but he made out! Tex Carleton has a no-hitter!" I didn't hold anybody up. I didn't know whether it was a pop-up or a grounder or a line drive, and I didn't care. It was a no-hitter, and that's all the listeners cared about. They didn't want me to delay things and give that last out the big dramatic hoop-la. When the details of the play came in a moment later, I passed them along. But the news was the no-hitter, and they got that first. That's how close we operated.

We kept as close to the actual play on the field as we could when we did wire reports of the games the Dodgers played in the Polo Grounds. We didn't have reciprocity with the Giants in the early years of the broadcasts, and we couldn't go into the Polo Grounds and do the games live. We had to do them by wire, the same as we would if the Dodgers were on the road in Boston or Philadelphia. The Giants broadcaster was doing the game from the Polo Grounds, and that meant we were competing with a live broadcast of the same game right there in the same city. That's pretty tough competition. All a listener had to do was switch the dial back and forth from their broadcast to ours to see how far behind we were.

I told Western Union how important it was for their man at the Polo Grounds not to waste any time at all. We worked out a code, a simplified version of the standard Paragraph One report. Instead of using pilot words, we used letters, and we didn't wait for details. He'd send S and immediately I'd say, "Strike" and then as I saw a second S I'd add, "Swinging." And so on. I told him not to bother to report whether it was strike two or ball three. That was up to us to remember. If the batter hit the ball fair he sent H, and I'd say, "He swings and hits the ball" and by that time he'd add G for grounder, or whatever, and I'd add that information. We were right on top of the play. It was tightwire walking; you were feeling your way. But it was effective. They tell me that you could listen to the Giant broadcast, hear a play, flip the dial to the Brooklyn broadcast, and by the time you got there we had broadcast the play, too. We not only survived doing Western Union wire reports opposite a live broadcast, we flourished.

What did I say when the wire failed, with the Dodgers playing in, say, St. Louis? I said, "The wire has gone out, west of Pittsburgh."

No extra foul balls.

STATION BREAK

Four men figured most significantly in Red Barber's broadcasting career in big league baseball. His happiest and most productive years were served under two of them; his unhappiest moments were under the other two. Larry MacPhail, Barber's first major league boss, has already been discussed in some detail. Now we turn again to Branch Rickey, under whom Barber passed through the most critical moment, spiritually, of his life. And then we go on to Walter O'Malley, who was the real reason why Barber left the Brooklyn Dodgers, and to Michael Burke, who dismissed Red from the New York Yankees.

RED	1	3	5	7	9	11	13		
BARBER	2	4	6	8	10	12	(14)		

In the winter of 1934–35, after my first season of doing play-by-play broadcasts in Cincinnati, I heard a man speak. I was attending a banquet they had there, the same kind of banquet they have just about everyplace you can think of during the Hot Stove League season. It was one of those dinners where they serve rubbery chicken and even more rubbery peas, where the place is too crowded and the service too slow, where dinner always begins late, where the people who get up to speak say obvious things profoundly or try too hard to get laughs, where somebody invariably speaks too long and makes the evening drag and drag, and where there is too much tobacco smoke, secondhand.

I was sitting out in the audience, because this was several years before I would be invited to sit at the head table. It had been, on the whole, a quiet year for me at Cincinnati. I had had the excitement and challenge of getting the job and making that Opening Day broadcast and getting established in the job, but after a while things settled down. The people around Cincinnati —those at the station, other friends of mine, the radio audience— accepted me as an announcer. I could do a baseball game, and that was that. Once they had accepted the fact that I could broadcast a baseball game, they didn't go out of their way to keep telling me about it day after day, week after week, month after month. I was accepted, that's all there was to it, and I settled quietly into the community.

It was a wonderful thing to be accepted like that, but in a way it can be very hard, too. The individual suddenly has a problem, way down within himself. He had received some flowers while he could still smell them, and some plaudits while he could still hear them, and some fan mail while it was still spelled with an "f" and not with a "p." And then he goes on about his work, and there comes a silence. The acceptance sets in. It is ordered and normal, but it is a silence.

That is when the individual—I know it was true in my case—is most apt to miss the applause, the audible congratulations. When a community—or anybody, for that matter—accepts you as a man who is doing good work, you in turn have to accept its silence, its unvoiced appreciation. Sometimes that is very hard to do, and I think it is precisely that which accounts for the terrible hold that the theater, the stage, the nightclubs, any place you can perform before a live audience, has on the individual who performs before the public. Bill Robinson, the old tap dancer, kept going into his late sixties. He'd dance by the hour, just as long as people would applaud. You see a George Jessel, in his seventies, always going to any function, any benefit, any audience he can tell a joke to. Milton Berle is always performing, still a top man but always looking for an audience. Chevalier is eighty. It's the hypnotism of the stage. I believe it's all wrapped up in the simple fact that an individual wants and needs to hear thanks for what he is doing. He wants to be appreciated. And once he begins to hear it, it becomes a terrible prison. He must hear it. He must hear it again. The world of entertainment is filled with stories of the great artists who had one farewell tour after another. They couldn't stand the silence.

So, I was sitting in the audience, not feeling sorry for myself, but feeling perhaps a little unappreciated and restless. The evening was dragging on as all these winter sports evenings do. If you are looking for an answer as to why they have these evenings and why they are always so well attended, it is simply because the majority of men live routine lives and for the bulk of them it is a big night to get out to a winter sports dinner. For most of us who are in the business, who are around the athletes all the time and in and out of crowds all year long, it is a heavy chore. We know all the people who are going to speak. We have heard all the things they are going to say. And to have to stand and have strangers step on your toes and blow their breath in your face and hold you by the arm or the lapel of your coat or by the hand for long minutes after they have shaken it, and ask innumerable questions and argue with you over your answers . . . it adds up to a long, weary evening. It is work. The stale tobacco smoke becomes staler and heavier. The chicken and the peas, and the cold coffee, the inevitable dab of ice cream. . . .

Well, anyhow. This night in Cincinnati in the winter of 1934–35 a man got up to speak, and I forgot all about my unappreciated self and the chicken and the peas and the length of the evening. I had heard about him before, but I had never met him. I had never been in the same room with him before. But from the moment he began speaking he captivated me. There was a strength. There was a magnetism. There was a depth. There was great art. Above all, there was purpose. You sensed that this man—as Larry MacPhail used to tell me years later, even after Larry had had his bitter falling out with him—that this man, when he had made up his mind, would walk through a twelve-foot brick wall to get to where he wanted to go.

Branch Rickey took that whole evening up in his hands. He spoke of his St. Louis Cardinals, of Dizzy Dean, Frank Frisch, Pepper Martin, the Gas House Gang, the 1934 pennant, the World Series they had won over Detroit. He told how Dean, during the World Series, had come out to Rickey's house and interrupted a big dinner party with some exorbitant demand for more money immediately. It was a marvelously funny story the way he told it. Oh, how he could speak. What charm and warmth there was in that great rolling voice of his!

I learned a great deal about speaking right then, listening to him. I learned something every time I heard him speak, and I heard him a great many times. I heard him on baseball. I heard him on deep, serious, spiritual things. He could sway people. During the two years that I was Fund Raising Chairman for the Brooklyn chapter of the American Red Cross, Mr. Rickey, busy as he was and not as young as he had been, was my number one speaker. He was my public relations chairman, and he did a superb job. There is no way of knowing how much blood he secured for the Red Cross blood bank, or how much money he raised almost by himself. As busy as he was during those troubled years with the Dodgers and other matters, he would be there with his coat off working for the Red Cross. Because of him, I had no trouble getting any other important person in Brooklyn I needed to do a piece of work. With Rickey setting such an example, they had to come through. If Rickey could find time, they had to find time. His strength and his value and his use went far beyond calculation.

I am not naïve. I know that a man of Mr. Rickey's many facets and complex nature aroused different reactions in different people. There were some who could not abide him. But I know, too, that in hearing Mr. Rickey talk that evening in Cincinnati I realized that I had been in an unconscious quest for the things he could express. He was perhaps thirty years older than I was but something flowed from him to me, and it never stopped flowing. He took a long time dying, a year or two ago, out in Missouri. He was in a coma for weeks, hanging onto his life. I was in our new home in Miami then, and I was tired from all the strain of moving and getting settled, but I left word at the television station where I was working that winter that I wanted to be called when the word of his death came, no matter what hour it was. There wasn't a thing I could do—I knew that—but I wanted to be called. I wanted to know. He was such an extraordinary man that it was only right that you should be aware of it when he died. They called me at one in the morning. I had known him for more than thirty years.

After that dinner where I first heard him speak, I got to know Mr. Rickey slightly, not right away, but gradually over the next few years. The broadcasters did not travel then and I never got down to St. Louis, but he would come in to Cincinnati. Rickey was a man who worked at his trade, and he was in Cincinnati a lot. He was *everywhere* a lot. He never bothered to take a suitcase. If he was in his office in St. Louis and suddenly there was something about his minor league farm team in Rochester, New York, that required his attention, he went straight to the airport and caught a plane to Rochester. When he had time he'd buy a toothbrush someplace and the next day he would call down from the hotel and have them send up a clean shirt. Later that day, after he had straightened out the problem in Rochester, he might be on his way to Keokuk, Iowa. He might not come home for six or seven days, though before he left on the trip he had not been planning to go anyplace. He'd come home with six or seven ball clubs straightened out and six or seven dirty shirts.

This man moved, he just *moved*. He moved as the spirit willed him, and he had great spirit. One of the finest things I ever read was what Dick Young of the New York *Daily News* wrote in a flash of inspiration after he had learned that Rickey had died. Young had had his differences with Rickey in the years when the old man was running the Dodgers and Young was covering the ball club for his paper. But the burden of his story was that Rickey was so indomitable that, as the weeks went by and he refused to die, it began to look for a time as though he was going to defeat death. Young recalled a New York Baseball Writers' dinner—and that is the great dinner in the baseball world, my earlier comments on dinners notwithstanding—at which Arthur Mann did one of his famous parodies of Rickey. Mann had been a sportswriter with the New York *Times* and later was an assistant to Rickey with the Dodgers, but he had considerable skill as an actor and his takeoff of Rickey was warm, funny, and accurate. In the skit, Young remembered, St. Peter stopped Rickey at the Pearly Gates and explained that he had to leave his money behind, that when you die you can't take it with you. Mann, speaking for Rickey, looked at St. Peter in outraged incredulity and roared, "Then I won't go!" And Young, in his story, made the point that during those weeks that Rickey lay in the hospital in Missouri, it looked as though he wouldn't go. He was unconscious that whole long time, too. (The day Rickey died, MacPhail wired Mrs. Rickey: JANE, THE REASON BRANCH GOT THINGS THROWN AT HIM WAS BECAUSE HE WAS SO FAR OUT AHEAD OF THE REST OF US.)

In 1942, Rickey and Sam Breadon were at the crossroads in St. Louis. It was in the papers, clear enough to understand. These two strong men had come to a parting. St. Louis just wasn't big enough for both of them any more, and Breadon owned the ball club. Nobody knew exactly when Rickey was going to leave, or be asked to leave, but it was apparent that he would be going, and soon.

The Cardinals won the pennant that year, coming on with a great drive in September to catch the Dodgers, and then they went into the World Series against the Yankees, who had not been beaten in a World Series since 1926, and they caught the Yankees too. That was a stirring Series. The Yankees won the first game out in St. Louis, and Red Ruffing set a new World Series record for hitless innings when he went as far as two outs in the eighth before he gave up a hit. That was a record, and it stood until Bill Bevens went to two outs in the ninth in 1947, and Bevens' record, of course, stood until Don Larsen's perfect game in 1956.

But in the game Ruffing pitched, the Cardinals in the last inning gave the Yankees a premonition of what was coming later in the Series. They kicked up their heels in the ninth, though no one really thought too much about it at the time. They were behind 7–0, but after going hitless into the eighth, they ended up with seven hits in all, scored four runs in the ninth, and drove Ruffing out of the game. They never stopped after that. They won the second game, came to New York, swept the next three, and practically ran the great Yankees out of their own ball park. They won four straight after that opening defeat to take the Series. One of the Cardinal victories at the Stadium was pitched by a left-hander named Ernie White, who throughout his career was plagued with a sore arm. It was almost as if he spent two or three months getting ready to pitch one ball game, and it would be a whale of a game, and then he would not be able to pitch again for a long while. But he was ready that day at the Stadium. I had talked to his wife before the game and I asked her if she kept score when Ernie pitched. She said, "I try. I start out keeping score, but if he stays in there for a few innings I chew up my pencil and I haven't got anything left to write with." I saw her after the game in the Stadium—White pitched a 2–0 shutout—and she smiled and said, "I chewed up four pencils today."

Afterwards—I was broadcasting the Series—I came out of Yankee Stadium and started to walk down the street, and I just happened to fall in step with Branch and Mrs. Rickey. I had never met Mrs. Rickey before, and Mr. Rickey introduced us.

"Jane," he said, "I want you to meet Walter Barber, who is

not only as fine a man as I know but is by far the finest baseball broadcaster we have ever had."

I didn't realize that Mr. Rickey had any idea what my first name was, and to have him introduce me to his wife by my first name and then give such glowing compliments dumbfounded me. Rickey put his arm around my shoulder as he spoke and gave me a bear squeeze. It was precisely the sort of gesture that my father often used; just put his arm around my shoulder, squeeze, and turn me loose. He did that and said those kind things about me to his wife, and then we parted in the crowd.

About then—the fall of 1942—Larry MacPhail announced that he was leaving the Dodgers to go into the Army. It was one of the few things in his life that Larry did quietly. He announced that he was leaving, and he left. He was commissioned a colonel, and he did a superior job during World War II. He worked for General Marshall and General Summerall at the Pentagon, and I understand that it was very sensitive work. He was around fellows like Winston Churchill. I mean, MacPhail didn't go into the minor leagues in the Army. He was a full colonel, with that bird flapping his wings.

But he was gone. No more Larry MacPhail in Brooklyn. I was no party to the high-level discussions by the Brooklyn board and I had no idea what was going to happen, but the next thing I knew Branch Rickey had severed himself from his job with the Cardinals in St. Louis and was installed as MacPhail's successor at Brooklyn. I was delighted. Rickey came east and with Mrs. Rickey took a furnished apartment in Bronxville, in Westchester County, only a few miles from where Lylah and I were living in Scarsdale. I don't know why he wound up there, but I guess it was the first place he could find. He stayed there only a couple of months until he got the lay of the land, and then he went over to Long Island, to Kew Gardens, and after that for as long as he stayed with the Brooklyn club he always lived on Long Island.

He had not been in the apartment in Bronxville very long before he called up and asked us to come visit. Lylah had never met the Rickeys. We were happy to go. We went down for Sunday luncheon and it was very pleasant. Unless you were around the warm magnetism of Mr. Rickey in the bosom of his family in his own home, you really don't know what charm is. Mrs. Rickey was a doll, a living, breathing doll. She was just as much a personality in her own right as he was. Rickey, with all his strength and ability, never got one step ahead of Mrs. Rickey in all of his life, never once. I think maybe one of the reasons why Rickey went so far and so fast was because he had to set a gait according to his wife, and that was a pretty fast pace.

Lylah and I were captivated by them. They were genuine human beings, people of sensitivity, gentle people. And wise. It was not until we were getting ready to leave Sunday afternoon that anything pertaining to the business of the ball club came up. Certainly, the principal reason for the luncheon was that Rickey wanted to know me better. He wanted his wife to know me better, too, because I don't think he ever made a big decision in his life that he didn't talk over with Mrs. Rickey first. I remember hearing once that the two of them required very little sleep, that they used to sit up and talk things over late into the night. Mr. Rickey was very intelligently vocal. He didn't go to motion pictures, and I'm sure he didn't spend much time looking at television. He did not drink. He had his own life to live. He didn't have to be entertained. He liked to talk. He loved conversation.

So he would talk things over with Mrs. Rickey. She was his sounding board. She would listen, and then she would give her reactions. She had strong opinions and she was not the least hesitant about giving them to this man. He did not always follow her advice or agree with her opinion. For instance, she told him not to start the Jackie Robinson thing. She told him that he had no business getting into that at his age, stirring up all of baseball and all of the country and maybe getting into a thing he would never get out of until he went to his grave. As we used to say in Brooklyn, she left him have it about breaking the color line and bringing a Negro into baseball. She detailed the complications, the complexities, and ramifications, of what he planned to do. This was a long time before anybody knew Jackie Robinson's name—and I mean even in the Rickey household. Branch Rickey decided to bring Jackie Robinson into baseball two years before he knew who Jackie was. Jackie was the individual who emerged from the principle.

Mrs. Rickey was against the idea, and their six daughters and their only son asked Rickey to leave the thing alone, that he had enough going, that he was too old to take this problem on his hands. That was something, to have opposition, and reasonable opposition, from the people closest to him, the ones he loved, the ones whose opinions mattered beyond all others. But he went ahead anyway. Rickey wasn't headstrong much when he got that bit in his teeth, was he?

Now here he had come into Brooklyn and he found himself with a radio announcer on his hands, a fellow named Barber. Barber was a popular man who had broadcast through those formative, turbulent, exciting years of MacPhail and Durocher, through the pennant in 1941 and the near-miss at a pennant in 1942. Rickey knew without ever having to talk to anybody that I was not to be dismissed lightly. He knew, more than I did, the significance of my position. His intelligence was such that when he knew he was going to have to live with something, he decided that he was going to live with it on the best terms he could. He wanted to know how the thing operated, how it thought. Bear Bryant, the Alabama football coach, wrote at great length in *Sports Illustrated* about motivating football players, and I guess Bryant is pretty good at it. But compared to Branch Rickey, he's an amateur. Rickey motivated everybody. He would make a baseball deal one full year or two full years ahead of time. He could tell you—he'd say, "I'm going to trade so-and-so to such-and-such a club, and I'll do it in sixty days." The other club didn't know a thing about it. But, by George, you could count up to fifty-eight, fifty-nine, sixty days, and there was the story in the paper, just the way he told you. He set things in motion. He motivated.

Rickey wanted to find out about me, and more than that he wanted to begin his own motivation of me in his own way. I didn't know that then, but it doesn't bother me thinking about it because his motivation was a blessing. He never did anything for me that wasn't positive—up. I started with Larry MacPhail, was strengthened by Branch Rickey and was left alone by George Weiss, and that's pretty heady wine. Walter O'Malley and Michael Burke gave me a different vintage.

Rickey wanted to know me better, and he wanted Mrs. Rickey

to know me better. Now we get to something else about Mr. Rickey. He wanted to know my wife, who she was, how she felt, what she was like. He knew good and well that, over and above what I thought, the wife I was married to had an influence over me, and he wanted to know what the influence was. He wanted Mrs. Rickey to know my wife. I know now that after we left their apartment in Bronxville that day, Mrs. Barber was probably talked over more by the Rickeys than Mr. Barber was. Rickey was always aware of the wife. He would have a ballplayer who wasn't playing up to the way Rickey knew he could play. He would send for the ballplayer's manager, and he'd say, "What's the matter with him?" If the manager could not tell Rickey to his satisfaction, or if between them they couldn't get the ballplayer going again, he would send for the trainer. The trainer is closer to the ballplayer than anyone else. The trainer's room at Yankee Stadium used to be a refuge for ballplayers hiding from the press after a bad day. The trainer is a confidant, a friend. Here is the ballplayer lying on the training table getting a rubdown, and he's all soothed and relaxed, and there is often quiet talk going on as the trainer works on those muscles with his sensitive, skillful hands. There's a nearness, a proximity, a closeness, and the player is just liable to tell the trainer things he hasn't told anyone else. Rickey knew this, and if he couldn't find out what was wrong with the ballplayer from his manager he'd send for the trainer and ask him, and more often than not he'd find out the trouble.

But if he couldn't get it from the manager, and he couldn't get it from the trainer, he would send for one other person, and then he *would* get it. He would send for the ballplayer's wife. He would have her come to see him in his office, and he would give her plenty of time. Rickey never pulled a watch on himself. He always gave all his time to whatever he was doing right then. He did not wear a watch, and I think he did not wear or carry one so that he would not even think about time. Whenever he finished what he was engrossed with and needed to know the time, he would have to ask somebody. They would tell him and, almost invariably, he would say, "Oh, my goodness, I've blown the airplane. I've blown the train. I have three appointments that I've missed." But whatever it was he had been working on, he got it done. There is a line, "Do whatever your hand giveth you to do"; he always did whatever was at hand to do at that time.

He would get the ballplayer's wife in his office. He wouldn't mince matters. He would say, "Now, we have got something that we have to work out about your husband, your meal ticket. The manager can't tell me what's the matter with him, and the trainer can't tell me. But I know that something is the matter, because he is not playing up to his ability. You may not have thought about this, but whatever is the matter with him is going to be the matter with you, and sooner than you think. Because *your* career is inextricably coupled with his, *your* happiness is coupled with his success. Now, Mrs. so-and-so, you sit right there on the other side of this desk, and let's you and me get into this thing. Now, you tell me." And it didn't make any difference where that telling went, into the bedroom or anywhere else, whatever it was, he found out. He found out what was troubling the ballplayer, and if it could possibly be straightened out, he straightened it out. Talk about motivating somebody. He motivated people by going back and finding out who they were and what they thought and what they wanted and what troubled them.

And don't ever think that the success of a ball club isn't hinged to a very great extent on the ballplayers' wives. You could write a book about that and it would be a stunner. About how women have affected the outcome of ball games, the ball games they have cost a club—and for any reason you want to mention. They are still costing ball games.

So Mr. Rickey wanted to see who I was married to and he wanted Mrs. Rickey to see. And after he had looked us over and Mrs. Rickey had looked us over, and just before we got ready to leave, he finally got around to the more obvious business. He knew his ground now. He said, "Well, now, you know we have the winter ahead of us, months of it. And we have this war going on. We don't know—nobody knows—where we are going to have our spring training camp. We don't know *if* we are going to have spring training. We don't know anything about next year." He said, "I have never gone into a situation before in which I knew nothing about anything. *You* are going to have to go along with me. I'm going to count on you a great deal. You are going to have to guide me at Brooklyn." Then he completely won me. He said, "I am going to lean heavily on your advice."

And the thing about Rickey was, he *did*. He didn't just snow people with words. He motivated. He would call me up and ask me things. He would say, "Listen. Mr. so-and-so has brought up a point. What do you think of it?" Because I knew that the man wanted answers that were as accurate as I could give them, I would tell him honestly what I thought. I don't mean that he asked me about ballplayers. Rickey never had to ask anybody about a ballplayer. He never had to ask his managers, his coaches, his scouts, anybody. He told *them* about ballplayers.

Listen. During the war years the Dodgers trained at Bear Mountain on the Hudson River, about fifty miles from New York. We were quartered at the Bear Mountain Inn, and the club worked out on the playing fields next to the inn except on cold, rainy, snowy days, when we went over and used the fieldhouse at West Point. John Martin was running the Bear Mountain Inn then, and he was so kind to the Dodgers in so many ways that Rickey gave him a gold pass in perpetuity to Ebbets Field. But even so, there wasn't a great deal for the players to do around there—it was wartime, and there were restrictions on using gasoline.

So in the evenings at Bear Mountain, Rickey used to give lectures on baseball. He'd gather the players together and simply talk to them about baseball. Some of the writers went, and I always did, too. I didn't have to, but I went because I found them so interesting. At them I always learned something about baseball that I had never known before. These talks by Rickey would run on for an hour, an hour and a half, two hours. It depended on how he felt and what he was talking about. He would lecture on the play of the shortstop, or the play of the second baseman, or the play of the center fielder. Or he would discuss the sacrifice or the stolen base. One night he spoke on pitching. He had never been a pitcher himself—he had been a catcher and from all that I ever heard, not a particularly gifted one—but he got to talking about pitching anyway, and he went into the fine points of it, little things, important things. This was before the days of the tape recorder, which was a shame. I wish I had those lectures on tape. I could sell them. *How Baseball Is Played,* by Branch Rickey. It would be the definitive book on baseball.

There was a veteran pitcher on the Dodgers at that time named Curt Davis, who must have been close to forty then. Davis was a real head—and by head I mean he was an exceptionally intelligent ballplayer, a shrewd, smart pitcher. He knew how to pitch. Davis was long and lean and quiet, a mountain man. He never spoke unless it was absolutely necessary. So we got this lecture on the fine points of pitching from Rickey, and there was old Curt Davis sitting in the audience listening. After the lecture was over and we were leaving the room, I happened to be walking along with Davis. I didn't say anything to him. I knew better. I had been around Davis when I was in Cincinnati and again after I had moved to Brooklyn, and I knew him pretty well. I had learned not to make idle conversation with him, because he would rather be left alone in his silence. We walked along together—we didn't have too far to go, as I remember—and then, all of a sudden, Davis spoke. "I've spent my whole life pitching," he said, "and that man told me things tonight that I never even thought about."

Rickey ask *me* something about a ballplayer? No, never. He knew so much about ballplayers that all the smart guys in baseball went broke trying to trade with him. Everybody would tell everybody else, don't ever trade with Rickey. He'll skin you. But they couldn't resist him. They figured they would beat him sooner or later. They *had* to trade with him again, and they got skinned again.

He sold Dizzy Dean with a sore arm to the Chicago Cubs, back when he was with the Cardinals. He told the Cubs that Dean had a sore arm, but the Cubs bought him anyway. The reason they took him was simply that they said to themselves, *this* is Dizzy Dean. He can't have that bad a sore arm. We've got to beat Rickey in a deal sooner or later, and maybe we'll beat him with Dizzy. Rickey warned them. He said, "This man has trouble with his arm, and I will not make the deal until you acknowledge publicly that you are buying a bad-armed pitcher."

The Cubs were so sure that this time they were getting the better of the deal that they went ahead. They took Dean. They paid Rickey $185,000 for him, which was a tremendous price in those days; it was equivalent to, I'd say, half a million now. And Rickey got them to throw Curt Davis into the deal. He gave them Dean, and he got $185,000 *and* Davis. In the next four years, Dizzy won only sixteen games, and he finally had to quit. Davis won twelve the first year and twenty-two the next, and then he was traded on to Brooklyn where he won sixty-six games more before his career ended.

No, no one could advise Rickey on players. But during his first year with the Dodgers he would ask me about things that concerned the ball club and Brooklyn. I was his unofficial public relations man from the start, though it did not take very long for him to orient himself. And I like to look back and think that I didn't send him down any one-way streets backwards.

Between Innings: ASSOCIATE BROADCASTERS

I believe I was the first play-by-play announcer in baseball to have a full-time associate—or colleague, as I learned to say after I had been around Ed Murrow at CBS. At Cincinnati I worked alone at first, and then in my second year two or three fellows came and went. Nobody took it too seriously. The broadcast was still growing, still coming into being. But in my third and fourth years I had a full-time colleague, Al Helfer, who had been on radio at Pittsburgh before he joined WLW. Al had not been hired by WLW to do baseball, but he was assigned to work with me and we fitted together well. He grew restive in Cincinnati and went on to New York in 1938. When I got the Brooklyn job I asked for the right to pick my associate broadcaster and I named Brother Al. He shared the Dodger broadcasts with me from 1939 through 1941, but he had a reserve commission in the Navy and after Pearl Harbor he was called into service. Alan Hale, a former FBI man who had been broadcasting in Chicago, was with me for one year, 1942, but his wife's health was not the best and he left to move his family back to their original home in the Pacific Northwest, where he went into advertising.

Then we got Connie Desmond. This is interesting. Cliff Samuelson represented General Mills in New York, and Cliff fancied himself as something of a negotiator. Some people have to negotiate everything; they can't say just yes or no. General Mills had sponsored the Brooklyn broadcasts for three years, but they had not come to an agreement with MacPhail for the fourth year, 1942. They continued to negotiate. I told Samuelson, "Cliff, I want to warn you about something. You better quit fooling with that man. When you start this complicated negotiating, you're challenging him. You're making a contest out of it. And when you start playing games with MacPhail, he's going to beat you." Cliff said, "What should I do?" I told him, "I think you should say, 'Larry, we're partners. Let's see what you want and what we can pay, and let's agree on it.'" Samuelson said, "Oh, no. I couldn't do that. We'll wait and see." Cliff's great technique was: you wouldn't hear from him. He figured if enough time went by the thing would ripen and fall like an apple into his hands. MacPhail didn't ripen. Samuelson waited, and MacPhail charged off, made a separate deal with Old Gold cigarettes, and notified General Mills that he was no longer interested in their offer.

Naturally, that got Samuelson mad. He was going to show MacPhail and the Dodgers. General Mills still had the Yankee-Giant broadcasts, and they hadn't been going too well. They had had trouble finding broadcasters after Arch McDonald had gone back to Washington. A lot of fellows tumbled in and out of there. Jay C. Flippen was one. Richards Vidmer. Mel Allen was in there. The impression later was that Mel had always been the principal broadcaster, but when he started out he was simply one of the fellows hanging around doing odds and ends. Samuelson brought in Desmond, who was a fine young broadcaster out of Toledo, but at the end of the year their broadcasting plans were up in the air again. Alan Hale had left us after that season, and I was in Toots Shor's one day when Connie Desmond came in. I knew Connie only to say hello to, but he came over and said, "Red, can I talk to you a minute?"

"Certainly."

He said, "I'll come right to the point. I just heard that Alan Hale has left you and won't be back next season. I'd like the job. I'm not unhappy with the Giant-Yankee broadcasts—I'm awfully glad to be in New York—but they don't have any plans yet for next year, and nobody knows when they will have plans." He had a pretty good intimation of things because it turned out that the Giants and Yankees didn't broadcast at all that season. "If I can have the job with you, then that's it with the other broadcast. I don't have a contract with them, I don't have anything. Nobody over there can tell me what day tomorrow is going to be."

I got in a taxi and went over to the ad agency to talk to a fellow named Spencer. We called him Spence so much that I've forgotten his first name, but he and I got along beautifully. I told him about Desmond and said, "I don't see how we can find anybody any better." Spence said, "I think you're right. I've heard him. He's our man." Spence called Connie, and that was it. Desmond stayed with me through all the years I was at Brooklyn and I would say that before his illness he was the best man I ever shared a microphone with.

We added a third broadcaster to the team in 1948, when I collapsed with the bleeding ulcer in Pittsburgh, and Rickey brought Ernie Harwell up from Atlanta. Harwell stayed with us through 1949, but then he jumped to the Giants and we brought Vin Scully in for 1950. It was Barber, Desmond, and Scully from 1950 through 1953, and then I left to go over to the Stadium and the Yankees.

Scully was just a boy, fresh out of college, when we took him on. He came to Brooklyn because of an attempt of mine to establish a principle. I had had a feeling for years—it was like a woman who has never had a child. I guess I had never gotten over my early ambition to teach. I always had the dream of taking an untutored kid who showed some promise and of putting him on the air for what he was, a neophyte learning the trade. Scully was a perfect choice. He was a green pea, but he was a very appealing young green pea. It was obvious that he had something on the ball; you didn't know precisely what it was, but he had it. It's as Bob Zuppke, the old Illinois coach, said when I asked him what made Red Grange great. Most times a coach or a manager will let you know, subtly or not so subtly, what they did to help a player achieve greatness. Zuppke was too honest for that. He said, "The thing that made Red Grange great he brought with him." The same thing precisely holds for Vin Scully. Whatever made him the fine broadcaster he is, he had when he started. He'd had almost no experience. He had done campus radio work at Fordham and had worked a summer at WTOP in Washington. In the fall of 1949 he did some work for us on the football roundup. Ted Church had brought him in to talk to me at CBS one day and, while I was impressed by him, I didn't even get his name. I had no job for him. But later that fall we needed an announcer in a real hurry to go up to Boston to do a football game, and we tracked down Scully and put him on it. His game turned out to be the best one we had that day, and Vin did a sound job, even though it was bitterly cold and he had to work with a hand mike on the exposed roof of the ball park. The wind even blew his papers away, but he didn't complain.

I told Rickey of my idea of hiring this fellow Scully to be the third broadcaster and he said, "Send the young man around to see me." Scully went over to Rickey's office at eleven o'clock one morning, and at eleven forty-five my phone rang. "Walter," Rickey said, "I don't wish to trespass on your time, but you have found the right young man. Good day." And that was the start of Scully.

Vin and I had only one dispute in the four years we were together at Brooklyn. I feel strongly that while people may not like me or my voice or my thinning auburn hair, they do have to give me two things. The first is that nobody has ever worked harder in preparing for a broadcast than I have, and the second is that I have always been sober on microphone. I don't have anything against drinking. I don't believe anybody ever enjoyed a drink more than I did, the relaxing feeling, the sheer pleasure of a good drink properly made. But I never had a drink before I went on a microphone.

When Scully came to Brooklyn I told him, among a few other small rules we had, that I did not want him ever to have a drink before a broadcast. I had no idea whether he drank or not; it was a routine warning. If you take a drink and then make a mistake on a broadcast, the thing is amplified and blown up out of all proportion. Broadcasters aren't like newspapermen who have rewrite men and copy editors and proofreaders going over their stories and catching mistakes before they get into print. There is no recourse on the air. You can't take it back. It's gone.

But one day, about an hour and a half before air time, there was Scully in the press room having a sandwich and a glass of beer. I called him over and we went down to the booth and I shut the door. I said, "I thought I told you not to have a drink before you went on the air." He said, "Red, it was only a glass of beer. That's not a drink. That's a beverage." I said, "It's alcohol. Don't you know that one glass of beer smells just as strong on your breath as four or five highballs, and maybe even stronger? When you were having that glass of beer every newspaperman covering the game saw you. That fact is now catalogued in the back of their minds. You start making a mistake or two on the air, and they'll start saying, 'I wonder how much he had to drink?' Now, I'm telling you, Vinnie. You are not to have a drink, not even a glass of beer, before a broadcast."

Well, Scully is Irish and he was young, and he didn't want to give ground. He got stubborn. He said, "I still contend a fellow can have a glass of beer with a sandwich." I got just as stubborn. My mother was Irish. I said, "I'm not going to argue with you. But if I see you have one more glass of beer before a broadcast, you will never come into this broadcasting booth again."

Vinnie didn't like me very much for a month or so after that. But neither did he have a glass of beer again before a broadcast, at least not while I was still there. I don't think it hurt him.

RED	1	3	5	7	9	11	13	(15)	
BARBER	2	4	6	8	10	12	14		

At the end of that pleasant luncheon meeting in Bronxville, Rickey said he was going to count on me. He said, too, "You think I don't know much about you. But there is more about you that I know than you have any idea." He said, "You have a potential for civic value that has not been touched."

I look back now and I realize that up to then I had never been involved, or been asked to get involved, in any sort of fund-raising campaign or even been asked to solicit for any, not even for the Community Fund on my own block. I had never even thought about it. But when Rickey told me I had a civic value that had not been touched, he added, "And I'm going to do something about it." I don't know exactly what he did, but before long things began to jump and I was right in the middle. Sometime I'll take my shirt off and show the backful of scars I got trying to raise money for the Red Cross, for the Episcopalian Church, for St. Barnabas house, for the new St. Christopher's on Key Biscayne.

But that was all right. Rickey was at Brooklyn, and we had a warm relationship, and that meant much to me. After I became Fund Raising Chairman for the Brooklyn Red Cross, he became *my* public relations man. One day during the war there was a Red Cross meeting in the office of John Cashmore, the borough president of Brooklyn. It began in the late morning, and like so many meetings, especially those populated largely by volunteers, it dragged on. Volunteers like to be heard, and at this particular meeting all the volunteers wanted to say something. They spoke and they were heard, and as a result the meeting did not break up until considerably after lunchtime.

Mr. Rickey and I left Cashmore's office in Borough Hall and walked around to Joe's Restaurant, which was an old landmark in Brooklyn. It was just around the corner from the Dodger offices at 215 Montague Street. When we went in the place, it was practically empty because it was well past the luncheon period. Mr. Rickey walked to a table way in the back of the restaurant, and I followed. We sat down and gave our order, and the waiter left. We were completely alone.

I recall very distinctly that he picked up a hard roll and broke it into pieces, and that he kept jabbing his knife into the butter and dabbing the butter onto the pieces of roll and then eating them.

He said, "I'm going to tell you something. I'm going to tell you something that even my board of directors doesn't know. No one knows outside of the family."

He chewed another piece of roll and then he said, "When I was baseball coach at the University of Michigan—I coached baseball there while I was getting my law degree—the best player I had one year was a catcher. He was a splendid young man. He was a Negro from Upper Michigan, and his family was the only Negro family in that area. When he came to Ann Arbor he was, by and large, unaware that he was a Negro in a white world. He had had no unpleasant experiences.

"Early in the season we went down to South Bend, Indiana, to play Notre Dame. We were staying at the Oliver Hotel. I stood at the desk registering my players, saying this is so-and-so, and this is so-and-so, and getting their room keys for them and sending them off to their rooms. When the catcher came up, the room clerk pulled back the register and he said, 'We do not take Negroes here.'

"I was stunned, and the boy didn't know what hit him. I explained to the room clerk that this was the catcher for the University of Michigan team, and that the University of Michigan team had complete reservations. We were guests of the University of Notre Dame.

"The room clerk was blunt and rude and vocally firm. He said they did not register Negroes, and that they were not going to register this one, and he didn't care if it was the University of Michigan baseball team or football team or what. Quite a crowd had gathered around by now, listening and watching. I said to the room clerk, 'Well, now. We have to have some way out of this. He has to have a place to sleep. Would you object if he slept in the extra bed in my room, as long as you don't have to register him?' And the clerk said, 'All right. You can do that.'

"He turned and got the key and handed it to me, and I gave it to my catcher. I said, 'Now you go up to the room, and you stay there until I come up. I'll be up just as soon as I can finish registering the rest of the team. It won't be but a couple of minutes. You go ahead.'

"When I finished registering the rest of the team, I went up to the room, pushed open the door, and went inside. And there was this fine young man, sitting on the edge of a chair, crying. He was crying as though his heart would break. His whole body was racked with sobs. He was pulling frantically at his hands, pulling at his hands, pulling at his hands. He looked at me and he said, 'It's my skin. If I could just tear it off, I'd be like everybody else. It's my skin. It's my skin, Mr. Rickey.' "

There in Joe's Restaurant in Brooklyn, this bear-shaped man with the dark, bushy eyebrows broke another hard roll, spilled crumbs all over the place, jabbed at the butter. He was angry all over again. He was back in the Oliver Hotel in South Bend.

Then he leaned forward across the table and said "You know, I have formed a Negro baseball team called the Brooklyn Brown Dodgers."

I said, "Is that the team that's going to go into the Negro League?"

He said, "Yes. I have all my Dodger scouts out looking for Negro players. They're scouting them all over the Caribbean. They're scouting them all over the United States. I've got Sukey [he meant Clyde Sukeforth, who was his best scout] and all the others out working on this. They are scouting Negro players only."

He chewed on a piece of roll. "They think they're scouting them for the Brown Dodgers."

I didn't react at all. I really didn't understand what he was talking about.

Abruptly, he said, "I have never been able to shake the picture of that fine young man tearing at his hands, and telling me that it was his skin, and that if he could just tear it off he would be like everybody else. As the years have come and gone, this has hurt me inside. And I have made up my mind that before I pass on I am going to do something about it."

He looked at me. "What I am telling you is this: there is a Negro ballplayer coming to the *Dodgers*, not the Brown Dodgers. I don't know who he is, and I don't know where he is, and I don't know when he's coming. But he is *coming*. And he is coming soon, just as soon as we can find him."

Again, I didn't say a word. I couldn't.

"Needless to say," he went on, "I have taken you into my confidence in telling you this. I have talked about it only with my family. Jane is utterly opposed to my doing it. The family is dead set against it. But I have got to do it. I must do it. I will do it. I *am* doing it. And now you know it."

This was a year before I heard the name Robinson. It was a full year later—Rickey never talked to me about it again—that I picked up the paper and saw that Jackie Robinson had been signed and was going to play that season with Montreal, Brooklyn's number one farm team. I said to myself, "Well, he said he was going to do it."

I have often wondered why this man told *me* about his earth-shaking project that afternoon in Joe's Restaurant. You could argue that the thing had become so much a part of him, and the opposition of his family was so complete, and he was carrying all of this inside himself, that he had to have some human being to speak out loud to, that he had to have some other human being hear him say what was inside him. You could say he paid me a high compliment in choosing me as the human being that he would trust to listen to him and respect his confidence.

But Rickey's strength was such that he could walk his way

alone. I don't think he needed me as his confessor. And, certainly, when he spoke to me about it, I gave him back no support. I gave him back 100 per cent silence, because he had shaken me. He had shaken me to my heels.

And I think *that* is why he told me, because he knew it would shake me. He always told me that I was the most valuable person in Brooklyn to him and the ball club. He never let me forget that I had a great public relations worth to him and the Dodgers, and that I was doing valuable work. He saw to it that I was left alone, that I was free to do my job the way I wanted to do it. I don't believe anyone was able to go to Rickey and say something critical of my broadcasting. He stopped them. He wouldn't listen to them. He would say, "You don't know his job and his problems. He does. He handles things in his own way. You leave him alone."

Rickey saw to it, in other words, that I had sole occupancy of the catbird seat, but he shook me that afternoon in Joe's Restaurant. He needed me in Brooklyn, or he *wanted* me in Brooklyn, which is more accurate. But he knew that the coming of a Negro ballplayer could disturb me, could upset me. I believe he told me about it so far in advance so that I could have time to wrestle with the problem, live with it, solve it. I was born in Mississippi. I grew up in Florida. My father was from North Carolina. My mother's people were long-time Mississippians. My entire heredity and environment was of the Deep South. Florida is not Deep South in the sense that Mississippi, Alabama, Georgia and South Carolina would be considered Deep South—Florida has always been a more cosmopolitan state—but make no mistake about it, it is still a southern state. So I was raised southern. I was raised by wonderful, tolerant people who taught me never to speak unkindly to anyone or to take advantage of anyone. The Negroes who came and went through our lives were always treated with the utmost respect and a great deal of warmth and a great deal of affection. But there was a line drawn, and that line was always there.

I know that it gave me great pause when I first went to Cincinnati, the first time I went north to live. I wondered how I could get along in a northern city. Well, I got along all right, because I tended strictly to my own business. But what Mr.

Rickey told me in Joe's Restaurant meant that this was now part of my business. I would still be broadcasting baseball, with all its closeness and intimate friendships and back-and-forth and give-and-take, but now a Negro player would be part of all that. And if he meant one Negro player, he meant more than one. He meant that the complexion (and this is no play on words) in the dugout and the clubhouse was going to be drastically and permanently changed.

I went home that night to Scarsdale and as soon as I got in the house I told my wife what Mr. Rickey had said. (That was in no sense a violation of confidence: Rickey believed in wives and husbands sharing each other's lives.) I told her about it, and I said to her, "I'm going to quit. I don't think I want— I don't know whether I can— I'm going to quit.

She said, "Well, it's your job and you're the one who's going to have to make the decision. But it's not immediate. You don't have to do anything about it right now. Why don't we have a martini? And then let's have dinner."

So time went by and, as I said, Mr. Rickey never referred to it again. But the thing was gnawing on me. It tortured me. I finally found myself doing something I had never really done before. I set out to do a deep self-examination. I attempted to find out who I was. This did not come easily, and it was not done lightly.

I had to face the economic side of things. That was a great job in Brooklyn and, other things being equal, I did not want to leave it. I was very happy in my work, very happy at Brooklyn. (That's why I left in 1953, when I found I could not be happy broadcasting in Brooklyn under Walter O'Malley—the happiness that I had in Ebbets Field was too precious to me to dilute and vitiate, so I left.) Even so, when I was thinking about the impending arrival of the man who turned out to be Jackie Robinson and saying to myself, "Don't be in such a hurry to walk away from a great job," I wasn't afraid of leaving. I was only thirty-seven years old. I still had the confidence of youth. I have always felt that I could make a living. My father used to tell me, "Son, don't let anybody ever tell you that the job you have is the *only* job you can have. And don't ever let a man make you afraid of your job." My father told me that when

I was a boy, and he repeated it during my adolescence, and whenever anybody has threatened me, his words come back and I react rather strongly. So it wasn't so much the loss of the job itself. It was leaving something I loved.

But then I had to ask myself, what is it that is so upsetting about the prospect of working with a Negro ballplayer? Or broadcasting the play of a Negro ballplayer? Or traveling with a Negro ballplayer? What is it that has me so stirred up? Why did I react the way I did when Rickey told me he was bringing in a Negro player? Why did I go straight home and tell my wife I was going to quit?

Well, I said, I'm southern. I'm trained. Of course, that answer came to me more clearly some years later when I saw *South Pacific*; I didn't know it at the time I was struggling to find the answer. In that great show there was a song, "You've Got To Be Carefully Taught." That was my problem. I had been carefully taught, and not just by my parents. I had been taught by everybody I had been around. I had been carefully taught by Negroes and whites alike. I was a product of a civilization: that line that was always there was indelible. All right, I said, I'm southern.

And then—I don't know why the thought came to my mind— I asked myself the basic question that a human being, if he is fair, ought to ask. How much control did I have over the parents I was born to? The answer was immediate: I didn't have any. By an accident of birth I was born to Selena and William Barber, white, Protestant, in Columbus, Mississippi, February 17, 1908. And due to circumstances over which I had no control, I stayed in Columbus, Mississippi, until I was ten and then I stayed in Florida until I was a grown man. The first time I had something to do with what I was doing was when I left Sanford and went up to work my way through the University of Florida. For the rest of it, I had some vote in the matter.

Then, of course, I worked out that but for an accident of birth I could have been born to black parents. I could have been born to any parents. Then I figured out that I didn't have anything to be so proud of after all, this accident of the color of my skin.

Just about that time, the rector of the church of St. James

the Less in Scarsdale asked me to do a radio talk for him out in Westchester County. You look back and you say to yourself, how marvelous it is the way things synchronize in your life, how they fit and mesh together, the timing. I had been brought up in a family that believed in religion. I had gone to Sunday School as a regular thing, and later, as a young man, I taught Sunday School briefly myself. But I lost the habit of going to church after I got involved in broadcasting, and it wasn't until after the birth of our daughter Sarah that I became interested again. My father was a Baptist and my mother was a Presbyterian, but I married an Episcopalian and when I went back to church I went back as an Episcopalian. And so, while I was trying to work out this thing of who I am, and this accident of birth, and losing a lot of false pride, the Reverend Harry Price, an Episcopal clergyman I had gotten to know, asked me to do this radio talk. The talk, built on a sentence from St. Paul, was to be called "Men and Brothers." And what the rector wanted me to talk about was a problem that was coming to a head then. It was just about the time that it was beginning to get attention, and later it got to be quite serious and it hasn't diminished. It was the problem of the relationship between the Jews and the non-Jews in the wealthy community of Scarsdale, New York. It was going pretty good—and it still is. A lot of people forgot that Jesus was a Jew. Some embarrassingly sickening things were beginning to happen. Sad things were being said. Things were being done to children. And so the rector asked me to talk about men and brothers, with the idea being that whether you were a Jew or a Christian, you were brothers. You were men, and you were men and brothers together, and you should get along together.

Well, when I worked out that talk I suddenly found that I wasn't nearly so interested in the relationship between Christians and Jews, Jews and Christians, as I was about the relationship between one white southern broadcaster and one unknown Negro ballplayer, who was coming. That talk—working it out, preparing it, giving it—I don't know how much help it gave to anyone who was listening, but it helped me a great deal. What was my job? What was my function? What was I supposed to do as I broadcast baseball games? As I worked along on that line, I remembered something about Bill Klem, the great umpire. Klem always said, "All there is to umpiring is umpiring the ball." When you think about it, that is the one thing you must tell a fellow who wants to umpire. Just umpire the ball. There are a couple of other technicalities that you have to know, of course, but the ball is the basic thing. Is the ball foul or fair? Is the ball a good pitch or a bad pitch? Did the ball get to the base before the runner did, or did it not? Did the ball stick in the fielder's glove, or did it bounce out? An umpire doesn't care anything about how big the crowd is or which team is ahead or who the runner is on third or whether this is the winning run that is approaching the plate. All he does is umpire the ball. It doesn't matter whether the man at bat is a great star or a brand new rookie. It doesn't even matter what color he is.

I took that and worked over it a little bit, and I said, "Well, isn't that what I'm supposed to do? Just broadcast the ball? Certainly, a broadcaster is concerned with who is at the plate— you're deeply concerned. You're concerned about the score, and the excitement of the crowd, and the drama of the moment. You do care if this is the winning run approaching the plate. But still, basically, primarily, beyond everything else, you broadcast the ball—*what* is happening to it. All you have to do is tell the people what is going on."

I got something else in my head then. I understood that I was not a sociologist, that I was not Mr. Rickey, that I was not building the ball club, that I was not putting players on the field, that I was not involved in a racial experiment, that I did not care what anybody else said, thought, or did about this Negro player who was coming and whose name I still did not know. All I had to do when he came—and I didn't say *if* he came, because after Mr. Rickey talked to me I *knew* he was coming—all I had to do when he came was treat him as a man, a fellow man, treat him as a ballplayer, broadcast the ball.

I had this all worked out before I ever read that Jackie Robinson was signed and going to Montreal. And when he did come, I didn't broadcast Jackie Robinson, I broadcast what Jackie Robinson did. Sometimes it was quite interesting. But it was what *he* did that made it interesting. All I did was broadcast it, which was my job.

There was another Mississippian involved in Jackie's start. When Robinson reported to the Montreal ball club, the manager of the Royals at that time was Clay Hopper, from Mississippi. Rickey had told Clay, "He's coming," and I don't suppose Hopper was any happier about the idea than I had been. But Rickey put it to him flatly: "You can manage correctly, or you can be unemployed." That's all he said. He didn't waste any time gentling Hopper, who was a professional manager. Rickey just said, "You manage this fellow the way *I* want him managed, and you figure out *how* I want him managed." And Hopper said, "Yes, Mr. Rickey."

Clay told me that he first saw Jackie when Robinson reported at the minor league camp Rickey had set up for his farm teams at an old naval air training station at De Land, Florida. It was 1946, the year the Dodgers trained at Daytona Beach. The minor league camp was an area that they could get inside of and spread around in, and the unregenerate southerners outside could look the other way and pretend it wasn't happening. Robinson reported at a moment when Hopper had the Montreal team in the clubhouse, getting ready to go over something with them. The door opened, and Jackie came in. Clay told me later, "I didn't need an introduction when he came through that door. I said to myself, 'Well, when Mr. Rickey picked one he sure picked a black one.'"

And yet the relationship between Hopper and Robinson was splendid. Jackie told me so. Hopper was fair. Jackie was surprised, he said, but pleased. He found that Hopper was a *fair* man. When you get around to life, isn't that what it's all supposed to be? Be a *fair* man?

I believe that's what I came around to in my own mind when I was wrestling with myself. If I did do anything constructive in the Robinson situation, it was simply in accepting him the way I did—as a man, as a ballplayer. I didn't resent him, and I didn't crusade for him. I broadcast the ball.

It was a sensitive, even delicate, situation. After all, I had the microphone, and I had the southern accent, and I had millions of people listening to every word I said. And this thing was not something that you were suddenly confronted with one day, and then didn't have to worry about any more. It had to be handled inning by inning, game by game, month by month. It was there all the time because when Robinson came, he came to stay.

I think I did it the right way. I know that Jack told me he appreciated what I did, and Mr. Rickey said he thoroughly approved. Other people were kind in their comments, too. It's been written about in newspapers and magazines and in a couple of books. I never had any backlash from my listeners, to use a word that has come into popular use but which no one ever thought of using in that context then. To my knowledge, the Brooklyn broadcasts never had any backlash, either white or black, in the slightest degree. I know I never heard of any.

And so I am proud—in that meaning of self-respect—of this. But I would like to say something else. While I deeply appreciate it when Jack Robinson thanks me, I know that if I have achieved any understanding or tolerance in my life, if I have been able to implement in any way St. Paul's dictum of men and brothers, if I have been able to follow a little better the second great commandment, which is to love thy neighbor, it all stems from this. That word "love," in the Biblical sense, comes from the Greek word, *agape*. In Greek, the language that the New Testament was written in, the word *agape* means "to have concern for." That is the sense in which Christ used it when he said the second great commandment was like the first —the first was to love God, and the second was to love your fellow man. It means that far from "loving" him, you can hate his guts, but if he's hurting, you're to help him. If he falls, you pick him up. If he's hungry, you feed him. You don't have to like him. It has nothing to do with love in the romantic, physical sense. Jesus dramatized this in his story about the Good Samaritan. A man was jumped on and beaten and robbed by thugs and left lying in a road. A rich man, of the same racial strain, came along and saw the wounded man and ignored him, left him lying there. A priest, a priest of the man's own religion, passed him by. But a fellow who was foreign and of a different religion and of a different color skin—there was fear and bitter hatred between the different peoples there in the Holy Land, and it continues to this day—when this fellow saw the man lying there he turned back from where he was going, helped the man to an inn, and had him bandaged and fed and put to bed. He told the innkeeper to take care of him and whatever the bill was, he would pay it. That is concern, that is love. It is a great thing to have.

So, if I have been able to implement to any degree the second great commandment, to have concern. . . . Well, what I am trying to say is, if there is any thanks involved, any appreciation, I thank Jackie Robinson. He did far more for me than I did for him.

Between Innings: BURT SHOTTON

When Leo Durocher was suspended in 1947, Rickey brought Burt Shotton in to manage. Shotton was an old friend of his—Burt called Branch "Rick" and they used to go hunting together. Shotton had managed in the major leagues years before, and he had been an important instrument of Rickey's in the Dodger farm system. When Rickey needed somebody in a hurry to take Durocher's place, he turned immediately to Shotton.

Burt came in and did a superb job, and I don't think he has ever been given sufficient credit for what he did. When he took over the club it was two games after the season began, its manager had been snatched away, and it had on its roster the first Negro player in major league history. The Dodgers that spring were as troubled as a ball club could be, but that old man—he was well into his sixties and white-haired—put his hand on it very quietly and very surely. Some of the players had said they would quit before they would play with a Negro. Rickey stepped on that fast, and the would-be rebels discovered the force of Rickey's principle and decision. They found out he was not joking. When he said Robinson was going to play with the Dodgers, he left the dissident players with a choice—they could either play with Robinson, or do as they threatened and quit. They didn't want to quit.

So, Rickey established the policy, but it was Shotton who, in practice, had to execute it. Durocher would have done it, too, I am sure, but it was Shotton who found himself in the job. It was touchy. Robinson was harassed and beleaguered by opposing ballplayers, and for a time there things grew quite serious. There were threats from the St. Louis Cardinals that they would go on strike if the Dodgers insisted on using Robinson. Ford Frick, who was president of the National League then, stated flatly that if there were any such incidents, he would suspend the players involved. And that stopped that. It was one of the rare times that Frick showed strength. There was great trouble with the Phillies. Robinson and the Phils' manager, Ben Chapman, almost came to open blows in the dugout. There was a good deal of fear and apprehension and antagonism that season. But Shotton controlled the ball club and kept it together, and he won the pennant with it. He handled Robinson well enough so that Jack was named Rookie of the Year. All in all, Shotton did a magnificent job. And then he came back and won another pennant in 1949 and barely missed a third one in 1950, when Dick Sisler hit a home run against the Dodgers in the tenth inning of the last game of the season.

RED	1	3	5	7	9	11	13	15	
BARBER	2	4	6	8	10	12	14	(16)	

MacPhail and Rickey left me alone. They gave me the responsibility for the Brooklyn broadcasts and they let me exercise that responsibility. Rickey said, "You're closer to it than any man alive. You do it." This may explain in part the difficulty I had with Walter O'Malley, who was a man of different outlook and different temperament and different philosophy. I never had a quarrel with O'Malley, but I had been used to going along one way and he had a distinctly contrasting point of view. Whereas MacPhail and Rickey gave me my head, O'Malley wanted to cut me down to size. He tried to do it subtly. O'Malley is a devious man, about the most devious man I ever met.

But I had no reason to complain. You don't ask lightning to strike three times. You really don't ask it to strike twice. MacPhail brought me to Brooklyn and we had a close relationship. He put me up on a pedestal as far as broadcasting was concerned. When MacPhail left and the Brooklyn club brought in Rickey, he treated me the same way. Even the fact that I maintained my friendship with Larry after MacPhail and Rickey had their bitter parting of the ways didn't affect Rickey's attitude toward me.

However, when O'Malley took over the Dodgers, my continuing friendship and regard for Rickey bothered him. To Walter, I was a "Rickey man." I felt that I was a professional broadcaster, but Walter really couldn't accept that. He and Rickey had had a bitter difference, too—though on a business level rather than a personal one. They had never been close friends the way Rickey and MacPhail had been before their split.

O'Malley and Rickey and John Smith, who was president of the Pfizer Drug Company in Brooklyn, had formed a triumvirate that managed to buy 75 per cent of the Dodger stock. The remaining 25 per cent was still held by Dearie Mulvey, old Steve McKeever's daughter. Her daughter, incidentally, married Ralph Branca, the Dodger pitcher, and her husband, Jim Mulvey, is on the Dodger board of directors. Along with his 25 per cent, Rickey also had a contract to run the ball club. That contract was due to expire in October of 1950. But before that, John Smith died, leaving his 25 per cent to his widow. O'Malley, as the lawyer for the Smith estate and with Mrs. Smith's approval, voted her 25 per cent as well as his own. He and Rickey had been skirmishing for some time, and now it appeared that O'Malley had won. Rickey had a provision in his contract that gave him a certain percentage of the money the club got from player sales. He had had that arrangement with Sam Breadon in St. Louis, he had received the same deal from the Brooklyn board of directors when he came in 1943 and it had continued under the partnership, or triumvirate. O'Malley wanted it stopped. He didn't like Rickey getting all that money. He wanted to keep Rickey around for his baseball brains, but he wanted to curtail his power. Now, voting 50 per cent as he was, it seemed that O'Malley had Rickey trapped. And Rickey did appear to be in a tight spot. He had borrowed heavily to buy his 25 per cent, and now that he had lost the fight to control the club, he wanted to sell out. O'Malley did not want to buy him out, at least not at the price Rickey was asking, which was $1,000,000. There were several reasons why O'Malley did not want to buy, one being that Smith's 25 per cent had been bought for $350,000, and if a 25 per cent interest now went for $1,000,000, it would mean that the ball club would be appraised at that much higher value for tax purposes. So O'Malley sat back. He figured, logically, that Rickey would have a hard time finding a buyer who would pay $1,000,000 for a 25 per cent share in that setup, where

O'Malley was voting 50 per cent and Dearie Mulvey in her corner had another 25 per cent.

Moreover, Smith, O'Malley, and Rickey had made an agreement when they formed their partnership that if any one of them wanted to sell, he had to offer his 25 per cent to the other two at whatever firm price he had been offered by a valid buyer. Rickey sought the advice of his friend and fraternity brother, John Galbreath, who owned the Pittsburgh Pirates. Galbreath suggested that Rickey talk to William Zeckendorf, a real estate man who was famous at that time for the size and scope of his business deals. Zeckendorf was a freewheeler, and the deal intrigued him. He said, in effect, "You betcha I'll buy Mr. Rickey's stock for a million dollars." Thus, Rickey had a buyer, and a willing buyer. Zeckendorf naturally was informed that Rickey had to allow O'Malley an opportunity to meet the price. Zeckendorf said, okay, but I want something for my trouble. He and Rickey signed a contract in which Zeckendorf agreed to pay Rickey $1,050,000 for his 25 per cent. They further agreed that if Rickey's partners (which meant O'Malley) met the price, Rickey would get $1,000,000 and Zeckendorf would get the extra $50,000.

This sent O'Malley through the ceiling. He didn't want an operator like Zeckendorf coming into the Dodgers. Zeckendorf might form an alliance with Dearie Mulvey, and then where would O'Malley be? He *had* to meet Rickey's price, including the $50,000 on top that went to Zeckendorf. The tax people now had a specific market price with which to reappraise the ball club. And Rickey, instead of being trapped, was out free with $1,000,000, and his friend Galbreath promptly hired him to run the Pittsburgh club.

Now you can understand why O'Malley's feelings for Rickey were not of the warmest. When all this came to a head late in 1950 I still had a year to go on my own contract with the Dodgers. In the off-season, after O'Malley had had a chance to get settled, I called for an appointment and went in to see him.

"Walter," I said, "I have a year to go on my contract here, but I've come to tell you that I don't intend to hold you to it. You're the new head of the ball club and you're certainly entitled to have the broadcasters you want. If you prefer someone else, I'd just as soon tear up the contract and walk out and let you pick your own man."

"Oh, no," he said. "No, no, no. We want you." And so on.

I said, "Walter, be sure now what you're talking about. I had nothing to do with this thing the two of you got into. I took no sides, and I have no opinion about it. If I stay here, I'll do the best I can for you and the best I can for the ball club. I don't know any other way to broadcast. But I was a close friend of Rickey's, I still am, and I intend to remain one. So I'm putting it up to you. I'd be happy to keep this job, and I'll do everything I can for you. I won't be talking about Rickey all the time. But if I stay here I do want you to let me keep my friendship with him."

"Oh, yes," he said. "Yes, yes. Of course."

But he couldn't. The thing festered. It never was anything you could put your finger on, but it was there. The atmosphere was different. It was different immediately. For instance, before that meeting was over I should have realized how changed everything was. I should have quit right then. I shouldn't have stayed the three years I did. We were going along in our meeting, talking about this and that. O'Malley had assured me that he thought it was great, about being Rickey's friend. He said he admired a fellow who kept his friends, and that I was a great civic figure, an asset to the ball club. With that heavily arch humor of his, he added, "I'd say a lot more nice things about you, but you'll be renegotiating your contract in another year and it might cost me money."

Then, abruptly, he said, "Who's going to be my manager next year?"

I said, "You've got the best manager I know of right now."

"Shotton?"

"Sure."

"Well, we won't get into that, but I think we'll make a change." That was because Shotton was Rickey's man. So Burt was out. It was the first I knew about it, but I really wasn't surprised. You knew it was going to happen. Shotton was too close to Rickey. I mean, that was asking too much of O'Malley.

He could keep the broadcaster but he couldn't keep the other fellow's manager, too.

"So," he said, "who's going to manage my ball club?"

"Walter," I said, "I have never given an opinion on a ballplayer or a manager or a coach. You know that. I do play-by-play. I don't make judgments. I just wait until the play happens and I try to describe it. I haven't got anything to do with your manager. I don't even think about it."

"Oh, come on," he said. "I just want your opinion." He went on and he argued and he insisted that I give him a couple of suggestions on men who could succeed Shotton as the Dodger manager. He valued my opinion, he said, my judgment, my experience. I kept arguing that it was not my business, that it was beyond my province. But he finally convinced me that for his own private information he genuinely wanted to know what man I thought would make a good manager. I gave in.

"Well," I said, "there's a fellow available right now who is an excellent manager. Eddie Dyer." Dyer had been managing the St. Louis Cardinals, who were owned then by Fred Saigh.

O'Malley shook his head.

"Fred Saigh doesn't like him," he said. "He fired him, you know."

"Walter," I said. "You asked my *opinion*. I don't care about Fred Saigh. You asked my opinion, and I told you I liked Dyer."

"Well, that's good. I'll put that away in the back of my mind. Fine. I shouldn't have said that."

"All right."

"Give me another one," he said.

"There's a fellow who managed very successfully down in Atlanta this year. Dixie Walker. He was the most popular ballplayer that was ever around Ebbets Field. I think it could be a ten-strike if you brought him in."

"I hadn't thought about him," he said. "Of course, he hasn't had much experience."

"Walter, I'm just giving you my opinion."

"Well, I'll tell you what," O'Malley said. "This has been very interesting and very informative. Always interesting to know how a man's mind operates. But, you know, I've been talking with Harold Parrott and the boys, and we've decided that we're going to hire Charlie Dressen. We're going to announce it tomorrow."

This, after he had taken all that time to make me say who I thought would make a good manager. He played me like a cat with a mouse. For what? For why? I should have known *then*, when he said they were hiring Dressen. I should have said, "Walter, tear up the contract. Good bye." It took me three years.

Later on O'Malley objected to something I said in a broadcast of a Dodger-Phillie game. I remember this episode keenly, because it was one of the first real straws in the wind. Late in the game the Dodgers had a couple of men on base, and Carl Furillo came to bat. Philadelphia played the infield at double-play depth, and without even thinking about it I said that Furillo was not a fast runner and that the Phillies were playing the infield back in order to get the double play. That was not exactly a scoop that I was giving my listeners. Everybody in baseball knew that Furillo was a fine outfielder with a great and accurate arm, and that he was a very dangerous hitter. They knew he could hit to right field. They knew he was difficult to pitch to carefully because he was an anxious hitter; he was up there to swing. And they knew he was slow. Everybody in baseball knows everything about everybody else in baseball, and when I said the Phillies had the infield back because Furillo was not fast, I was saying nothing that everybody on both teams was not already aware of. It happened that Furillo did hit into a double play, and it cost the Dodgers the ball game. Maybe that's why O'Malley jumped me the next day in Brooklyn. In that sort of cute, fun-making-but-I'm-serious-about-this way he has, he said, "What were you trying to do yesterday? Tell everybody how slow Furillo is?" In other words, why was I deprecating a Dodger ballplayer, why was I pointing out his weakness?

But when you think about it, that is the very heart of the work of the play-by-play announcer. He has to apprise his audience of these things—a man's abilities and his lack of abilities. Otherwise, how can they understand how the game is really being played?

O'Malley and I never had an argument. We never had anything open. It was just a combination of small things that kept growing and growing. I bothered him. I irritated him. There was the time I came back from a trip to Europe with a *boina*, a little Spanish beret-like cap. I wore it in spring training, and he tried to get me to take it off. He really did. Once he tried that, I stood on my constitutional rights to wear it. Word got around. After it was announced that I was joining the Yankees I ran into John Royal of NBC.

"I see that you're going with the Yankees," he said.

"Yes, sir."

"Well," he said, "I'll tell you this. They don't give a damn what you wear on your head."

But I will say one thing for O'Malley. He could be as kind as he was devious. There was a man with the Brooklyn club— a good man, too—who drank up his career, drank up his marriage, drank up everything. O'Malley had more patience with him and did more for him than anybody else. The man was washed up, through, but O'Malley overlooked everything, took him back, and gave him a second chance. The fellow blew it again, but O'Malley took him back and gave him the chance, and I know that that's more than I would have done. Also, I had begun talking with Rickey about a sizable advance on my salary to build a house. O'Malley gave it to me. He stood up for the money—one hundred cents on the dollar.

I finally left the Dodger job at the end of the 1953 season. The Dodgers won the pennant that year, and as their principal broadcaster I was supposed to work the World Series. But I turned down the assignment, and then I quit at Brooklyn. I had been growing increasingly unhappy with the way Gillette, the World Series sponsor, handled the broadcasters at the Series. They didn't negotiate with you about the job. They tapped you for it. They told you that you had been chosen to broadcast, and that was it. You didn't even know what your fee was going to be. They sent you a check afterwards, and that is when you found out what you had made. When they first started doing it, they paid AFRA scale (it's AFTRA now, for American Federation of Television and Radio Artists), which was thirty-five dollars a game. Or they might double that and pay you seventy dollars a game. For a World Series. That's the first pay I got for doing a Series radio broadcast.

In 1952 the World Series was fully televised for the first time. There had been television coverage of the Series as early as 1948—I was on that—but TV was still feeling its way then, and the telecast was limited to certain areas. But in 1952, World Series TV went national—full coverage all over the country with enough stations to make it really important. It was a full seven-game Series, and it was exciting, beautifully played. Seven games on national television, each two to three hours long, watched by a huge, attentive audience. Television is a lucrative business, but when I received my check from Gillette two weeks after the Series it was for fourteen hundred dollars—or two hundred dollars a game. In television, that is peanuts. And for televising the biggest sporting event in the world—not for one day but for seven —it was worse than peanuts.

I sat at my desk at home looking at that check, and I said to myself—I told my wife and my agent later—that next year things were going to be different. I decided that I would not do the Series the following year, assuming that Brooklyn was in it again, unless I had the right to negotiate with Gillette *before* the Series and to know *before* the Series what I was going to be paid. I didn't know how much I wanted, except that I was ashamed of how little I had been getting. The amount was not the sticking point; it was the attitude. I had negotiated contracts with advertising agencies and with big companies. I had negotiated with CBS and NBC, and I had negotiated with ball clubs. We hadn't always seen eye to eye, but at least they had treated me as a responsible party to a contract, and they had paid me good money. I was ashamed of the way I had gone along with the Series broadcast. I decided that I simply would not take it any more. Gillette didn't like me much anyway. They had tried to get me to leave Brooklyn and switch over to the Giant-Yankee play-by-play back when they had bought into those broadcasts, and I wouldn't do it. They had kept after me and really put the heat on me. They liked to have their own way.

The Dodgers clinched the 1953 pennant in St. Louis the last week of the season, and the following morning I was having breakfast in the Chase Hotel there with Tommy Holmes, who was writing sports for the then Brooklyn *Eagle*, another one of the many fine newspapers that have since died. I was called away from breakfast to the phone, and it was Ed Wilhelm of the Maxon agency, the agency for Gillette. Wilhelm was sort of a front-runner for Craig Smith, vice president at Gillette and the big man in their broadcast operations.

"Red!" he said, all happy and energetic. "You and Mel Allen are doing the Series. You're on the television side. We announced it last night in New York. I meant to call you, but I didn't get around to it last night."

That was enough to get me mad, right there. Here it had already been announced to the newspapers that I was going to be doing the Series, and nobody had mentioned a word about it to me. I didn't need any strengthening in the resolve I had made a year earlier, but if I had needed any, that would have done it.

"Ed," I said. "You know Bill McCaffrey, don't you?"

"Sure." His voice sounded funny. "What about him?"

"He's my agent."

"Yeah, I know." And then he started talking about something else.

"Wait a minute," I said. "Will you call McCaffrey and make the arrangements?"

"You want *me* to call McCaffrey?"

"Yes. That's the way I do my business."

We hung up, and I went back and finished breakfast with Tommy Holmes. Then I went up to my room, and after about thirty minutes McCaffrey called.

"Red, listen. Is your mind really made up about what you want to do? Do you want to go through with this?"

"Why?"

"Wilhelm called, and, boy, he is mad. I just wanted to check with you before I drop the spot on him. Be sure now, before he calls Craig Smith in Boston."

"I'm sure," I said. "I told you a year ago, and I haven't changed my mind."

"Okay."

In about an hour Bill called again.

"Wilhelm phoned Craig Smith, and he's raging." Smith was

incensed because I had the temerity to want to negotiate, to discuss what I was going to get paid. "Wilhelm said that Craig Smith sends you this word: you will get the same as you got last year. Take it or leave it."

"Call him back and tell him we leave it."

So that is how I resigned the Series. That day was my daughter's sixteenth birthday. I had arranged for her to go see what was then known as the Sadler's Wells ballet with her mother and two friends. They were to see the big one that has Aurora's wedding in it, and the blue birds. Tschaikovsky's great ballet. *The Sleeping Beauty*. That's what it was. We played in St. Louis in the afternoon, and I flew back into New York that night. Sarah had often said how much she would like sometime to go to Birdland, which was then in existence, and I had reserved a table there. That was to be her surprise on her sixteenth birthday, and I was going to join them there if my plane got in on time, which it did. And I remember afterwards as we were driving home in the night, I said to Sarah, "You don't know now and you won't know for some time, but I gave you the best sixteenth birthday present I could give you today. I gave you your father's self-respect."

I meant that. I had my self-respect back. I regained some of it that I had lost. I knew that night I would not be on the Series. I knew that Ford Frick, who was then Commissioner of Baseball, could have done something about the situation, but I knew he wouldn't raise a finger to help me. Nor did I anticipate any help from O'Malley, though I admit I did not expect the chilly climate I ran into immediately. The next morning, after I got back to New York, I went down to the office at CBS, and McCaffrey came over. We were talking about this thing, and I said, "Bill, I have to call O'Malley. He's entitled to know what his principal broadcaster is doing about the World Series." I phoned Walter, though not to ask him for any help, because I didn't think it would be there. And I don't go around asking for help. The only help you get in this world is not the help you ask for but the help that people see you need and volunteer and give to you. It's like asking for thanks. You don't ask somebody to say thanks. Thanks is meaningless unless somebody genuinely volunteers it.

I called O'Malley and said, "Walter, I just want to bring you up to date about a position I am taking." I told him briefly what had gone on about the Series fee, that Gillette had said take it or leave it, and that I had instructed my agent to tell them that we'd leave it. I told all this to O'Malley, and he said, over the phone, "That's your problem." When he said that, I hung up.

I said to myself, "Well, now. Anything connected with O'Malley and the Brooklyn club is—as soon as my contract expires after the last game of the season Sunday in Philadelphia—*his* problem."

Between Innings: I'M SORRY THEY LEFT

The fifteen years I had in Brooklyn were wonderful. The Ebbets Field we've been talking about was a part of America that's gone, and there never again will be anything to equal it. I don't criticize O'Malley for moving the Dodgers (and, because of that, the Giants, too); that was a most complex situation, and certainly the introduction of major league baseball to California was a boon to baseball. But, personally, I was very sorry when the Dodgers left and moved to Los Angeles. I regretted seeing a unique institution die. There was never another ball park like Ebbets Field. A little small, outmoded, old-fashioned—well, Mac-Phail stuck a lot of paint on it and spruced it up, but it was still a dirty, stinking, old ball park. But when you went in there as a fan, it was *your* ball park. You were practically playing second base, the stands were so close to the field. Everybody was in touch with everybody else at Ebbets Field. There have been other small old parks in the major leagues, but none quite like this one—with its double-decked stands across left field into center and that big wall in right. And the people. And the rivalry with the Giants. When you add that in, it clinches the argument. There never was before or since, and probably never will be again, two teams in the same town in the same league. Those great rivals met *twenty-two times a year* in the same city. Whenever the Dodgers and the Giants played—whether it was at Ebbets Field or the Polo Grounds—you had both factions in the stands. In other words, it wasn't a rivalry just on the ball field, with a home crowd rooting for their team and booing the visitors. At the Dodger-Giant games in Ebbets Field and the Polo Grounds, you had a constant back-and-forth roaring from the first pitch to the last, *for* both teams and *against* both teams. I think there was a reluctant affection down underneath for the rival team; that is, there was no team a Brooklyn fan would rather see play the Dodgers than the Giants, and the same thing went for Giant fans as far as the Dodgers were concerned. It was an invigorating, emotional rivalry, and I think that emotion explains a good part of the success of the New York Mets. When the Dodgers and

Giants pulled out of New York and went to California and left the Yankees as the only team in New York, the Yankee attendance did not go up. It stayed at about the same level where it had always been. The National League fans—the Giant fans, the Dodger fans—did not care about the Yankees and the American League. Their ball clubs had left them, and they were bereft. But when the National League came back into New York with the Mets, and put this clownlike ball team—so like the old, old Dodgers of the Babe Herman-Uncle Robby era—in the Polo Grounds, the old home of the Giants, those bereft fans were back in business. Or at least enough of them were to form a strong nucleus for the so-called new breed of Met fans.

Those were great days, those days of the Dodger-Giant rivalries, and I miss them. I miss the Polo Grounds, which was torn down after the Mets moved into Shea Stadium, and I miss Ebbets Field, which was torn down before that. I pride myself on being an objective, professional baseball reporter, but down inside I'm an emotional human being, too. Ebbets Field meant so much to me, even after I had left it to go to Yankee Stadium, that I never went back to look at the place after it became a ghost park. I never have gone back because I can still see Ebbets Field. As far as I am concerned, it is still standing.

RED	1	3	5	7	9	11	13	15	(17)
BARBER	2	4	6	8	10	12	14	16	

My contract at Brooklyn ended with the last day of the season in 1953. No options, no nothing. Finished. Everything was to be renegotiated by all parties concerned. There were no strings, nothing implied. I was a completely free agent. When I quit at Brooklyn, I had no other job, no prospect of a job, no idea of a job. All I knew was where I did not want to stay, and where I did not intend to stay. I did things one at a time. I resigned the World Series, I quit at Brooklyn, and then I found a job.

The World Series was between the Yankees and the Dodgers, and now that I was out of it they named Vin Scully to take my place. I was delighted. After all, Scully had nothing to do with what happened. And, bless his heart, Vinnie phoned me from his home over in New Jersey. He said, "Red, I've just been called and they said they want me to do the World Series in your place. I told them I wouldn't do it until I had talked to you." I said, "Well, you have my 100 per cent blessing, because you are *not* doing it in my place. You're doing it for yourself. I'm out of it. I've been out of it for a couple of days. Keep that in mind, Vinnie. You're not in any way interfering with me. I quit for my own reasons. It's too long a story to tell now, and I won't go into it. But I want you to know that I'm very pleased and delighted that you've got it, and I'll give you my scorebook and, if necessary, I'll come up to the booth and rub you down before the first game."

Nothing could have pleased me more than his calling me then, saying he wouldn't take it—and he meant that—until he had spoken to me. He was wonderful. You appreciate somebody feeling that way.

I needed some tickets for the games at the Stadium. I always bought two tickets to the Series for Lylah, and she would bring a friend along to sit with her. This time I would sit with her. I had already arranged to buy tickets to the Ebbets Field games before the denouement and, ordinarily, I would have gotten tickets to Yankee Stadium from those that the Yankees allotted to the Dodgers staff. But I wasn't of a mind now to ask O'Malley or anybody else at Brooklyn for anything, not even the time of day. I had paid back the salary advance. I was even. They could keep their Yankee tickets. I went over myself to Yankee Stadium and looked up Arthur (Red) Patterson, who was their publicity man and an old friend. He later moved over to the Dodgers and he's still with them out in Los Angeles. I said, "Arthur, I need two tickets to the games at the Stadium for Lylah and myself." By this time, everybody knew that I was off the Series. It had been in all the papers.

Patterson looked at me sort of funny, but he said, "Sure, Red. I'll get them out of George Weiss's allotment."

"Fine," I said. He went into Weiss's office and in a few minutes came back with the tickets, and I gave him my check. There are no free World Series tickets. When I turned to go, he walked out to the elevator with me. It's funny how little things can turn your life. Just as the elevator stopped and its doors began to open, I turned to Red—I don't know what prompted me to—and I said, "Arthur, I own myself." With that, the elevator opened and I stepped in it and left.

A few days later the Series got under way, and before one of the games at Ebbets Field, Lylah and I were sitting at a table in Hal Stevens' kitchen under the stands, having a bite to eat with Mr. and Mrs. Bob Carpenter of the Phillies and Buzzie Bavasi of the Dodgers. George Weiss and Dan Topping of the Yankees came in and when they saw me Topping stopped and Weiss came across the room to our table. In front of Bavasi and

Carpenter he said, "Red, Topping and I want to talk to you."
Bavasi's face went white. I said, "Okay," made my excuses to the
table, and walked over with Weiss to the corner where Topping
was waiting.

Weiss said, "We want to talk to you about coming to work for
the Yankees. From what Red Patterson says, we understand you're
free."

"I'm completely free," I said, "and I'm completely interested."

"All right," he said. "When can we talk to you? How about
coming over to the Commodore Hotel tonight?"

I shook my head.

"I'd do it," I said, "except that I have an engagement tonight
that I can't change. A friend of mine is celebrating his seventy-
fifth birthday out in Westchester, and as much as this job means
to me and as much as I'd like to talk to you, I'm going to go
to his seventy-fifth birthday party."

Weiss said, "What about tomorrow at the Stadium before the
ball game?"

We made a date for eleven in the morning, and the next day
Weiss and Topping and I met and talked and I agreed to take
the job. Then I went out and watched the ball game. I didn't
know who was going to win the game or the Series, but I knew
where I was going to be working the next year. And it wasn't
going to be Ebbets Field any more.

A funny thing about that seventy-fifth birthday party. Here was
a big job that I wanted very badly, and I held off the man who
had the job in his hands offering it to me because I had to go
to somebody's birthday party. We drove from Ebbets Field up
into Westchester to the man's house, and when we got there the
house was dark. Absolutely dark. We found out later that they
had forgotten that they had invited anybody to the house, and
they had gone off around the neighborhood calling on people.
I thought to myself, "If this isn't the way things go. If this isn't
something." I wasn't angry. I had another feeling—I was aghast.
Look, you can't do much more to express your regard for someone, can you, than to say to George Weiss, who is offering you
the Yankee baseball job when you are out of work, "No, I can't
see you tonight, I have to go to a friend's birthday party?" That
job meant a great deal to me. It meant that I was going to the

big ball club, that I didn't have to sell my house and leave a part of the country I had gotten to know and like, and leave the friends we had made. It meant that now, after a week or more of turmoil, things were suddenly settled. And—no party.

Listen. It was painful for me to refuse the World Series and to be in that situation. It hurt. It hurt to be leaving the Dodgers after all those years. I didn't like it. People looked at me. Some people said things.

But then there were other people, like Bill Slater, the broadcaster. As I was going toward the ball park with Lylah for the first game of the Series, we ran into Slater on the sidewalk. He stuck out his hand and said, "Red, I want to congratulate you. I know what you did, and you're the only guy in our profession with guts enough to do it."

That made me feel good. That made me feel *good.* I remember before the Series started having luncheon in Louis and Armand's in Manhattan, and some guy from the Maxon agency —I forget his name; Freud says you forget the things you want to forget—came over to my table and said, "Red, how could you do this to Craig?" Meaning Craig Smith. "How could you do this to Craig?" He was practically crying. Boy. How could *I* do this to Craig?

I'd rather remember old Ted McGrew, who at eighty-seven is still scouting for the Dodgers as this is written. He had scouted for a lot of clubs, and I knew him well. The story that I would not be on the Series broadcast was in the papers the day I went over to Brooklyn to pick up my tickets for the Ebbets Field games. I was waiting for them when McGrew came into the office. He chuckled when he saw me and he said, "Well, kid, I see where they couldn't make you cut the mustard."

I said, "What do you mean?"

"You wouldn't cut the price, huh?"

And I remember the thing that made me feel best of all. Casey Stengel was managing the Yankees then, and he won that World Series. It was his fifth straight World Series win, something no other manager has ever done. Casey was standing in the middle of the clubhouse surrounded by reporters and photographers and TV and radio people, holding court, when I came in after the last game of the Series. I wanted to congratulate him. He didn't know yet that I was coming to work for the Yankees. Nobody knew but Weiss and Topping and me, and my wife and my agent. We had just agreed on the job, and the Yankees weren't worrying about rushing down in the middle of a World Series to tell their manager that they had hired a new broadcaster. And I had not been down on the field or in the dugouts. During the course of that Series I was a civilian. I had no pass, no badge, no nothing. But after the last game I told Lylah to wait there in the seat for me for a few minutes, and I went down to the Brooklyn clubhouse to say good bye to my friends. After all, the ballplayers had done nothing to me. I was on good terms with them, and I wished them all a happy winter. Then I went over to the Yankee clubhouse to congratulate Stengel. It was a mob scene, as it always was around Casey. I came in through a door behind him and I waited until he paused for breath, or wasn't on a microphone, or wasn't posing for a picture, and I leaned forward and tapped him on the shoulder. I just wanted to speak to him, congratulate him, and then leave and get back to my wife. He turned when I tapped his shoulder and I said, "Casey, congratulations." His eyebrows went up and he grabbed my hand and he shook it, and he said, "Let me congratulate *you!* I want to tell you that a major league job is worth major league money."

Well, boy, Casey Stengel owned me from then on.

I never actually resigned formally from the Dodgers. My contract expired, and I was a free agent. The word got around, of course, that I was leaving. There are no secrets in baseball. Bavasi was there when Weiss spoke to me. O'Malley learned very quickly from various sources that I was leaving. But he did not choose to say anything to me about it, and I did not choose to say anything to him. He had told me, "That's your problem." And when he told me that, he signed me off. The news got into the papers, and it was verified, and that was it.

When I signed with the Yankees, the pre- and postgame baseball shows were a much more valuable commercial franchise than they are now. I understand that when Joe DiMaggio did pre- and post- at the Stadium he was paid a hundred thousand dollars, though, of course, Joe was hired as more than just a television announcer. There was the DiMaggio name and the fact that he had recently quit as an active player after Topping had offered him a hundred-thousand-dollar contract to stay another year. I don't know all the ramifications of the deal, but I do know that pre- and post- was big money. There was much more listener and viewer interest then. The idea of seeing and hearing major league ballplayers talk was still a fairly fresh thing. Now it's old hat, ballplayers coming on camera and talking. Television eats up everything.

When the Yankees first began their pre- and postgame shows they had Dizzy Dean handling the job. I never learned why Diz didn't stay there, or what there was between Diz and the sponsors and the ball club, but he went off and they gave the job to DiMaggio. That was a struggle, because Joe was completely out of his element. He is quiet and retiring by nature, and now he had to run an interview show in which he had to draw things out of other people. Jackie Farrell of the Yankee publicity staff used to write questions on a board and hold them up off camera, and Joe even had trouble doing it that way.

One year was enough, and DiMaggio left. Then the Yankees hired Joe E. Brown, who had the advantage of being a professional actor and who also had a real fan's knowledge of baseball. But Joe E. didn't go over. It is one thing to be an internationally famous comedian and act in a couple of baseball movies and be a big baseball fan, but it's quite another to move into baseball and television simultaneously and do two shows a day with all those ballplayers. It wasn't that Joe E. Brown failed. He was being asked to do something that wasn't his leather. It was as though Rudolph Bing at the Metropolitan Opera asked me—and I didn't have any better sense than to agree—to go out on the stage and sing Rhadames in *Aïda*. I love that opening aria, and I wish I could sing it, but I know I can't. Joe was asked to do something he couldn't do, but in his case he didn't know he couldn't do it until he got into it.

You see, when radio started it jumped right out of a laboratory—and so did television. There was no training school, no preparation. Anybody could come into it, and anybody did. Some survived and some didn't, but the listeners—and viewers, as far as TV was concerned—were pretty tolerant, if only from a subconscious standpoint. Because, after all, they had never *heard* anything on radio—or *seen* anything on television—and they had no standards to judge people by. That was how everybody got started. If it hadn't been for that initial tolerance back in 1930, I'd have never gotten very far. People put up with me because they thought, "Well, that's radio, I guess." I understand that the first incandescent lamps were pretty faulty, but that was all the people had at the time. The first telephone wasn't too good, but people oohed and aahed about it. They wouldn't put up with it now.

What I'm trying to say is, until somebody got into the specialized business of doing pre- and postgame shows interviewing ballplayers, they did not realize what it required. I am certain that when Joe E. Brown took the job there was no doubt in his mind but that he could do it in a breeze, and there was certainly no doubt in the minds of the Yankees and the sponsors. It seemed like a great natural thing. But in the working out, in the grinding, relentless day-by-day presentation of the show, in the need of keeping it pertinent and lively, it didn't work. Long before the Yankees knew that I would be available they had made up their minds that they were going to replace Joe E. Brown. Weiss told me that. If I hadn't come along, someone else would have taken his place.

And Weiss made it very clear to me that I was being hired specifically for the pre- and postgame shows. He said that Mel Allen would continue to do the bulk of the play-by-play, and that Mel and Jim Woods, who was the associate broadcaster then, would do all the traveling. Mel liked to travel, and he made all the road trips. Weiss told me that they did not want me to do any traveling at all, unless there happened to be a special event out of town, like a pennant clinching, where they thought there should be pre- and postgame interviews. Weiss explained, "When DiMaggio was doing it, the sponsors wanted him to go up to Boston once toward the end of the season, and Joe wouldn't go. Now, if such a situation comes up with you, and we want you to go on the road and stay with the club for, let's say, five, six, seven, eight days, would you go?"

I said, "Certainly. Look, George, I don't mind traveling, and I don't mind not traveling. And I'm glad to do the interviews show: it's a new dimension for me, and I'm looking forward to it. I only have one stipulation. I don't want to give up play-by-play broadcasting entirely. I don't want to take the job unless I can do *some* play-by-play—say, five innings or so on radio and TV together of home games at the Stadium."

Weiss said that was all right, that could be worked out, and that's the way things were arranged. But I had to push myself into the play-by-play there.

The thing of going on the road, traveling, was never a factor. But as the years went by and I didn't go on the road, people began to make their own judgments. They decided then that I had left Brooklyn because I no longer wanted to travel, and O'Malley gave them that little Mona Lisa smile of his which lent the report substance. Eventually, even before Mel Allen was fired, I did go on the road occasionally with the Yankees. Mel was sick once or twice, or there was a pennant clinching and they wanted an extra man waiting downstairs in the clubhouse. I traveled to Boston several times, I went out to Minnesota, Chicago, Los Angeles, Kansas City, Cleveland, Washington. I was always in and out, making a series, doing something extra. I wasn't paid anything extra for that; I was supposed to do it. It was understood between the Yankees and me that the broadcast came first. The Yankees called me one time when Mel was having foot trouble. They phoned me at two o'clock in the afternoon, and I caught a plane to Minnesota an hour and a half later. I was glad to go. I want this clearly understood. I have always, all of my life, gone where the work is. And that's all there was to it.

I want to make another thing clear, too. I did not go to the Stadium to challenge Mel Allen, as was written in several quarters when it was announced that I had the job. In no sense was there ever a contest between us. It never entered my mind, and it never happened while I was there. No one could have been more cooperative and agreeable than Mel was. He even sent me a wire of welcome. Mel behaved like a very large person through all of this, because he knew what people were writing and thinking. Here was Barber, a principal broadcaster of twenty years' standing, the last fifteen right there in the same city, now coming into his ball park. But he could not have been nicer to me, either then or all through the years we worked together.

Certainly, Mel was restive about me being there. I knew it,

though he never said anything to me about it and though we never had the slightest difference. We were friends. We had worked together on World Series and All-Star Games and other events for years. We liked each other, and we still like each other. But at that time, if I had pushed to go on the road and share the play-by-play, it would have bothered Mel considerably. He would have wondered, with considerable justification, what in the world is coming off here? After all, at Cincinnati and again at Brooklyn there had never been any question but that I was the principal man, so much so that I allocated the innings that my associates worked. When I had one associate, I did six innings and he did three. When television came along in Brooklyn, if I wanted to work on television that day I worked on television. I set things up before the ball game. I'd assign the innings and the commercials and anything else that pertained to the broadcast. If the game took a certain twist, if there was a big rhubarb or a fight or if a man got beaned—if a thing was serious enough—I didn't hesitate to take the air back. I felt that this was something the principal broadcaster should do once in a while, if he felt it was called for.

But when I went over to Yankee Stadium I knew that I was not going to be the principal broadcaster. This was an entirely different kind of a job with an entirely different emphasis. I was one of a team. When we were discussing the job, Weiss said to me, "How do you regard yourself in this setup in relation to Allen? After all, he's been here for years and he's our number one broadcaster."

"Well," I said, "Allen is your number one broadcaster and the Voice of the Yankees, and that's it. Whatever he has been, he is, and I don't question it. But I would like it understood that neither am I coming in as an assistant to Mel. I come in as a colleague, as an equal, but with different duties."

And Mel accepted me as an equal. He never once tried to direct me or show his seniority at the Stadium, and I was extremely careful never to step on any of the prerogatives that he had rightfully earned. But it was difficult doing that stop-and-go play-by-play; that is, picking up the ball club at home for a week or two and then dropping it again until they returned from their next road trip. It was like opening up the season again every two weeks. If you are going to do play-by-play and really do it right, you have got to stay with the club the bulk of the season. You can't come and go. I didn't enjoy broadcasting only at the Stadium. I liked the job all right, but I liked it a lot better when I eventually did go on the road full time in 1965, and play-by-play again became the major part of my work. The eleven years of stop-and-go broadcasting at the Stadium was the most difficult continuing assignment I ever had.

Between Innings: RADIO VS. TELEVISION

Most people don't realize it, but there is a profound difference between doing a play-by-play broadcast on radio and doing the same thing on television. If I had the choice—if I could ignore all questions of money and responsibility and advancement—I would much prefer to do a ball game on radio instead of TV, and I think any baseball announcer worth his salt would agree with me. On radio the play-by-play announcer is the show. He is the artist. There is nothing else but him, except for the crowd noises that are picked up by the field microphones. He sees the game for his listeners, he interprets it, and it is *his* skill, *his* preparation, *his* approach that are important. There is a direct relationship between announcer and listener. The announcer uses the listener's imagination. When a baseball fan hears an announcer on the radio describe a double with the bases loaded, he probably *sees* the play better than he would if he was watching it on TV. What you see on TV is big and explicit, but it is only a glimpse. A person with any intelligence has to go nuts watching baseball on television for the simple reason that there is so much more about every play that you want to see, and which the camera can't or won't give you. The radio announcer can balance his account, give you every necessary detail. He can bring in his little notes and added observations as he sees fit—the shading of the defense, what the manager said yesterday about just such a play as this. He can talk about the weather and the third-base umpire and the lady with the big hat in the first row of seats. He can use all these things when and how he wants to. The result—if he's a good announcer—is a creative accomplishment, and it's his.

On television, instead of being in control and broadcasting what *his* eyes see and what *his* brain thinks of, the announcer is the unquestioning servant of the monitor. When you do a TV game, you broadcast what you see on the monitor, and it is the director downstairs in the control room—who is not even at the ball game but who is looking at it through six different cameras simultaneously—who decides what is to be done and what is to be talked about. He says, "One," and Camera One's picture pops on your monitor, and you go with whatever that picture is. Then the director says, "Five," and you better be ready to broadcast whatever Camera Five has to show. It's a difficult technique. You can never start a sentence during a TV play-by-play and be sure you'll have time to finish it. You have to learn to speak in such a way that you can quit what you're saying in two words.

If you see something at first base that you'd like to mention (and which you would mention if you were doing radio) but the monitor is showing third base or home plate or the scoreboard, you can't talk about the thing at first base. Everyone thinks all you have to do on TV is ask the director to get you a shot of what you want, but that doesn't work. Suppose you ask for a shot and by the time a camera picks up first base, and the director puts it on the monitor, whatever was going on has stopped. Or suppose at that moment something far more important is going on someplace else on the field. Either way, the show looks bad. You're telling your audience that your director and camera crew can't even pick up a simple little thing at first base. It's insulting, telling your camera crew what to do. You don't know what's going on down there in the control room—a camera might be out, or the director may be chewing out a cameraman who was getting off the reservation, or perhaps there has been some trouble with the sound. That's a sweat, directing a telecast. It's a demanding job, and the director can't be worrying every five minutes about an announcer who wants a quick shot of a ballplayer fooling with his glove just as the pitcher is throwing the ball.

But that's the point. On TV it's the director's show, and the broadcaster is an instrument of his, like a camera. On radio, it's *my* show, where my knowledge and experience and taste and judgment decide what goes and what doesn't. On radio, you're an artist. On TV, you're a servant.

RED	1	3	5	7	9	11	13	15	17
BARBER	2	4	6	8	10	12	14	16	(18)

Now, about losing the Yankee job. As I sit here at this moment, talking, it is almost exactly twenty-four hours since Mike Burke told me that the Yankees "would not seek to renew my contract." That was a nice, gentle way to put it. The newspapers, which use a more earthy, accurate, blunt language, said I was fired.

Burke said the Yankees would not seek to renew my contract. It was beautifully put, and I hope—for his sake—that it was an instantaneous, spontaneous remark. I hope he hadn't worked on it ahead of time. The Yankees will not seek to renew my contract. That was to save my face, you see. It left the inference that the Yankees were aware of me, of my reputation, of my years as a broadcaster. It was almost as though I had decided that I did not want to work there any more, and that the Yankees were bowing to my personal wishes. That they had my well-being in mind and therefore would not disturb me. The way he said it, it was almost caressing: "The Yankees would not seek to renew my contract." It was as though Mike Burke was saying, "Red, listen. Not for anything in the world would we trespass upon you."

So, it's twenty-four hours later, and after twenty-four hours you begin to look back. There are two or three things that you have to understand, and which I have tried to understand. I never did feel that the New York Yankees or Yankee Stadium belonged to me. I always knew it all belonged to somebody else, and that all I did was work there. For a while, when I was first with the Yankees after George Weiss had brought me in, I had two-year contracts. Then it became the custom to have one-year contracts, and that was all right. I know that when you have a contract, it can or cannot be renewed. After all, what is the meaning of a one-year contract? All it means is that at the end of one year everybody takes a look to see whether they want to go around again. Maybe someone doesn't want to, or perhaps there has to be a readjustment, a refinement, some change that is indicated and proper and acceptable. When somebody says he is completely surprised when he is dismissed at the termination of a contract, he is not being completely honest. As long as you are working for people, you had better never be surprised to find that suddenly the fellow you've been working for is saying, "I don't want you to work for me any more." He can give you any number of reasons, and whether they are valid reasons or not has no bearing on the case. If the fellow doesn't want you, that's it.

What I am trying to say is, I wasn't *that* taken by surprise when the Yankees let me go. You remember things. No one has ever asked me, up to now, about what I knew about the situation when Mel Allen was fired by the Yankees. That was in 1964. Allen was not given the World Series broadcast, even though the Yankees had won and he was the senior Yankee broadcaster, and the rumors that were being printed in the papers kept getting stronger and stronger that he was all through, and finally, well after the season was over, the fact that he had been dismissed became evident. But I had known about it much earlier, well *before* the season was over.

In early September of that year, 1964, the Yankees were getting ready to go from New York to Cleveland, where they had three doubleheaders scheduled—three doubleheaders in a row, six ball games in three days. That was the year I had been ill a great deal. I had had a heart attack in Virginia as I was driving down to spring training camp, and I was in the hospital three weeks. When I finally got to the Yankee camp at Fort Lauderdale, I stayed down on the field level with the ballplayers. I did my background work, and I regained a lot of my strength, but I did not climb the steps to the top of the stands where the press box and broadcasting booth were because the doctors had said I should not climb stairs for a while, even though I had had no heart damage. What happened to me is called a fibrillation; my heart got out of rhythm. I received prompt attention, and with treatment and rest my heart came back just as strong as ever. Hell, President Johnson had a real heart attack, a massive one, and he did pretty well after it. The world is full of people walking around who have had heart attacks.

But I had had this fibrillation, and because of it I blew spring training. I didn't broadcast at all, and the fact was well publicized. That was all right. I gaited myself through spring training like a pitcher with a chronic sore arm, and on Opening Day I was ready. The Boston Red Sox came into Yankee Stadium, and I did my full stint. I did a pregame show. I climbed whatever ramps and steps had to be climbed at the Stadium to get to the mezzanine, where the press box and the broadcasting booths are, and I hopped back and forth from the radio side to the television side whenever I had to. I was ready. I didn't miss a regular broadcast.

But late in May, five or six weeks after the season began, I felt a soreness in the calf of my left leg. I thought it was a muscle I had pulled, or something like that, and I didn't pay any attention to it at first, but it got more and more painful. I had a blood clot. I don't know how I got it. Later, the doctor said that, as a general rule, people don't know. I hadn't had a blow or a knock or anything like that, but there it was. About four o'clock one morning I woke up with a tremendous pain in my chest, and, boy, I thought I was a goner. They called an ambulance and took me to the hospital—Doctors' Hospital in New York—and they found that the blood clot had broken loose in my leg and a piece of it had lodged in my lung. I was in the hospital three weeks, and two more pieces of that clot broke loose; I had three of them hit me in the lungs. It was a close call, and I had to stay off the leg and get complete rest. They kept a hot, wet pack on the leg, and they gave me all sorts of medication to change the content of my blood, so that it would be lighter. And they worked to dissolve the clot. I don't know what all they did, but I do know I was in the hospital three weeks. Fortunately, the Yankees were out of town on a road trip for two of those weeks, so I missed only a week of broadcasting. As I look back over the thirteen years I was at the Stadium, that was the only week of work I missed in all the time I was there. I don't call broadcasting spring training games from Fort Lauderdale work.

But this had slowed me down, this thing in May. I got back on my feet and returned to broadcasting at the Stadium, but I was convalescent. In other words, when you have twice within a few months been stretched flat on your back for three weeks at a time for complete rest, you lose physical vigor. Sometimes the cure is worse than the disease. Complete rest is the most debilitating thing that can happen to a human being. You lose your strength. You lose your muscle tone. I had almost forgotten how to walk. All you can do is fight your way back, step by step. And let me put it on the record: the Yankees were wonderful to me and to Lylah during both these hospital trips.

By August I was in good shape again, so much so that when September came around and I saw these six games in three nights coming up at Cleveland, I volunteered to go out and broadcast them. I suggested that I take Phil Rizzuto's place and give him a few days off. Well, all Phil Rizzuto ever needs is for somebody to wink an eye that he'll take his place for a day or so and Phil scoots out to the golf course. Nothing could have pleased him more, so I went to Cleveland, he stayed home, and both of us were happy. I wanted to go because this would be what you call a *tour de force*. It would be pretty positive practical public evidence that I was back in health. Red Barber went out to Cleveland and did six ball games in three days. That would do a lot to counteract all the "sickness" publicity I had been receiving. It would demonstrate that I was no longer a wheelchair case out of Doctors' Hospital.

The day before we were to leave for Cleveland was an open day for the Yankees, and I got word from Miss Doran, Dan Topping's secretary, that Mr. Topping wanted me to come over to his office about four o'clock that afternoon. That was fine with me. I wanted to talk about next year and about some trouble I had had behind the scenes with Ballantine Beer, the dominant sponsor at that time for the Yankee broadcasts and telecasts. The trouble went back to a year or two before when Ballantine had gotten it into their minds that they wanted to bring Jerry Coleman in as broadcaster and add him as a fourth man to work along with Allen, Rizzuto, and me. I was glad for Coleman's sake that they wanted him, but Ballantine said that the way they wanted to bring him in was for the Yankees to renegotiate my contract and cut my pay. They would then use the money they saved on me to pay him. In effect, I was to help pay for Jerry Coleman.

I wouldn't do it, and I told them so. I said, "I stand on my contract." The fellow who presented the idea to me at Ballantine was Len Faupel, their advertising manager, and he was ice water when he handed that one to me. It was a noon meeting at their offices in New Jersey, and I had gone over there that day with Bill McCaffrey. Faupel said, bluntly, "We want you to take a cut in salary, but for that you will get a two-year contract at the lower figure." In other words, they would give me an extra year for less money. Faupel said that Topping knew and agreed to this proposal.

"No!" I said. I was outraged. I said, "I'll worry about next year when I get to it. But I am not going to budge now. I have a contract for this year, and I am going to be paid every cent of it whether I broadcast or not." It was what they call in show business a play-or-pay contract, and if I didn't change it they had to pay me.

Faupel got mad, but I got madder. Oh, I was mad. This thing made me sick inside. I mean genuinely sick. They made an insulting, demeaning proposition and when I turned it down, *they* got angry. And the thing that made me particularly sick was that, aside from standing on the letter of my contract, there wasn't a thing I could do about it. There was no counterattack.

McCaffrey and I went back to New York and got into mid-Manhattan about one-thirty. "Come on," Bill said, "let's go over to the Casbah and get a cup of coffee." That's what he called Toots Shor's place. I said fine, and we went to Shor's. The Yankees had been giving some sort of press party—a small thing, some announcement or other—and there in Shor's was Roy Hamey, who was the Yankees' general manager before they turned him out to pasture and promoted Ralph Houk. I went over to him and told him what Ballantine had attempted to do.

Hamey said, "They tried to make you quit, huh?"

All of a sudden I realized he was right. I said, "Yes, I guess that's what they tried to do. They tried to make me quit."

Well, this thing stayed with me, and it bothered me. It was still bothering me in 1964 when I got off my back twice and came back to broadcast. It was down inside me, and it was pestering me a lot more than the fibrillation or the phlebitis. That was where the focus of infection was.

So when I went in to see Topping that afternoon in September, I had this in my craw. They had worked out something else to bring Jerry Coleman in, but the thing was still annoying me. I went into Topping's office, and Ralph Houk was with him. I hadn't expected Houk to be there, but that was all right. He had been promoted from manager to general manager and now he was sitting in a Fifth Avenue office in a gray flannel suit. Topping was in shirt-sleeves behind his desk.

Topping never was one to mouth pleasantries. He didn't play any games with you. He came out with whatever he had to say.

He said, "I don't know whether you want to talk about next year or not."

I said, "I don't know whether I want to talk about next year or not, either. If I talk about what I really want to talk about, I'd probably talk about quitting. This year. Just as soon as we finish this month and end the season."

He straightened up, and Houk straightened up, and they looked at each other. Then Topping said to Houk, "I guess we better tell him." Houk nodded.

Topping turned to me and said, "I had Mel in here this morning. I told him he was through." I stared at him. "I'm tired of him popping off. I called the Commissioner and told him that Allen was out, and I put Rizzuto on the World Series. If we win." Each team in the Series has the right to nominate a broadcaster.

Topping said, "Now you know why we want to talk to you about next year."

"Well," I said. "Did I ever talk to you about this thing with Len Faupel?"

Topping said, "You don't have to worry about Faupel. You're talking to me. I'm president of the Yankees."

Houk said, "Red, you know you're our man. We want you."

"In that case," I said, "I'd be very interested in talking to you about next year. Provided I'm talking with the Yankees and that I don't have to go over to Newark to the Ballantine Brewery and talk to Faupel ever again." And for one of the rare times in my life I used a little profanity, which made me feel immeasurably better.

The conversation there in the Yankee office left me with the impression that instead of being just one of the fellows around there, which I had been, Topping and Houk wanted me to step in as principal broadcaster. Up to this point I had been very careful never to trespass on any of Mel's prerogatives—he was the senior broadcaster, he was The Voice of the Yankees. Basically, up to this day, I was the pre- and postgame broadcaster. Now Allen was gone, or would be gone after the season. Topping and Houk asked me if I would be willing to travel now and do out-of-town broadcasts.

"Sure," I told them. "Look. I never said I wouldn't travel." I went over that with Topping again. I said, "Dan, with you and with Weiss, I never said a thing about not traveling."

"I know it, but we're spelling out some things now for next year. All right, you'll travel. How much will you travel?"

"Look," I said, "let's not try to get too specific. Why don't we say that I'll guarantee you that I will travel at least half of the season. That's the minimum, and I won't say it's all I'll travel. I'll respect the job. Whatever the job has to be, I'll do."

Topping said, "That's more than I thought you'd say. That's great."

"You're our man, Red," Houk said. "You're our boy. That's what we want to hear."

There was no problem about money. I said I'd like a raise, and Topping said, "How about five thousand dollars?" I said, "Fine." I never had any problem with Topping about money. I don't think anybody could ever say they had trouble with Topping about money.

So, I left the office with the understanding that I would travel, I would step up, I would be the principal broadcaster. Topping had said, "I think we ought to have four men." I said, "I do, too." With Allen gone, there would be only Rizzuto, Coleman, and me to do all that had to be done—radio broadcasts of all games home and away, telecasts of all home games and a great many telecasts of those on the road, and pre- and postgame interviews, which were being done on the road now, too. Topping asked, "Do you know anyone who could be a fourth announcer?"

"No, I don't. But I would recommend that we get a young professional announcer who is on his way up, someone who would be fresh and new. This would be the greatest job in the world for him. People would know that he is new and that he has come in from Terre Haute or Arizona or someplace, and they'd be interested in him. They'd watch his progress."

"That sounds pretty good," Topping said. "That sounds fine. How are you going to find him?"

"There's a fellow here in New York who knows broadcasters all over the country. He knows their work. That's Gordon Bridge, director of sports over at Armed Forces Radio. In his job—they pick up broadcasts and relay them overseas—he hears more sports announcers than anybody. He probably knows somebody."

"That sounds good. Will you talk to Gordon and get some names?"

"All right," I said.

"There's no rush. We can wait on this until after the season. You've got this trip, and Mel is going to finish out the year, so there's no hurry. We left it up to Mel to make his own announcement whenever he gets ready. We decided to let him do it his way."

That was the end of the meeting, and I left and went to Cleveland and watched Mel Allen sit there. I worked six ball games with him in three days, and I knew something that he didn't know I knew. It was painful to sit there and watch him, watch him broadcast, watch him *try* to broadcast. You talk about somebody being knocked galley west. He was in a state of shock. He didn't know if he was in Cleveland or Paducah, Kentucky.

We got the season finished, and the news about Allen finally got out. But I never had another meeting with Topping and Houk. That was always to come, there wasn't any rush. I was going over in my mind the things I had to do. If I was going to be doing the work of the principal broadcaster that I did at Ebbets Field, I was going to have to have some say over the announcers. Not only who they were, as in the case of the yet-to-be-named fourth man, but in *how* they worked and their approach to the job.

Then a few things began to happen. I still hadn't seen Topping or Houk to discuss the next season when Topping sent word to me that the Yankees were bringing in a man to take over the radio and television end of things. He would run it, sell it, do whatever had to be done, and in effect he would be supervisor of announcers. His name was Perry Smith, and the Yankees were bringing him in from NBC, where he had been assistant director of sports. That came as a little shock.

Then they had an affair at Shor's, a press party, and there they made the announcement that Joe Garagiola had been hired. He would be one of the Yankee broadcasters the next season. That came out of the blue as far as I was concerned, particularly after that September meeting I had had with Topping and Houk. Nobody had ever said a word to me about Garagiola.

As I look back now, I can realize that a warning buzzer sounded then. A few weeks before everything looked one way, and now, all of a sudden, *pow!*, there's Perry Smith, *pow!*, there's Garagiola. As you look back you can see how things were set in motion.

We went into the 1965 season, four broadcasters again, but now it was Rizzuto, Coleman, Garagiola, and Barber. Joe and I never had any trouble, except for one thing. From the time he began broadcasting in St. Louis it was difficult for Joe to let his associate broadcaster finish a sentence. Joe would cut in on him. Apparently, Garagiola felt that whatever he had to say was so much more important or interesting or pertinent or colorful or funny that it didn't make any difference who it was he was working with. He ran over fellows. He seemed impervious to the fact that the other fellow up there was a human being. I would say that he demonstrated a public lack of concern for his colleagues.

Before Joe came to the Yankees, he announced the 1964 World Series with Phil Rizzuto (that was the Series Allen got busted off). I was working on the Armed Forces Radio broadcast with Gordon Bridge, doing color for them between innings of their pickup of the regular broadcast, and Gordon and I were both flabbergasted at the way Garagiola cut in on Rizzuto when Phil was trying to do play-by-play. Phil took it, and when Garagiola was doing the play-by-play Phil never bothered to cut in on him.

In 1965 I was traveling with the club, and we went to Boston. Until that trip I had been working with either Rizzuto or Coleman, and this was the first time Garagiola and I did play-by-play together. Joe was consistent. He cut in on me. It was the first time in my life that I had sat in a radio booth with a fellow who moved in on my broadcast. I couldn't finish what I was saying. He cut in on me in the middle of sentences. I would start to tell some little anecdote about a player, and I could never get it finished.

I never wanted to have any sort of unpleasantness over the air with anyone, and I never have had. But when I got back to the hotel that night, I realized that Garagiola and I had to have this thing out. The next morning I phoned him in his room. I said, "Joe, I want to talk to you. Either I'll come up to your room, or you come down to mine."

"I'll come down, Red," he said. "Mine is all messed up. I slept late."

"Fine."

He came in a few minutes later and after we exchanged pleasantries I opened up my scorebook and, as gently and as nicely as I could, I said, "Joe, do you see those words up there in the upper left-hand corner of my scorebook? Those are to indicate little things I wanted to talk about during the game last night, when I got the opportunity. But I never got to say one of them all the way through, because you kept cutting in on me. Now, Joe, I don't know about your relationship with other broadcasters, but you are not to cut in on me. If you feel that what you have to say is so much more important than what I am saying, hold your hand up where I can see it, and when I get around to it, if I feel like it, I'll bring you in. But don't cut in on me."

Joe said, "Oh, no, Red. Gee. I don't mean to cut in on you. I'm sorry." And he took it. At least, he took it on the surface. But I know he didn't like me saying that; he didn't like it at all. People who cut in on you don't like to be called on it. But Joe didn't do it to me any more, and that was the important thing to me at that juncture. Yet it was all part of a pattern that was developing.

Now we go along, and in the middle of 1965—Garagiola's first year, Perry Smith's first year—the ball club was doing very poorly. It was pretty evident that it wasn't just a slump; the team was foundering, foundering badly. Everybody was trying to blame Johnny Keane, and I don't mean only people on the outside. But this was no doing of Johnny Keane. It was his first year, too, and he had been handed a club that was coming apart. It was a team that not only was not going to win the pennant again; it was not even going to challenge. If there was any hope left, it ended in Minnesota on the Sunday before the All-Star Game. Harmon Killebrew hit a home run for Minnesota in the last inning of the last game before the All-Star break, and that was it. If he had gone out, the Yankees would have won, but he hit a homer in the last of the ninth and it turned a Yankee victory into a Yankee defeat, and they were all through. That was the moment, the final, definite *coupe de grâce* that ended the long run of great Yankee teams.

I could see it. Anybody who had been around baseball any length of time could see it. John Keane became ill on the bench. The Yankees were a losing team. They were disappointing their fans. By this time CBS had bought a controlling interest in the franchise, and that didn't sit too well with the public either.

All this meant, to me at least, that the problem of broadcasting the Yankees had changed. You couldn't sit back and wait for the big home run, the inevitable rally, the strong pitching effort. You had to bring something extra to the broadcasts. I don't mean that I was trying to change the play of the game, hoke it up, alter the outline of what was happening down on the field. You can't do that. You have to broadcast the ball. But I tried between batters and between innings to put in extra things, interesting things. I dug hard. I did a lot of background work. I talked to the players. I went out of my way to get new information, new material. I widened and lengthened my preparation, and I had always done a great deal of preparation in the first place. I worked. I worked hard. Maybe I worked too hard.

But at the time, I felt good about what I was doing. We came back from a road trip, and I was in a glow, feeling that I had done a pretty solid two weeks of work for a club that needed it. I was in the press room at the Stadium before a game, sitting around a table with four or five other fellows, fellows from the TV crew, the assistant director, people like that. Perry Smith came in. He was my superior; he was in charge of the broadcasters. He sat down at the table and said, "Red, you know, you were really talking too much out there on this trip."

I said. "What?"

"We've been getting letters. Topping has been getting letters. People are saying you talk too much. A sportswriter from up in Buffalo, or someplace up there, phoned me and he complained about it. He said you were talking too much."

I looked at him. He would talk like that, in front of this group of people, here in this public press room? A lot of people heard him. I didn't trust myself to answer. I got up and left.

I walked out of the press room and up the stairs, and I ran into Ralph Houk. I wasn't looking for Houk, but he was standing there in Joe Cousins' office, the auditor, and the fury I had felt at this thing suddenly spilled over. The impropriety of those remarks in front of those people. What it amounted to was a public dressing down.

Angrily, I told Houk what Perry had done, and Houk immediately and profanely exploded. He said, "I don't want to hear anything about you and your blank problems. I got enough blank problems of my own." Houk has a vocabulary mules can't stomach.

So, I guess another seed was planted, another buzzer buzzed.

The next year—1966—things came faster. The Yankees opened the season looking even worse than they had the year before. They lost something like sixteen of their first twenty games and were stuck in last place. Johnny Keane was fired, Houk went back to managing, and Dan Topping, Jr., was put in the general manager's job. Things picked up briefly, and then sagged again. The Yankees weren't going anyplace. Early in the season, in May, Dan Topping, Sr., in his irritation sent a memorandum to each of us announcers. The memorandum was mimeographed and Perry Smith distributed it. Nobody knows how many copies were made. He handed it to us with cameramen there, engineers there, everyone there. The memorandum said that each of us had been horrible. I think if Dan hadn't been so upset by the way things were going on the field, he would have admitted that it wasn't the four announcers who were horrible, it was the team. But he said now that the team was getting straightened out—this was just after Houk had succeeded Keane, when the club had gone on its brief winning spurt—it was time for us to get on the ball.

But the good streak ended and the team sagged again. In the middle of summer one of the columns in *Radio Daily*, a trade paper, had a statement declaring that two of the four Yankee broadcasters would not be back the next year. That was the first time, so far as I know, that anything was printed about all this. I took the column to the Stadium that night and gave it to Perry Smith. I didn't ask him for any reaction. I just gave it to him.

"Oh," he said, "I want to show this to Dan."

Off he went, and he came back about the second or third inning, when we were on the air. He handed it back to me and leaned over and whispered into my ear, "I showed it to Dan." That was all he said. He didn't make any comment, then or later, and I never heard from anybody about it.

Later, we were out in Detroit when the same sort of thing appeared in the New York *Daily News*. Bill McCaffrey called me in Detroit to tell me about it, and then he said, "I hope I haven't done the wrong thing, but I've already called Perry Smith about this. I asked Perry what he knew about it, and he said, 'Nothing.' He said he didn't know how these fellows got these things." And then Bill told me that Perry said he knew Topping had seen it because he, Perry, had put the column on Topping's desk that morning.

Then we were in Boston, on our last trip there, and a column in the Boston *Traveler* said, "Don't invite Red Barber and Jerry Coleman to the same party with Phil Rizzuto and Joe Garagiola. They're feuding. And as for next year, Barber and Coleman are out." He named us.

I hadn't seen the column, but Joe Garagiola did and he brought it over as I was getting ready to sign on on the radio side. About one minute before air time Joe stuck it in front of the microphone and said, "Look at that."

When I got back to New York I brought *that* column to Smith's attention. Perry said, "Now, Red, I'll tell you. All I know about this thing is—I don't know where these writers get these things—all I know about it is that they had a meeting over at CBS. Topping was at it, and Paley and Stanton were there, and Mike Burke. They phoned me here at the Yankee office and they asked me, 'Can you get along with three announcers next year?' 'Well,' I said, 'if I have to, I can get along with two.' Later, after the meeting, young Dan Topping went to his father and told him, 'Dad, I think you'd be making a serious mistake to change the announcing staff. I think you ought to leave the four of them alone.' And that's the way it stands."

That was all I heard until Saturday, September 17, which was Bobby Richardson Day and my daughter's birthday. Barney Kremenko had a column in the *World Journal Tribune* in which he stated, in the second paragraph, that it looked for a time as though the Yankee broadcasting situation was going to be one way but now it's been changed again, and Red Barber is out for next year.

The next day, Sunday, I was sitting in the press room with Bob Fishel, who is in charge of public relations for the Yankees. He said, "I don't know where these fellows get these things." I saw Barney Kremenko, and I went over to him. I said, "You know more about it than I do." Barney got a little red in the face, and he walked away and never said another word.

On Monday I was having lunch with Sidney Fields, the columnist for the *Daily News*, and he said, "Red, the fellows down at the paper tell me that unless Kremenko can prove what he wrote, it is occupational libel."

"Who wants to think in terms of libel?" I said.

"You might think in terms of money."

"No," I said. "Let's let it go."

Things were really popping now, day after day. On Tuesday CBS announced that it had taken over complete, active control of the Yankees, had bought out Dan Topping 100 per cent and had moved Mike Burke in to take over. I thought to myself, "Well, this ought to settle things." I would not have been surprised at being let out had Topping remained but, I thought, CBS, that's different. I had worked for CBS as director of sports and had had a very happy association there for nine years. I had left for a legitimate reason—television was getting so big I felt they needed a full-time director of sports, and that was something I did not want to attempt to be. I wished to remain a broadcaster. I had had a fine personal relationship with Dr. Stanton, the president of CBS, and when I left he thanked me for thinking of the company ahead of myself. Stanton said he hated to lose me, but he agreed that it was the right decision and gave me his blessing. I had always felt that CBS was *my* network.

And, of course, Joe Garagiola had had an intense association with NBC. Every day he was singing the praises of NBC all over the Stadium, all over the league. It was NBC this and NBC that and the fellows he knew at NBC and the tapes he was doing for NBC. I thought, "Well, now that CBS has taken over and Topping is gone, I might have an even better job in this setup next year. Maybe the thing I thought was going to happen when Topping and Houk talked to me in September 1964, when they gave Mel Allen the black spot, is going to happen now. Maybe CBS will say, 'You've got a real value to us. You've got all these years in the city. You've got your standing in the community. You have the background of your work in the Red Cross and in your church. You did the Jackie Robinson thing. You were in Cincinnati under MacPhail when a ball club had to be rebuilt, a last-place ball club. You were at Brooklyn with MacPhail when a second-division ball club was rebuilt. You were at Brooklyn when World War II reduced the Dodgers to the second division again, and you were there with Rickey when he rebuilt that ball club. You have a particular value for CBS now in our dilemma.'"

Thursday night, my daughter Sarah—who is teaching in New York, the second grade in a school in Harlem—and I went to the opera, the second night of the opera at the new Metropolitan at Lincoln Center. During the first intermission, who did I run into but William Paley, chairman of the board of CBS.

"Hello, Bill," I said.

He turned, saw me, and said, "Hello, Red."

I introduced Sarah and then I asked him, "How is your father's garden?"

You may have read that Paley bought the land where the Stork Club used to be on East Fifty-third Street and was turning it into a small public garden in the memory of his father. I had written to him about it because I thought it was perfectly wonderful for a man to so honor the memory of his father. It was an admirable and expensive thing he was doing.

"They're putting trees in now," he said, "but I don't plan to open it until next year."

I said, "Well, let me tell you again, I think it's one of the most sensitive, thoughtful things I have ever heard of a man doing in memory of his father."

And then he did something that I saw but did not comprehend until Mike Burke dropped the black spot on me. I remember now that Paley was a little restive. I don't mean that anyone of his position and prominence would be uncomfortable, but he *was* restive. He did not wish to prolong the conversation with my daughter and me. After he had said he didn't plan to open the garden until next year, and before I could finish my sentence on what a fine thing it was, he turned and walked away.

My thought at the moment was, I guess he's in a hurry to go find whoever he had come with. My daughter thought he was rude. Now I know he wasn't in a hurry to go find anybody. He was in a hurry to leave talking to whom he was talking. He knew what was going to happen, because CBS doesn't dismiss a fellow getting fifty thousand dollars a year without Mr. Paley knowing. And approving.

Saturday morning—that was quite a week—I suddenly awoke to the fact that on Tuesday I would be leaving the city for the year. The Yankees were finishing the season on the road, and their home schedule was ending the next day, Sunday. Monday was an off day, and Tuesday night we opened in Washington. I had asked and received permission from Perry Smith to skip the last three games of the season in Chicago. I planned to leave New York on Tuesday in my car, drive to Washington, do the three games there, and then drive on south to Miami and home.

I realized Saturday morning that in three days I would be gone, and I realized, too, that before I left on Tuesday I wanted very much to talk to Mike Burke, the new Yankee president, especially in view of all that had been going back and forth. I wanted to talk to him personally, to see if he would ask me if I had any suggestions about things to be done—things I had learned from MacPhail and from Rickey, ideas I had picked up in the thirty-three years I had been around the majors.

I phoned his office, and his secretary was there. He wasn't in yet, but he would probably be there in another hour or so. I told her that I would like to make an appointment to see him, and I explained my schedule to her. I said, "Would you tell him that

I have a night game tonight, so all day today is free. I have only a single game Sunday afternoon, and while I'm to read the first and second lessons at the Church of the Epiphany at eleven o'clock, I don't have anything else interfering on Sunday. I'll be completely free all day Monday except for an early-morning appointment just to check in with my doctor. And I can change that. But I would very much like to sit down and talk with Mr. Burke at his convenience sometime between now and Tuesday, when I leave. I want to talk about the work on the broadcasts next year, and I think it would mean a lot more if I could talk to him across a desk instead of over the telephone. If I could see him now it would save me flying back up from Miami later on."

"Oh, yes," she said. "I'll get in touch with him, and I'll call you back."

She phoned a little later and told me that he was not coming in to the office until late in the afternoon and that his schedule that day was simply impossible. She said he wanted to talk to me, too, but at a leisurely pace when there would be plenty of time, and would breakfast Monday morning be all right?

"Good," I said. "Where would he like to have breakfast?"

"He said he could meet you in the lobby of your hotel at eight-fifteen. He said for you to pick someplace where you can sit and talk."

"I tell you what. I'm not just in a bedroom here at the Hilton. I have a little suite, with a sitting room. Why don't you ask Mr. Burke if he wouldn't get on the elevator and come up to Room 4355. We'll send out for room service and have breakfast up here."

"That sounds fine," she said. "If you don't hear back from me in half an hour, that's what it will be."

I didn't hear back, and that pleased me very much. The suite I had was very pleasant, with a lovely view of midtown New York and Central Park. It was a very nice place to sit and talk in. And I felt, from the way his secretary had relayed his comments, that it was going to work out splendidly. Here was a young, new man. We had had luncheon once during the summer, but we hadn't discussed baseball or broadcasting. We had merely gotten to know each other a little. But now, I thought, we can go over some things about the Yankees and see what can be done, see how the situation can be improved.

I went over things in my mind. I asked myself, "What would Larry MacPhail do? Right now?"

Well, I thought, the first thing Larry would do would be paint the Stadium. He'd say, "I'm stuck with this place. It's grand old Yankee Stadium, but I'm stuck with it. Whether there ever is a new one or not, I'm stuck with the old one for now. But if I'm stuck with it, I'll make the best of it. I'll paint it. I'll paint it inside and outside."

I went on, dreaming of what I would do. I'd strip all the advertising signs off the outfield fences. I'd let the people know that, wealthy as CBS is, we can afford to take those signboards out. We'll paint the outfield fence a nice restful green. We don't have to say this publicly, but the people will see it for themselves and they'll say, "Gee, they're not trying to squeeze every dollar out of things. They've made it more pleasant for us to sit here." It gives a certain dignity and class to take down all that indiscriminate stuff about soft drinks and shirts and deodorants that you see all over the signboards. Whenever you see signboards in a ball park, it is an indication that the ball club is being run either by someone struggling so desperately that he has to grab every last dollar, or by someone who is just plain greedy. Or else by a person who doesn't think, who does things a certain way because "that's the way we've always done it."

Oh, yes, I said, I'm certainly going to suggest that. And I'm going to tell him that a thing about Yankee Stadium that is more upsetting to people than they realize is the sight of those three old pieces of granite in center field. They look like tombstones. Granted, they're only stone markers with plaques on them, but they *look* like tombstones. And when you have a tenth-place ball club, you don't need three tombstones in the outfield. I was going to say to Mike Burke, we have got to get rid of those tombstones. And because there are some people who are sensitive about sentiment and who won't want you to come in there and rip those tombstones out, the way you get rid of them—well, you can't get rid of them; you just want them out of sight; you don't want people to be staring at them all the time—and the way to get them out of sight ties in with another change I'd make. It is a mistake to have the bullpens at the Stadium out of sight of the fans back in those runways in left field and right field. Baseball is a game of anticipation and development, and one of the exciting things about it when things get a little uncertain is to see the fellows in the bullpen warming up. Not only do you see them, but you see who they are. That's part of the game, and it should be. But in Yankee Stadium you can't see it.

What I would do is rebuild center field. The center field area at the Stadium is too large anyhow. It's too vast. I'd run a wire fence across from left-center to right-center, and I'd put the bullpens behind the fence. That way, you'd improve the dimensions of the outfield, bring the bullpens out in the open, and get those tombstones behind the bullpens and out of sight. People could still walk through the bullpens and past the plaques on their way out of the ball park, which is the only time they can read them and see what they say anyway.

In center field, where there is an old, dirty, frayed canvas that they use as a backdrop for the hitters, I'd take down the canvas and build a permanent backdrop, and I'd paint it a deep green. I'd rip out the bleacher seats behind the backdrop. They never use them anyway; the only time they ever did use them was in the past when they had a complete sellout, and then they had to roll down the backdrop. If that isn't self-defeating, what is? I'd take out the bleacher seats behind the backdrop and put in some sort of a small cafeteria for the bleacher fans. It would give them a little plus.

I'd do something about ladies' day. I'd make ladies' day an occasion. Every lady would get a little Hawaiian orchid as she came into the park, or a carnation. I'd always see to it that there were gate prizes for the ladies—maybe three of them each time. Nice prizes, something you'd talk about even if you didn't win them. I'd vary them, but they'd be given away after the seventh inning to the ladies who held the lucky program number or lucky seat number. I'd see to it that a movie star or a television personality or some well-known person would be there to step up to home plate while we held up the game for a minute or two, and he'd present the prizes to these three women.

I'd do something about the seats with obstructed views, the bad seats behind posts that are sold for the same price as good seats. I'd have the seats and the tickets for them in a sharply different color, so that everyone who bought an obstructed-view seat would know it. I'd cut the prices on them, too. If he buys it anyway, he knows what he's getting and he can't go around complaining that "they stuck me behind a post."

I had a lot of ideas I wanted to talk to Mike Burke about, and a lot of thoughts about how the broadcasts could be set up and worked. Yes, I thought, it's going to be a nice Monday morning. We'll sit up here and look out at this lovely view, look up there at Central Park, and we'll talk. I was getting excited. If there is anything that is stimulating, it is taking something that is at the bottom and building it up again. I've been around three times when that has happened in baseball, and it's tremendously exciting. It's something like having a child to raise again. It gives you something to do, something to watch grow, something to take pride in.

I kept thinking about things. I would tell Burke that one of the first things he ought to change was the company box. Topping had put a high enclosure around the mezzanine box where he sat, and that was a direct affront to every fan. He cut himself off from the public. He had his private domain. Rip the enclosure down. Let the president of the ball club sit with the folks. Let him move around. Sit a couple of innings in the bleachers, just to listen to them talk. Find out what they think about things. Do what Bill Veeck did: move around with the crowd, be available, sign autographs. Let people be able to say, "I talked to Mike Burke at the Stadium today, and I told him what I thought." The Yankees had a survey thing going on. You don't need a survey. Do your own survey. Go down and talk with the people. They'll talk with you.

Oh, I had a list. It was a pretty darn good list, and it was important. Because you cannot develop new stars rapidly in baseball. It's going to take a few years to build the Yankees up again, and the people are going to have to have something else to hold them. They are going to have to understand that the new owners care about the people, that they're *giving* the people something, that the Stadium and the Yankees are not cold corporate images.

When I spoke to Burke's secretary, I didn't mention that I

had a little kitchenette in my suite at the Hilton, and that I always prepared my own breakfast in it. There was a refrigerator, a stove, a coffee pot—and I make very good coffee. Saturday afternoon I went over to a grocery store and I bought the finest Casaba melon they had. I paid $3.50 for it. I had them cut it. I wanted to be sure it was an excellent melon, and it was. I bought some fresh cream and I got a new can of Brown Gold all-Colombian coffee and some Thomas' English Muffins. And I bought some butter—one of the fads today is worrying about cholesterol, and I've been using margarine, but I thought for this occasion I'd get a stick of butter. I got some orange marmalade, too, and I brought everything back to the kitchenette in the little suite in the Hilton.

I said, well now, when he comes up here, instead of ordering room service, I'll have breakfast ready. I'll have the table in the sitting room overlooking Central Park all set. I'll use the china that I bought earlier in the summer at Takashimaya, the Japanese store on Fifth Avenue, lovely blue-and-white china. I had some stainless steel flatware that I had bought at the Japanese store. In other words, this small suite in the Hilton had been my home all through the season, and because I respond to the things around me I'd prefer to have my own china and my own stainless steel and my own food and my own coffee rather than deal with the necessarily impersonal service of the hotel. Again, this goes back to my father and his kitchen and his rocking chair.

I had been using paper napkins, but I went downstairs to the Seven Hills, a restaurant in the hotel, and I borrowed two or three linen napkins from the headwaiter. I wanted this breakfast for Mike Burke to be perfect, because in a very real sense he was coming into my home. I thought, too, that it would give him an extra insight into this creature named Red Barber. He doesn't know me, or how I live. He might find out a little more about who I am. He might find that I'm a bit more sensitive and aware of things than he thought. My goodness, he might be pleasantly surprised to find the personal china and the table-ware and the linen and the beautiful melon, with a piece of freshly cut lime to squeeze on it. And real good coffee, right off the stove, fresh and hot. It wouldn't take but a minute to plug in the electric toaster and hot up the English muffins and bring out the butter and the marmalade.

And we'd talk. We'd put this thing back on its wheels. We'd make it move again. Boy, I was going back to MacPhail, going back to Rickey. I wanted to give everything I had, everything I knew. I wanted to lay it right in his lap. I wanted to point it out to him. I wanted to say to him, "Look, you're in this job one week today, seven days. There are great things to be done. All the public wants to feel is sincerity, an interest in them from you and the Yankees. They want to feel that maybe for the first time in the history of the ball club, this is now a people's team and not a team entrenched wealth."

Oh, I had ideas. I anticipated that breakfast meeting.

I made all my plans and did my shopping on Saturday, broadcast the game Saturday night, went to the Church of the Epiphany Sunday morning, broadcast again Sunday afternoon, and then went back to the hotel. Everything was ready for Monday morning.

About ten-thirty Sunday night the phone rang in my room. It was Perry Smith. He said, "Red, about your breakfast with Burke in the morning."

That was a jar to begin with. I didn't know Perry Smith knew anything about my breakfast with Burke.

Smith said, "Burke wants you to meet him in the Edwardian Room of the Plaza Hotel at eight-thirty."

That was another jar.

I said, "All right." He hung up, and that was that. But a bell was going off now, because I know that every time somebody says something or does something it *means* something. The problem was to find out what it meant. I kept saying to myself, what does it mean that 1. Perry Smith knows about this; and 2. Perry called me to change the meeting place? Why didn't Burke call? Why did Burke have Perry Smith call? What does the change in the meeting place mean?

I got up early Monday morning—I am by habit a very early riser—and I left on schedule to walk the few blocks to the Plaza to meet Burke at eight-thirty. As I reached into the closet in my room to get my coat and hat, I saw something on the shelf. I had a large stack of books there, and on the top of the stack was a copy of *Best Sport Stories of 1966*, a splendid collection of the finest writing done by newspaper and magazine people in the field of sports for the year. The 1966 volume covered the year 1965, 1965 covered 1964, and so on.

I was always interested in the annual volumes of *Best Sports Stories*, but I was doubly interested in this one because I had been one of the three judges. I had been asked to succeed Quentin Reynolds, who had died. I felt honored, and I enjoyed the assignment. When I saw the book on the shelf, I remembered that Mike Burke had a young son of school age. I didn't know exactly how old, but I knew that he was in school. I had several copies of *Best Sports Stories* lying around that the publishers had sent me, and I decided to take a copy along with me and give it to Burke for his son. Be nice reading for him, no matter what age he was.

I got to the Plaza, checked my hat and coat, went into the Edwardian Room, and asked the captain if Mr. Burke was there yet. He pointed, and there was Mike sitting at a table by the window. I went over.

"Hello," he said.

"Hello, Mike." As I sat down I said, "Mike, here's a book that I thought you might want to take to your boy. It's excellent writing, and I'm especially pleased with it because I had to read everything in it from a particular point of view. I was one of the judges this year."

"Oh? Well, thank you."

"There is a great story in here by Dick Young on the death of Branch Rickey, a marvelous piece of writing. I voted it first, and I was very glad that the other judges felt the same way about it. It's really superb. And there's another story in here that's absolutely inconceivable. I cannot understand how a sportswriter watching the ebb and flow of a big football game can turn to his typewriter the minute it is over and in the clamor of the press box immediately write a story for his morning paper like this one." And I turned to the story that had been written by a man in Texas, about the tremendous Arkansas-Texas football game, which begins, "Like a mighty sword, Arkansas struck."

"Look at this," I said. "This is writing. This is literature. And the lead was written only minutes after this exciting, uncertain football game had ended."

He was saying, "Umhum," and "Yes," and "I see," and two or three other little pleasantries. Then he mentioned something about the philosophy of broadcasting, and I started to tell him the thing about Bill Klem umpiring the ball and the way I tried to broadcast.

But he interrupted. He said, "There's no reason for us to be talking about these things. What I have to say is not very pleasant. We have decided not to seek to renew your contract."

He looked at me, and I looked at him.

I said, "Why?"

"Well," he said, "there has been a growing feeling that you were getting disinterested—bitter. No, bitter is not the word. At any rate, Topping had made up his mind that you were to go at the end of last season. Then there were some other thoughts on the matter at CBS, and it was decided that you would stay another year. The decision not to renew your contract for next season was made some time ago. It was made, to be exact, two weeks ago today. Topping was supposed to have told you, but he didn't. So I am telling you."

"It's not a very pleasant assignment for you," I said. "I realize that. But let me tell you something. I have *not* been disinterested. These past two years, broadcasting for a ball club that was crumbling on the field and off, I regard as the best two years of work I ever did. I tried to help this ball club *and* its broadcasts. I went out of my way, every way I knew, to try and help. I have *never* been more interested in broadcasting in my life."

"Well, that's the way it is."

"Look, now that the decision has been made, that's it. I would have preferred that it had come out differently, but I want you to know that if *you* don't want me to be there, *I* don't want to be there. I only work for willing buyers. But I'll tell you one more thing. You have made a mistake. You have fired the wrong broadcaster."

He said, "Maybe. If you had your say as to which one was going to be fired, who would you have picked?"

I told him whom I would dismiss—I'm not going to mention which one; that's neither here nor there—but I told him I would keep the broadcasting team at four. I would search around the country and bring in a young professional who was not a ballplayer. I'd keep each of the professionals paired with one of the ballplayers.

After I had said that, Burke asked, "Are you going down to Washington to do those three games, as you planned?"

"Yes, of course."

He said, "I have been told that you have said at various times that when you knew a broadcast was going to be your last broadcast, it was going to be a lulu. You were going to rip everybody to shreds."

I smiled.

I said, "Mr. Burke."

"Michael."

"I know what your first name is. I am using this for rhetorical emphasis, *Mr.* Burke. I have said that, yes, but I like to think I have a sense of humor. The demands upon a broadcaster during a ball game are great—the care he must exercise, the constant editing he must do in his mind before he glibly pours forth these so-called ad lib descriptions—what you can say, and what you can't say. The things you know about a ball club and its ballplayers—dames, debts, dumbness, drunkenness—that you don't talk about. You walk a tightrope to do your work, and you do it for the best interests of all. Yes, sitting around a table I have said, 'Fellows, after all these restrictions and all this being careful and being protective, if some day I knew it was going to be my last broadcast it might be fun to really have a ball and talk about all the things that have been bottled up all these years.' I said it and laughed. And everybody around me laughed, too, and they said, 'Oh, boy. Wouldn't that be a beauty? I'd like to hear that one.' Now, *Mr.* Burke, let me say this to you. I like to feel, too, that I have a certain sense of dignity. I have done thirteen years of excellent work at the Stadium, and I had fifteen excellent years before that at Brooklyn, and five excellent years before that at Cincinnati. I haven't the slightest intention of throwing the least bit of discolor on those years. I'm a professional broadcaster, and I'll broadcast these three ball games in Washington the way I'd broadcast any other three games in Washington."

"I apologize," Burke said. "I should have known."

"Let me say this, too. You'd better put it in the back of your mind that whoever told you that is a light, dangerous person. Don't believe everything he tells you."

"I already have put it in the back of my mind."

We got up then and walked out of the Edwardian Room. That was all the breakfast I wanted, a half cup of coffee. We got to the steps of the Plaza. I was going to get a taxi and keep my appointment with the doctor, and I suppose Burke was going to walk over to the Yankee office just around the corner. We shook hands.

"Good luck," I said. "In fact, in all sincerity, God bless you."

"Well," he said. "God bless *you.*"

And I left.

Leaving Mike Burke on the steps of the Plaza, Red Barber hailed a cab and went off to the doctor's office. It was really not much more than a courtesy call before Barber went south for the winter, but the doctor did check Red's blood pressure. He read the figures aloud, and Barber asked him what they meant. "They mean your pressure is all right," the doctor said. "It's exactly where we want it."

Red laughed and said, "Thank you very much. I didn't tell you this before, but twenty minutes ago, just before I came here, I was fired from my broadcasting job with the Yankees."

The doctor looked startled, glanced at the reading again, and declared, "Then it's better than just right. That's a damned *good* pressure."

Red left the doctor and went to the office of his agent, Bill McCaffrey, at Madison and Fifty-second. He told Bill what had happened, and then he put a call through to Lylah in Miami. "She was great," Red said. "She has always been great."

After he finished speaking with Lylah, he told McCaffrey in detail what had gone on at the breakfast meeting with Burke. Then he said, "I'm going to leave your office now and walk across Fifty-third Street to the Hilton Hotel and go up to Room 4355. While I'm walking over there, you call all the newspapermen you want to call, because I'm not going to have happen to me what happened to Mel Allen. I'm going to have this thing out, and I'm going to have it out right now. The Yankees have dismissed me. The move is now mine, not theirs. They have no more moves in my life."

He told McCaffrey that there were two newspapermen uppermost in his mind. One was Val Adams of the *Times*, and the other was Jack O'Brian of the *World Journal Tribune*. There was no rush to call Adams, since the *Times* is a morning paper, but he asked McCaffrey to phone O'Brian right away so that he could get it into that afternoon's *World Journal Tribune*. O'Brian is a personal friend of Barber's, as well as a professional friend. Red had been on O'Brian's radio show only a few days earlier, discussing English words and the beauty of the language with a professor. "Call Jack," Barber told McCaffrey, "and tell him that if he's interested, he can reach me at the hotel."

O'Brian *was* interested, of course, and he phoned Red immediately. The story was on the front page that Monday afternoon, and by nightfall everybody knew that the Yankees had fired Red Barber. The dismissal aroused extraordinary interest, and criticism of the Yankees steamed on for days. I know that I read every story and comment that I could find, and while one or two maintained a neutral attitude toward the Yankee action, none justified it.

On Tuesday morning, after Red had finished telling me about his breakfast with Burke, he smacked his hands together and said, "Now, Robert. I have got to go to Washington. As David said on the death of his infant son, he will not return to me. I will go to him. My future won't come to me. I will go to it."

He drove to Washington for that last set of three games, and I eagerly tuned in the radio to hear his last broadcasts. Not for the reasons Mike Burke had expressed concern about, but simply to hear Red. I had listened to him when he came to New York City twenty-eight seasons earlier; I would listen to him now that he was leaving New York.

But the games in Washington were rained out, all three of them, so that Red Barber never did make a "farewell" broadcast. A man from WNEW in New York did go down to Washington with a tape recorder for a farewell interview. It was broadcast the following Sunday night, and it got widespread publicity in the New York papers. Red was amiable and direct and not at all bitter during the interview, and he ended it on a pleasingly sentimental note when, after briefly reviewing his career and especially the days with the Dodgers, he said he would like to blow a kiss to Brooklyn.

To Washington also, during those three rainy days, came a telegram. Addressed to Red Barber, it said: YOU ARE A MAN. MAY THE WIND BE ALWAYS AT YOUR BACK. It was signed: Michael Burke.

Mrs. Barber has never cared much for that telegram.

AFTERWORD
Bob Edwards

Red Barber was not idle in retirement. After writing this book with Robert Creamer he wrote four more very fine books on his own. He wrote newspaper columns for the *Miami Herald, Tallahassee Democrat*, and *Christian Science Monitor*. He continued his work as a lay reader in the Episcopal Church. And in January of 1981, he began the final chapter in his broadcasting career, one that would endear him to a whole new audience.

National Public Radio was shopping for commentators to fill two hourly sports segments of our daily newsmagazine program, *Morning Edition*. We invited Red to join *Morning Edition* after he had given us a wonderful interview about Jackie Robinson. But Red didn't want to write and narrate a script as commentators usually do; he preferred to have a live conversation with the host of the program. He was seventy-two years old and would have to be up pretty early to chat for four minutes at 7:35 A.M. every Friday. Neither of us imagined our Fridays together would continue for twelve years and become the most popular feature on NPR.

I was excited about the opportunity to work with a broadcasting pioneer, but also worried that I might not measure up to his standards. We had never met, so he had no idea what he was getting into. I knew all about him, but he didn't assume that. In fact, he sent me an autographed copy of this book so that I'd be ready. Once again he was teaching another broadcast partner about preparation.

Friday is a good day for a sports commentator, providing an opportunity to review the week's events and set up the weekend matches. I'm sure we anticipated that Red would give us the historical perspective. He had seen Red Grange, Lou Gehrig, Sammy Baugh, and Babe Ruth. He had traveled with teams led by Casey Stengel and Leo Durocher. He had worked for Larry MacPhail and Branch Rickey. He knew Jack Dempsey, Jesse Owens, and Babe Didrikson. Red provided NPR listeners with eyewitness accounts of some of the great moments in twentieth-century sports. But he gave us so much more.

He told the stories with the folksy expressions so familiar to those who heard him in his play-by-play career. We heard about games that were "tighter than a new pair of shoes on a rainy day," and how an infielder struggled with a ball that was "slicker than oiled okra." He talked about the clutch pitching of Lefty Grove and hitting genius of Ted Williams. There were examples of character (Ben Hogan) and characters (Babe Herman). The stories delighted the sports fans in the audience and probably also appealed to others because they were delivered with the engaging style of an entertaining raconteur. What grabbed all the listeners was not Red's recollection, but Red himself.

Trips down memory lane were easy for Red, but he didn't like to live in the past. He believed in living each day to the fullest. That's all very nice, but talking with a man about his life in retirement in Florida doesn't sound like great radio. Only Red Barber could make that interesting. Red told us what was growing in his garden in Tallahassee and what adventures his cat had encountered. He reviewed the opera he had seen on public television that week. And he always included Lylah. Listeners loved that. Red talked about what was important to him. An audience will respond to anything said by someone with Red's wit, charm, and intelligence. Red's commentaries were less about sports and more about the celebration of the human spirit. Red became the listeners' friend, a favorite uncle with stories to tell. He lightened their troubles and put them in a good mood to get through one more workday. Awakening to Red's voice on *Morning Edition*, a listener could smile and think, "Ah, it's Friday." Red's segment on the program was the one feature no listener could miss. Morning showers and shaves were delayed until the Ol' Redhead had said his piece. None of our member stations dared to preempt those four minutes for fundraising pitches for fear they'd be answering protest calls until noon.

Listeners appreciated the fact that Red kept sports in perspective. Many of them have recalled a conversation I had with Red in November of 1991 when Florida State narrowly lost a football game to Miami. The loss probably cost the Seminoles a national championship that year, and on the following Friday I asked Red if hearts were still heavy in Tallahassee. "Well, I'll tell you something," Red replied. "I was around the Ohio State–Notre Dame game in 1935, and the Bobby Thomson home run, and the Mickey Owen dropped third strike and the Chicago Bears 73–0 win over the Redskins. And I saw the FSU–Miami one-point game, and you know what happened the next morning? The sun rose right on time."

Another appeal of the broadcasts was their conversational nature. Listeners were sharing in Red's developing relationship with his younger partner in Washington. He called me "young fella." No one calls me "young fella" anymore. He also called me Robbitt, which is southern for Robert. And he called me "the Colonel," a reference to my membership in the Right Honorable Order of Kentucky Colonels. He did this to give me some charisma and establish our common southern brotherhood. He would challenge me and ask me questions. News interviewers are comfortable with asking questions, not answering them. He seemed to delight in making me squirm. It was all part of the teaching process and I owe much of my maturity as a broadcast journalist to Red Barber. And like any good mentor, he did not withhold the praise when he felt I had earned it.

Sports journalism changed dramatically at about the time Red Barber retired. In Red's day, the personal lives of ballplayers seldom made the sports pages and broadcasts unless there was something positive to be said. Today it seems we know every human failing of our star athletes. I could never get Red to talk about gambling or substance abuse even when it was the week's lead story in sports. Instead he would offer a psalm, a reflection of his spiritual side. I always marveled that his psalm recitals never drew protests from listeners. They seemed to realize that such acts of faith were totally in character for Red.

In October of 1992, Red gave us the last of his more than six hundred NPR broadcasts. He died three weeks later, during the World Series. Red had been an eighty-four-year-old man in frail health, but the *Morning Edition* audience was stunned. They were not ready to let him go. Thousands wrote to console me and to console themselves. They told me about meetings with Red in ballparks long ago. They recalled kindnesses he had shown to children and notes he had written (always in red ink). Favorite *Morning Edition* conversations were mentioned. A few listeners said I should write a book.

I took a four-month leave of absence from NPR and wrote *Fridays with Red—A Radio Friendship*. The focus of the book was Red's NPR career and the long-distance partnership between two radio broadcasters of different generations. I meant it as a sort of valentine to my mentor and a keepsake for listeners so touched by his words.

Some listeners suggested replacements for Red. Obviously we knew the day would come when Red would no longer be with us, but we resolved that we wouldn't try to replace him. It seemed disloyal to even think about it. And we wouldn't have done a favor to anyone by suggesting he try to take Red's place. The 7:35 segment of a Friday *Morning Edition* is just another place for a news story now.

The memory of Red Barber endures. This new edition of his book is testament to that. The newsroom of the University of Florida bears his name, as does a street in Tallahassee and an end zone at Florida Stadium in Gainesville. My book is still in print and is being adapted for the stage. But I miss him so much. I have stories to share with him and more questions to ask. I just hope he's tuning in from up in his catbird seat.